ONCE IN A LIFETIME

# ONCE IN A LIFETIME

An Improbable Voyage

by Nicholas Auger and Donald Lyon

*Best wishes.*

*Nick*

**LIFETIME
PUBLISHING**

Copyright © Nicholas Auger and Donald Lyon 2003
Illustrations © Gordon Redrup 2003
First published in 2003 by Lifetime Publishing
235 High Street, Acton
London W3 9BY

Distributed by Gazelle Book Services Limited
Falcon House, Queen Square
Lancaster, England LA1 1RN

British Library Cataloguing in Publication Data
A catalogue record for this book is available from the British Library

ISBN 0-9543731-1-1

Typeset by Amolibros, Milverton, Somerset
This book production has been managed by Amolibros
Printed and bound by T J International Ltd, Padstow, Cornwall

## DEDICATION

I DEDICATE this book to my sister in law, Margaret Truran and the nuns at Stanbrook Abbey Worcestershire who I know prayed for me and the rest of the crew throughout our voyage.

This may well explain the divine intervention that I allude to at various stages during the trip.

I know that they were all only too well aware of the trials and tribulations of living cheek by jowl with a complex mix of personalities cut off from the world for long periods and with no means of escaping!

And as Margaret quite poignantly puts it when trying to surmise the reasons for embarking on such a venture:

> 'Perhaps deep down we are all engaged in a search for the meaning of life. It is a strange search that involves losing our life in order to save it, facing death to find life!'

# CONTENTS

# by Sir Chay Blyth

NICK RECALLS how he was not sure how he found himself as a Crew Volunteer on the BT Global Challenge Round the World Yacht Race.

What Nick was sure about though was how he completed his training and the voyage for this major event described as "The World's Toughest Yacht Race".

He was also sure that he had a story to tell on such an event and dealing with the rigours of the Southern Ocean. Also with the team dynamics of thirteen other Crews all being confined for very long periods of time on an ocean racing yacht. Not to mention worrying about his family/business and how they would cope without his assistance.

It is a story about life, challenges and an opportunity of a lifetime. It is a real story about real people in an unreal life situation.

# Foreword

## by Sean Blowers

NICK AUGER is one of the nicest, most generous men I know and I couldn't think of a more entertaining and loyal companion to sail halfway round the world with. A mild-mannered gentleman with a penchant for "lolly-stick humour" (bad jokes), Nick was always there in a crisis, the first to offer his support. Always cool, calm and collected, he had an uncanny knack for never losing his temper and never, ever swearing. In fact, there was always the suspicion among the crew that Nick hailed from another galaxy!

I look back very fondly on my time with the BT Global Challenge. A great adventure that brought together a great diversity of people from all walks of life. Whenever I need to escape the pressures of everyday life or rise to meet a certain challenge, I look back and remember wrestling with a headsail in pitch black, sub-zero conditions on the foredeck of a forty-ton, sixty-foot yacht in fifty-foot waves with Nick Auger by my side. When you've shared that kind of experience with someone and trusted your life to them in the process, you don't forget it in a hurry.

There have been and will be many things written about the BT Global Challenge. This is the true story of one man's adventures and, entertaining as it may be, take it from me: you really had to be there!

Cheers Nick!

# PROLOGUE

COME WITH me on a trip to the fairground. I know I'm supposed to be telling you all about sailing in this book. But just bear with me. I know what I'm doing. Honest.

The fair has come to town. And everybody is clamouring to visit it—from the smallest children through to the biggest parents. Because this fair has something for everyone. A thrill at every kiosk.

For the children there are impossibly coloured giant swathes of candy floss. There is a Haunted House reputed to have real ghosts in it: a freak show with real freaks: and a daredevil motorcyclist who rides a Wall of Death. Literally.

There are the bumper cars with hourly updates on deaths and casualties. There is the insect and reptile house where nothing is kept in cages. And a real jungle plantation where you can roam at will meeting tigers and black mambas, anacondas and cobras, pythons and panthers. Here you live, or die, according to your own wits.

There is a diving pool where you can swim amongst sharks and electric rays. Here you are positively encouraged to dive as deep as you can go: right down to the "addicts' level", where your consciousness starts to twist into euphoric visions of heaven or hell, paradiso or inferno: where you can make love to an angel of death, or be violated by an eternal tormentor.

Truly, as you wander through this fair, everybody you encounter has a blood adrenaline level to break all known records in the real world. You can see it in their faces. It shows as a crazed ecstasy shining out through masks of terror.

Right at the end of the fairground, if you dare penetrate that far, is *The Worst Ride You Will Ever Experience*. It has large red neon signs around it:

"WARNING: THIS RIDE IS NOT FOR WIMPS"
"THIS RIDE IS EXTREMELY DANGEROUS AND
YOU COULD EASILY DIE"

And, right beside the place where you step right up and pay your money, an almost plaintive final notice:

"HONESTLY. YOU DO NOT WANT TO DO THIS.
YOU REALLY OUGHT TO GO HOME INSTEAD.
NOW."

And then, in small print:

*"Don't Say We Didn't Warn You."*

But in spite of these warnings, (or it may be on account of them) a reasonably large group of people is queuing up, faces glistening with excitement, to book their places on the ride.

And I have come to the fair today for that very purpose.

As I walk towards the end of the ground, I pass a young child writhing on the ground, a discarded stick of candy floss beside him. His parents stand over him, wringing their useless hands, shaking their helpless heads. "I warned him," the mother wails, "but he's so strong-willed. He just had to try the Deadly Nightshade flavour."

As I pass the Haunted House, I see people streaming out of the exit. They are all either gibbering and shaking, holding onto each other for comfort and support, or walking in a kind of shocked trance, expressions of horrified wonderment on their faces.

Similar scenes greet me outside the freak show. But as I approach the Wall of Death a silence louder than lamentation thunders in my ears. A crowd of leather-clad figures stands limply over something lying on the ground. The urge to rubberneck is almost irresistible. But I manage.

As I pass the carnage that is the bumper cars, I fix my eyes solidly before my feet. I close my ears to the sounds coming from the insect and reptile house, and muffle them against the groans and growls that float heavenwards from the jungle enclosure. There is a smell in the air that has the freshness of fear about it. And there is an incense taste on my tongue, already stale, from the heavy air, humid with myriad red vapour droplets.

At last I arrive at the kiosk for *The Worst Ride You Will Ever Experience*. I pay my money, and take my place in line. This is what I have come for, and I'm not going to miss the experience for the world.

There are fourteen of us, including one chap who looks as though he's done it many times before. He has a swashbuckling air of authority, and is encouraging some of the faint-hearts who look as though they might be having second thoughts. I feel rather like one of them, but I'm not about to let everybody know. After all, they call me Mr Brave. I fix my adrenaline mask in a confident smile and start circulating, giving out my own brand of encouragement. If I'm going to do this, I want to be on this guy's side. I suck in reassurance from his bravado and, in a perverse way, from the palpable fear of the others.

The experienced rider wanders round the little group of punters. He cajoles, he grins. He bobs enthusiastically on his heels and jingles the change in his pockets. Some of the punters are beginning to look very doubtful about the whole idea, but he presses their arms and pats them on the back. Smiling a confident smile, he gazes into their eyes and communicates scrawled messages of hope and invincibility.

Suddenly, as if realising that he cannot keep this up for much longer, he turns towards the kiosk. He taps on the glass and gestures at the man inside. He smiles one of his broadest smiles as if to say, "Here is one happy rider ready for the off. What are we waiting for?"

The attendant looks very bored. He's seen people like him before. He's seen them go in confident and happy, only to emerge the other side with their personalities shattered like rotten eggshells. Eventually, however, he sighs and shrugs. "Well, if that's what he really wants," he seems to think, "so be it."

The barrier lifts. We all file in. We're ready to go.

# Introduction

FIFTEEN MINUTES into the watch and I no longer have any feeling in my hands. They clasp the helm like mechanical tools. Vices, or mole grips. I know that they are attached to my body, but even that is becoming for me a very vague description of the situation. Truth to tell, I think I've almost lost all sense of having a body.

My mind knows that it is contained in a body whose every muscle is at this moment impossibly strained in holding the helm doggedly facing into the weather. There are sixty-foot walls of water rising in front of the boat every ten seconds, and my body's job is to keep the boat facing as square on to those waves as possible. A split second's relaxation could result in the boat turning broadside to the waves. That would be fatal. The boat would roll over and we would lose what minute degree of control we have over our situation immediately.

Heading straight into these waves is a bit like being on a roller coaster ride. But one devised by God when he's drunk. Or in a particularly malicious bad mood.

Think of the worst roller coaster ride you have ever been on. Now pull a canopy over the car so that it is almost pitch black. You can hardly see where the car is heading.

Now imagine that all the crests are at least sixty-foot high, and that some are as high as eighty feet. Imagine that, no sooner do you reach the bottom than you start riding up the face of the next one. And there is always another crest beyond the current one. The car is also subject to violent sideways movement, and it is down to you to try to minimise this as much as possible.

Now imagine that you won't be on this ride for just five minutes or so. You'll be on it for at least forty-eight hours. During that time you will be swamped with freezing water and whipped by razor winds. You will steer the car for half an hour at a time, following which you will be allowed half an hour's rest – if you're lucky. But sleep? Not likely.

Finally, realise that there is no guarantee that you will get off this ride alive. The car could simply be overcome by the volume of water and you could drown. Or, just beyond the next crest, the car could smash straight into a towering wall of solid ice, killing you and everybody else in it.

Imagine this, and you might have a fraction of an inkling of what I was experiencing. I was standing in a Force Ten storm in the Southern Ocean in the middle of a moonless night with a broken radar. There was therefore no warning of when I might have a date booked with an iceberg just past the next wave.

Small wonder I was feeling a little disorientated.

As I stood anchoring our course firmly against the waves, I became aware of a door to my left on the deck. As I look back I obviously recognise it as a hallucination, no doubt induced by the extraordinary levels of adrenaline that were washing around in my blood. But at the time it was real. It had substance and sensation, and I was very surprised at not having noticed it before.

It was a lovely door. It was a white door, but it glowed softly with a light orange glow. The colour of the neat Codeine pills I used to have when ill as a child. When I saw it, my tongue leapt with the bittersweet tang of the healing medicine. "In here," it seemed to say to me, "in here you will find warmth and succour."

I thought about doctor friends who had told me about their own secret doors. They conjure them up at will, whenever the stress of dealing with one too many life-or-death situations overcomes them. They can walk through these doors and find a place of quiet within which to compose themselves before facing the world again.

I turned to grasp the door handle and looked back at the helm. There was Nick Auger. Mr Brave, standing facing the weather, grim-faced. I laughed happily and gave him a wave as I passed through the door. But I don't think he noticed. Certainly there was no sign that he had.

Through the door, I entered a very warm room. There was a blazing fire in the hearth and I suddenly felt very comfortable. I couldn't understand why I had spent so long standing on that freezing deck. Seated at a wooden table in the centre of the room was an old man. He looked as though he was dressed up for a children's party.

He had on a green paper crown, and he held a trident in one hand, obviously made up from an old broom handle and some cardboard. "Hi," he said. "Good to see you. Bit blowy outside, eh?"

I agreed. "You must be God," I said.

"Right first time," he replied, with obvious delight. He slapped His knees and let out a billowing laugh. "How do you like the disguise?"

"Neptune?" I queried. "It's a bit tacky, isn't it?"

"Oh, it'll do for the children. They look as though they're having a whale of a time out there on that boat. They'll never even notice. I know Ulysses used to love it!"

So saying, he looked down at His feet. There was a hole in the floor through which I could see our boat thrashing around on the sea, with Mr Brave doggedly holding course. Nonchalantly, God reached down and stirred the waters violently with His broom handle.

"There, that should shake them up a bit." He leant back in His chair with obvious satisfaction.

"Now, what can I do you for, young man? How about a joke?"

I pulled up a chair. "All right then."

God gestured to the corner of the room. I followed His indication, and immediately had to look away again. There was a baby sitting in

7

the corner, eyes staring. It was obviously dead, and caked from head to toe in blood. A cut-throat razor lay on the floor beside it.

"Oh, sorry," said God, "that's the punchline. I forgot to say: "What's red and sits in a corner?" He slapped His thighs again, and laughed uproariously.

I stared at Him in disbelief. Eventually I said, "You're sick. You're supposed to be a loving god and care for humanity and all that and you go around telling jokes like that? You're horrible."

"Oh, don't be silly. I've heard thousands of humans tell that joke, and worse. Whenever a disaster happens, humans delight in thinking up a joke about it. Princess Diana jokes, Freddie Mercury jokes, famine jokes, Ayrton Senna jokes, Louise Woodward jokes, they go on and on. At least when I make a joke, I try to make a point with it."

"Well, what's the point of the baby joke?"

"Isn't it amazing? That's my favourite joke. It's the one that says most of all about Mankind, my favourite (believe it or not) creation. And yet tell it to a human, and they just don't get it. Allow me to explain."

"You know about children. Put a year-old baby in a kitchen on the floor. Give it some toys to play with, including a set of well-sharpened cook's knives. Shut the door and go and read a good book for an hour or so. Come back and open the door. You can be pretty sure of what you will find."

"A dead baby."

"Quite. So my joke isn't really a joke at all. It's a simple statement of fact. Now take it one step further. Take some older children, and give them a deserted and very unsafe building site to play on. Make sure you put up lots of big red danger notices to warn them not to do various things with ropes, heavy stones, high scaffolding and deep foundations. But come back a few hours later and they will have done all the dangerous things, and in all probability come to serious grief."

"In fact, it is amazing how the human race has managed to evolve to the stage that it has at all, given the predilection that its members have for killing themselves."

"Well, that's not so surprising," I replied. "The adults have more of an idea about danger, and they pass on that awareness to the children by admonition and instruction."

God laughed again. "But that's just the point I'm coming to. Very often the adults are no better than the children are when it comes to dealing with danger. Look at all your friends on the boat, for instance," (Here He leant forward and gave the waters another stir with His broom handle.) "they all know that there is no greater force on earth to be reckoned with than a storm in the Southern Ocean. Particularly when there are icebergs floating around. They were all told this by their skipper during the initial training. But did it put them off? Did it hell! They just carried on with their preparation as if he'd mentioned that he'd got to go to the chandlers to get some cleats."

"In short, all you have to do is tell a group of human beings that something is very dangerous, and you can bet that a fair number of them will then rush off and do it as quickly as possible. It is, I have to say, a serious flaw in the design."

He mused silently on His own words for a few moments. Then He seemed to remember His visitor. He shook His head, as if to clear away the cobwebs of His ruminations.

"But really. I'm forgetting myself completely. You certainly didn't come here to listen to me going on about my problems. You've got enough of your own. In fact, that's the only reason you've been allowed in here. Nobody gets in to see me unless they are absolutely up shit creek without a paddle."

"The poor lambs are normally in a dreadful state. Beside themselves—quite literally! They pop out of their bodies and go wandering around, not knowing what to do. It's the least I can do to give them a little entertainment. Usually I offer them a complete rerun of their life—which I think is pretty generous considering they're normally just about to lose it! Gives them a sort of second chance to review all the triumphs and disasters, don't you know.

"And since they can't do anything about them, they have to treat them all just the same! Good old Kipling. He was always one of my favourites! He had just the right approach to human life. 'To see the things you gave your life to broken/And stoop to build 'em up with worn-out tools.' That's exactly the philosophy I've been trying to instil in them all from the beginning. Particularly the Jews. I must say their resilience has exceeded all my initial expectations!"

He looked at me roguishly.

"So. What's it to be then, eh? You going to go for the life rerun? It's good value, I promise."

Then His genial manner vanished. His face distorted in a vicious snarl and I saw the other side of His personality.

"Besides, you haven't got any choice. Don't forget who I am! What I say goes! That's what omnipotence is all about!"

So saying, He banged His broom handle on the ground. All the lights went out, and I found myself in a cinema, watching a puttering, flickering film play itself out on the screen. There was a large bucket of popcorn on my knee. It smelled like the most fantastic popcorn ever made. But something seemed to tell me that I shouldn't eat it.

The film played its way rapidly through my early life. In fact, sequences of it looked exactly like excerpts from the old Super 8 films my dad used to take when we went out on family picnics. I have to confess to a few lumps in the throat at seeing the colourless, ill-defined blobs that represented our family out enjoying themselves on a Sunday afternoon.

There was a sequence of us all sitting down on a rug and unpacking the picnic tea. And, wonder of wonders, unwrapping the very first Twix bars that had just come on the market. We were there at the birth of a world-conquering brand! I am still unable to taste a

Twix without being whisked back in time to those endless sunny afternoons.

A new car of my father's, of which I remember him being excessively proud. One of those models that was sufficiently rare for fellow-owners to flash each other in recognition when passing on the road. For it was an age when a man and his car had an almost brotherly relationship, like James Bond and his Aston Martin DB7.

Every boy wanted to be James Bond. And every father thought he *was* James Bond. Another lump-making sequence showed my father proudly exhibiting his name in the paper having won a small amount of money on the football pools. His name appeared next to the winning coupon number, which began "007". For weeks after that I confided to my closest friends that my father had a "licence to kill".

And I was all the more proud of him because I had never seen him exercise this privilege. Like Shane in the classic western, he obviously only used his power and lightning reflexes when under extreme provocation. I felt safe when sitting next to him in the front seat of his car, watching him expertly (as it seemed to me) changing the gears to overtake yet another slow-coach on a Sunday outing.

Then there was a sequence where I secretly put a bullet-hole transfer onto his windscreen. These had been distributed at garages as post publicity for the latest Bond film. He didn't comment on it, but one morning I woke to find that my bedroom mirror had been seemingly shot through with a series of five bullet holes. Underneath was the legend "I'm a wild one!" I loved him for that.

These early scenes were in black and white, but as the film worked its way through my teens the colour content gradually increased, so that my first sexual conquest (an incident of which I am not excessively proud) was delivered to me in full lurid Technicolor. I nearly threw up.

From there on, the cringe factor was very evident. Teenage lust, self-interest, know-it-all cockiness and bouts of guilt and angst.

Showdowns with parents over trivialities. Arguments with girlfriends over who was using whom in a current relationship.

Then came the onset of bouts of drinking, and coming home at all hours of the morning to yet more showdowns with parents. Here my father was pitifully stripped of all likeness to Britain's most famous agent, *sang-froid* melted in the heat of quivering, helpless rage at his son's irresponsibility. Of course, by now the "real" James Bond had mutated to a foppish dandy, prancing around on overpriced and improbable film sets. What chance had we of behaving in an honourable fashion with our hero so pitifully transformed?

Then there was reckless driving in the first flush of euphoria after passing my test. Incidents of egging on friends to do the same while knowing they were in no state to be in charge of a petrol lawnmower, let alone their father's souped-up Capri or whatever. And then being present while those same friends had showdowns with *their* parents in the small hours of the morning. Followed by *post mortems* in the pub the next day analysing the lack of understanding shown by parents for the legitimate activities of their children.

All this passed before my eyes, and I was feeling worse with every incident. But then the frame froze, and a caption appeared:

*"All this is past. Acknowledge it. Then let it go."*

I did so, and felt a relief as I have never felt before. It was intense, and I felt that, wherever all those people were now, whatever had passed between us was all closed. I smiled. And if you can imagine what it felt like the first time you ever smiled, that is how it felt for me.

There followed sequences of which I honestly felt proud. The gradual healing of relations with my parents as maturity dawned. No great confessionals or anything—just imperceptible acceptance of, and acceptance by, the adult world.

Perspectives, frames of reference, attitudes, all shifted and slotted into place. Where once there had been strife over political and institutional attitudes, there was now acceptance of other points of view as valid syntheses of personal experience.

And then my marriage: a truly happy occasion for Kate and me, with the birth of our four daughters following on in rapid succession. Here again there were showdowns and arguments punctuating the happy times. But they were in some sense honourable. Just two people going through the process of working out life's puzzle together in mutual love and commitment.

Suddenly the style of the film changed. A voice-over started, very much in the mode of one of those old Pathé News broadcast reels, but the film continued in colour:

> "So, how did Nick Auger, a happily married and settled father of four, come to find himself in this situation?" [Cut to sequence of Mr Brave holding course doggedly in horrific Southern Ocean conditions.] "With no previous sailing experience, he left his family and his steady life as a partner in an insurance brokers in sunny West London, to take part in the world's toughest round-the-world yacht race, the BT Global Challenge. A foolhardy decision if ever there was one, you might say. Yet here he is, battling the elements in a ten-month long odyssey of mental and physical tribulation."

A superimposed caption "***Once In A Lifetime…***" appeared, and the sound of the Talking Heads song of that name boomed out of the PA system:

And you may find yourself living in a shotgun shack
And you may find yourself in another part of the world
And you may find yourself behind the wheel of a large automobile

And you may find yourself in a beautiful house, with a beautiful
   wife
And you may ask yourself – Well...How did I get here?

Letting the days go by/let the water hold me down
Letting the days go by/water flowing underground
Into the blue again/after the money's gone
**Once in a lifetime**/water flowing underground.

And you may ask yourself
How do I work this?
And you may ask yourself
Where is that large automobile?
And you may tell yourself
This is not my beautiful house!
And you may tell yourself
This is not my beautiful wife!

Letting the days go by/let the water hold me down
Letting the days go by/water flowing underground
Into the blue again/after the money's gone
**Once in a lifetime**/water flowing underground.

Same as it ever was...Same as it ever was...Same as it ever was...
Same as it ever was...Same as it ever was...Same as it ever was...
Same as it ever was...Same as it ever was...

Water dissolving...and water removing
There is water at the bottom of the ocean
Carry the water at the bottom of the ocean
Remove the water at the bottom of the ocean!

Letting the days go by/let the water hold me down
Letting the days go by/water flowing underground
Into the blue again/in the silent water
Under the rocks and stones/there is water underground.

Letting the days go by/let the water hold me down
Letting the days go by/water flowing underground
Into the blue again/after the money's gone
**Once in a lifetime**/water flowing underground.

And you may ask yourself
What is that beautiful house?
And you may ask yourself
Where does that highway go to?
And you may ask yourself
Am I right?...Am I wrong?
And you may tell yourself
MY GOD!...WHAT HAVE I DONE?

Letting the days go by/let the water hold me down
Letting the days go by/water flowing underground
Into the blue again/in the silent water
Under the rocks and stones/there is water underground.

Letting the days go by/let the water hold me down
Letting the days go by/water flowing underground
Into the blue again/after the money's gone
**Once in a lifetime**/water flowing underground.

Same as it ever was...Same as it ever was...Same as it ever was...
Same as it ever was...Same as it ever was...Same as it ever was...
Same as it ever was...Same as it ever was...

The song faded out, and the only sound remaining was that of the wind screaming in the rigging and of the waves crashing onto the deck. Amidst it all, Mr Brave's face was set in a mask of ice. He offered no expression to the wailing of the storm, but as the camera closed on his rigid features, I fancied that his lips moved, and breathed out the words:

"*How did I get here?*"

The Pathé News voice came back again: "How indeed? A very good question. Let us try and answer it for him, shall we?"

And suddenly I was out of the picture theatre. I was back on the deck of the same boat, the *Commercial Union*, but several years earlier, in July 1992.

As one of the network of insurance brokers in the West End, I had accepted an invitation from the manager of the Commercial Union West End operation to go out for a day's sailing in the Solent. I had never sailed before, apart from a few childhood experiences on dinghies in very tame waters. It sounded like an interesting day's corporate entertainment, more exciting than another day at the races, or an outing to a test match. I accepted eagerly.

Chay Blyth, the famous round-the-world yachtsman, had grown bored of his own exploits, which nevertheless would have provided more than enough adventure for any normal man's lifetime.

So he had masterminded a race, then called the *British Steel Challenge*, in which ten crews, under corporate sponsorship, would race around the world. And just to make it difficult, he decided that they should go "the wrong way". That is, against the prevailing winds! This is typical of Chay's personality. He never does things the easy way.

The day's sailing had been organised as an introduction for those who had signed up for the race, and also for those who were casually interested, like me.

It was an excellent adventure for me. It was a rough day, and it was blowing force 6. But I thoroughly enjoyed myself. I was amazed at how easily I took to working in a team with all the other brokers who had taken up the challenge.

By the end of the day there was a tremendous sense of achievement amongst us. Like army recruits who naturally form into groups or "sabres" during the adversity of their initial training, we had reached a level of interdependence that day. I had certainly come to the point where I would probably have trusted any of them with my life.

And what's more, the feeling was mutual. Although I was a complete novice, I had pulled my weight and earned respect. After all, many of these other brokers were in the same situation as me. They had simply signed up for a day's excitement – and got it in spades.

We arrived back to a lavish dinner reception, completely worn out but feeling relaxed in the way that only strenuous exercise can achieve. We tore into our dinner with the appetites of Olympian heroes, until an ugly rumour started circulating in the dining hall.

The rumour concerned another boat that had been sailing in the Solent that day, unconnected with the *British Steel Challenge*. As the rumour circulated we began to realise that it must be true. Nobody would have leaked news like this without it being confirmed first.

Later in the evening the rumour was officially confirmed. Two crew had been washed overboard when they were hit by the boom. They had been knocked unconscious. By the time their bodies were recovered they had drowned.

This struck home to our table all the more forcefully because it sounded like a true novice's error. Experienced sailors develop a kind of sixth sense for what the boom is doing, and, more importantly, what it is capable of doing without warning. Although even they are not immune.

In rough conditions especially, a momentary error in helming can result in the boat crossing the line of the wind. The result is a sudden swing of the boom across the deck, felling anybody who has neglected to keep their head down. The effect is like being hit hard with a baseball bat – magnified about 100 times!

Later, when in training for the race, I was to recall this unhappy incident on a number of occasions when I myself experienced a number of close encounters of the painful kind with the boom on board the *Commercial Union*.

We were all a bit shaken up, to say the least. And an evening that would normally have turned into a late night marathon with these new friends (whom I now counted among my greatest, so powerful had been the bonding effect of the exercise) ended relatively early.

One by one, we each muttered something about having to be up early the next day, and retired to our rooms with our thoughts. And for the record, mine were that the day had been fun, and a great experience. But after hearing about the deaths I decided that sailing was the last thing I would take up as a hobby. I enjoyed life too much to put it in peril so easily, particularly with Kate and the girls back at home.

The next morning when we said our farewells, I little dreamt that when we next met, alone of our company, I would be the one to have signed up to take part in the BT Global Challenge Round the World Yacht Race 1996/97!

But that was some way in the future. At this stage I quite understandably went home and put sailing as far from my mind as possible. It was exciting, but strictly for the nutters amongst us. I put it quietly on my mental shelf of hazardous activities along with Himalayan bungee jumping and unarmed tiger-neutering.

But Fate, Hazard, God, Destiny or whoever was running the show at the time had other ideas. And they made sure I was put on the subscription list for the British Steel Challenge magazine.

Copies of this unholy publication started arriving shortly after the race began in September 1992. I read them with vague interest, but there was no way they were going to get me on a boat again! Besides, they didn't seem interested in getting me on a boat again. Particularly in view of the fact that there was no mention of a further race having been scheduled in any event.

After the race, further sailing-related magazines continued to arrive on my doormat. I think whichever deity was in fact in charge of things had arranged for my name to be released to several mailing lists under the classification "certifiable – would definitely make a good crew member for any hazardous enterprise"!

My interest level remained low. I had been severely shaken by the aftermath of that corporate day's sailing. But I will say that the deity in Direct Marketing certainly knows a thing or two about targeting. One day I received a copy of a press release – get this – on the day before it was officially released! It came through Commercial Union from Chay Blyth himself. It announced that another race was now scheduled for 1996/97 under the sponsorship of BT. All he needed was some crew volunteers!

I am to this day unable to say what particular switch was flicked, button pressed or lever pulled in my mental machinery. All I can say is that this was the point where my attitude turned completely around. I immediately rang Challenge Business, Chay Blyth's company, and asked them to send me an application form.

All I can think is that I needed a challenge in life. And the marketing genius behind the race (presumably the deity in Direct Marketing) had billed this as "The Ultimate Challenge". How could I refuse?

I said nothing to Kate about applying. I did mention it straight away to Zena, my business partner, but only to tell her that I hadn't told Kate and to try to stop her mentioning it to her if she found out by accident. At the time I told myself this was because I was sure I didn't stand a chance. But looking back, I think the opposite was probably true. Hazard seemed to be steering me in the direction of this adventure, and deep down I was probably afraid that I would be talked out of it.

In due course I heard from Challenge Business. An interview was arranged with Chay Blyth personally during October 1993, but this was rearranged several times because of Chay's other commitments. I think this was the celestial marketing department using "backing off" tactics, as it simply made me think how I would rue my missed opportunity for ever if I didn't get chosen.

It was at this stage that I told Kate and Zena. Zena was very relaxed about it. After all, we reasoned, she had taken a one-year sabbatical on a Kibbutz prior to starting college. Kate was less accommodating. In fact, she blew her top. We had several heated "conversations". During these I couldn't stop the annoying twangs of Tammy Wynette singing D – I – V – O – R – C – E from running in the back of my mind.

She was not at all happy—largely because I hadn't said anything to her earlier on. But I know that if I had done, then there would have been so many reasons for not doing the trip that I wouldn't have applied. I think we both knew this. I also think that Kate thought at this stage that I didn't stand a chance. But she has since told me that deep down she knew that I would be chosen.

The whole thing was selfish and self-centred. But once you get something like that into your head, there is nothing for it but to do it. Otherwise you think about what might have been for the rest of your life!

I eventually managed to meet the elusive Chay at the Royal Offshore Racing Club in the West End. I was completely relaxed at the interview, because I basically didn't give a damn whether I was chosen or not.

If I was not chosen, at least I would have been true to myself. I would have done all I could to win my place. If I was rejected, however, I could go home to a very grateful wife and carry on in my secure situation. (But God only knows what I might have gone looking for afterwards to satisfy my newly kindled thirst for adventure!)

Chay was there to meet me in person. He was on the telephone when I arrived, and he was yawning at every other word of his conversation. He waved me towards a jug of coffee on the table in front of him. I poured myself a cup and waited. And waited! It was one marathon of a conversation, but he eventually finished and shook my hand, yawning copiously.

I was a little peeved. I said something like: "Charming. I've obviously impressed you already!"

He looked a little embarrassed, and immediately apologised. He had apparently not managed to get a wink of sleep on the overnight sleeper from Cornwall the previous night.

He went on through the interview, asking a whole screed of questions of which I could not catch the relevance. But at the end of the interview all became clear. This very British character was suffering from that most British of conversational afflictions – talking about money! His main concern turned out to be whether I was going to be able to finance my berth aboard ship (a matter of some £18,000).

I told him that I was married with four children, that I had set up my business four years previously, and that I wouldn't be going in for something like this if I thought I couldn't handle the finances. Looking back on it, this must have made me a pretty attractive prospect in his eyes. Like a tenant who turns up with a rent deposit in used fivers. He could tell that I was very keen, was willing and able to finance my berth, and was unlikely to drop out once I was committed.

He went off into another one of his yawning fits, then sat staring into space. I sought to lighten the situation with a little comical aside. One of the questions on the application form had read "Do you have any sailing-related qualifications, e.g. diver's licence?" I had misread this in my haste to fill in the form, and thought it had said "driver's licence". I had answered "Yes," and written my number in the relevant space.

After sending the form, I had spotted my mistake. I now drew his attention to this, joking that at least I would be available to drive the team bus when we put in at Rio!

I thought this wasn't a bad attempt at humour. But Chay showed no emotion whatsoever. He carried on yawning and ruminating on other things in a world of his own. But if I had known him then as I came to know him later, I would have said that this was just his little interviewing tactic. Just as Albert Einstein found it convenient sometimes to take refuge in the rôle of unworldly nutty professor, I think Chay was playing with ways of impressing me with his mystique.

The interview came to an end. I thought selection would now follow the course of most job interviews. There would be a shortlist, with perhaps second interviews (at which one would no doubt be asked to produce bank statements to support one's claim to a berth!)

We stood up, and in my mind's ear I heard him say, "Thank you, Mr Auger. We'll let you know."

What he actually said stunned me into silence. He shook my hand warmly (the most emotion I had detected in him all through the interview) and said, "Welcome aboard, Nick. I am pleased to tell you that you have been accepted to train for the race."

How did I get here? That's how I got here.

I was back in the picture studio. God was there at my elbow.

"Well, what d'you think?" He grinned.

"Very interesting," I said.

"Sorry if I startled you earlier," He said. "I just can't help it sometimes. Mysterious ways and all that."

"That's all right."

"The big thing with me is," and here He lowered His voice to a whisper, "don't say I told you so, but you shouldn't take me *too seriously*."

"Thanks," I said. His voice was so kind that I almost cried. But I didn't. Whatever would Mr Brave have thought?

"Don't worry," He went on. "It's not your time yet. I brought you into this world with nothing, and you've done all right so far."

I said nothing.

"You hear me? I said you've done all right. That's high praise coming from me."

I looked up at Him. And suddenly we both laughed. Then I stopped. I could see the Codeine-coloured door behind Him. Suddenly I was riven with fear.

"D-Do I have to go back out there again now?"

"Yes, son. But I've told you. You've done all right. And believe Me, you're *going* to do all right. This silly little race of yours, you're going to come through the other end, and you're going to be really proud of yourself. Believe Me. And notice I didn't say, 'Believe *in* Me,' which is what a lot of people hear when I say that. I don't need to be believed in. I simply Am, as you will know if you've ever read your Bible. If you want to believe in someone, believe in yourself. You already have done so far. Just take it a step further."

"Thanks," I said, and reached for the door handle.

Then a thought struck me. "Oh, by the way. Are you in charge of Direct Marketing around here?"

He smiled, and gave me a wink. A moment later I was back on the icy deck. I climbed back inside Mr Brave's body. I shook my head and came back to consciousness. I glanced at my watch, and realised I had only been unconscious for what must have been a second. But I felt a glow inside me, a coiled-up confidence like an electric element.

"When I get back," I thought, "I'm going to write a book."

## The Storm Before The Storm

DURING THE last days before setting off on a ten-month round-the-world yacht race, it is very important to have a good time with the family.

Forget about what lies ahead, unwind a bit, make sure they know how much you love them. Make sure you leave them and yourself with happy memories for the long time of separation ahead: no insignificant squabbles, no vindictive blaming for minor errors, no snapping and shouting and condemning. After all (and this thought hangs in the air inevitably, though nobody dare give it utterance) they might never see you again.

And if they never see you again, it's nobody's fault but your own.

Some widows and orphans can say that their men died quietly and peacefully. Some can say that they died fighting for a worthwhile cause. Some can say that their men died at sea, but saving the lives of others. But if I didn't come back, all they would be able to say was that I died fulfilling a selfish dream, one that even I couldn't explain. That I just had this feeling inside me that sailing round the world was "something I had to do".

Pretty lame, eh?

This feeling coloured my last days with the family. We all knew that I was leaving in a few days, to set out on this great adventure. But it was a "great adventure" only for me. For those left behind, it would be a tedious ten-month heartbreak. For Kate, a long grind of managing four children without a father. For the children, just managing without a father.

And, of course, I could always turn back. Sure, I'd paid my race fee, but that was only money. There would be any number of keen young adventurers ready to take my place. And the family would readily forgo that money just to have me stay behind. But such a solution would be no solution. If I didn't do it this time, I'd have to sign up for it again, or something similar. Whatever it was that was in my system, it would have to come out in the end.

And on top of that, there was my insurance business. I was leaving my partner, Zena, to cope with everything. This was bad enough, but as I was only to find out when it was far too late, there was a powerful extra reason why I should not have been placing this burden upon her. There were so many things I had left undone. Clients I had meant to write to personally, but whose letters, as it turned out, never even saw the light of day. Forecasts and reports that I had never got around to preparing. Post-It notes full of unreturned telephone calls clamouring for space on my computer screen.

So the strain was there constantly. And of course I knew that the family were in reality hoping against hope that I would turn round and change my mind. They had listened patiently to my reasoning for taking part in the race over and over again. Every time I tried to explain what I was doing in rational terms, I tripped up on the basic fact that what I was doing simply wasn't rational! I had continually to try to convince them.

And the more I encountered difficulty in convincing them, the more difficulty I was having in keeping myself convinced. My every waking hour and, to judge from my dreams, a good number of my sleeping ones, were spent in an inner argument with myself that I was, if not doing the right thing, at least doing the only thing. That there wasn't a real choice any more.

It was thus continually hovering between Kate and me. Like a fragile glass balloon round which we groped fearfully for each other, afraid all the time that it would break and explode in a shower of lacerating splinters. And afraid that those splinters would lance deep into our souls, taking us over like the painted puppets of a Wagnerian tragedy, forcing us to enact our archetypal destinies, exchanging impassioned arias of betrayal as we inched towards the inevitable finale.

So, as you might have guessed, those last days did not pass happily. There was no way for me to unwind, and I oscillated between contemplative silence, distracted conversation and snapping at Kate and the children. Then, on the last night, we had a quiet meal in the hotel, over which we reached a kind of peace. They knew now that nothing was going to stop me getting on the boat the next day. We went to bed early, hoping for a bright and pleasant day for the send-off.

But the next day dawned dark and stormy. It was Force Eight, gusting Nine in the Solent, and the start was going to be chaotic. I could not help but remember that first day of corporate sailing that had got me into all this, when similar and if anything slightly better conditions had prevailed. Yet on that day two novice sailors had lost their lives.

And this was the Solent. This was home. But in the dark southern hemisphere of my mind there lurked the shadows of the future terrors that awaited me in the southern hemisphere of the globe.

But my overwhelming feeling now, on this morning of the start of the race on the 29th September 1996, was just that I wanted to get on with it. This was what I had trained for. I was super-fit. For months I had been out running every morning, and going to the gym four times a week. Now was the time to put it all into action. Kate and the girls were there to say their final goodbyes, but the race was the thing now. I was hungry for the off.

All the crews embarked on their boats, pulled out into the furious, heaving water and made their way to the starting line. Following in our wake came the dejected launches bearing the families to see us off. The planned festivities were obviously dampened somewhat. The jazz band that had been booked to play us over the starting line could hardly play for sea-sickness, and its sporadic attempts at ragtime came and went with the Force Nine gusts (I was quickly identified as one of the only two members of our crew with the proverbial "iron stomach" and therefore assigned to galley duty later that day).

And always mingled with this soggy jollity were the shouts of "Daddy, Daddy, Daddy" from my daughters, and "I got it, Nick, I got it!" from Raff as she waved the white teddy that they had bought for her.

# 1ST LEG —

## Southampton to Rio de Janeiro

WE CROSSED the starting line in eighth position, but before long we were accelerating well and picking off other boats. I felt so focussed. My body was doing things automatically, almost without intervention from the central nervous system. We had been through these drills and procedures so many times, and now our muscles were responding with their own memories of how to perform. Like concert pianists who play every note of a concerto without once thinking about what they are doing, for whom thinking about the process only gets in the way, for whom the brain works too slowly, labouring sluggishly in the wake of the nimbly dancing fingers.

Not far out I had my first of many feelings of gratitude for the rigour of our training. I was trying to retrieve the main halyard, which had come loose and was whipping around in the vicious gales. Suddenly I was swamped by a massive wave and washed the whole length of the deck. Had I not earlier unconsciously performed the essential act of clipping myself on to the guard rail, my race could well have come to an abrupt end there and then.

Pulling out into the Atlantic now, a school of dolphins took up with us, skipping playfully along beside us, almost mocking us. "Fourteen of you on a highly designed and expensive boat and you can't outrun us?" they seemed to be saying.

And then I caught a snatch of that old David Bowie song flashing through my head, mechanical metallic music that nevertheless chimed with the thrashing of the bows through the steely water, with a slow, mournful, yearning guitar line floating above it:

*"I*
*I wish you could swim*
*Like the dolphins*
*Like dolphins can swim*
*Though nothing*
*Nothing will keep us together*
*We can beat them*
*For ever and ever*
*Oh we can be heroes*
*Just for one day..."*

And I thought briefly of Kate and the girls as happy, joyful dolphins, skipping along beside me, guiding me, playing around the boat in the perilous water.

And I thought about heroes. I was confused. Were they the ones who went to sea, as I'd always thought? Or were they the ones that stayed behind?

That first burst of energy that took us out of Southampton was, I think, the most exhilarating part of the whole race. The rushing and throbbing of the wind, the thrashing of the sea and the whistling of the stays all conspired to convey an intimation of promise. The boat was singing, and our bodies and souls were joining in harmony with it. Spirits were high, in spite of the sad farewells to the loved ones left behind, and now we wanted nothing more than to get on with the job in hand. This was what we had been waiting for, training for, straining for, for months. In a few weeks I would meet my fears and confront them full on.

But not yet. That was still a long way ahead, and at this stage it just felt to me like we were just embarking on another training sail. But as the enthusiasm of the launch slowly crystallised into grimly determined racing, and, as watch gave way to watch, it began to sink in to my mind that this was it. This was the real thing, and I personally had made up my mind that for me there would be no turning back. I had signed up for the full Ten Months, the whole Nine Yards, the One Over The Eight, the Magnificent Seven, the Birmingham Six, the Renault Five, the Petit Four, the Three-In-A-Bed, the Tamworth Two and the Weatherfield One. I had paid my stake, and I was going to make sure I got my money's worth.

By the 2nd, things had calmed down and we had settled into the initial rhythm of life at sea. We sighted *Ocean Rover* heaving along in the distance just as I was beginning my first experience of what was to become an all too familiar phenomenon: the watch from Hell! Generally in this account, you will find this description applied to two types of night watch: 1) The kind where the boat would seem to forget that it was a £1m ocean-going racing yacht, and languish along through the sucking, sluggish sea; and 2) The opposite kind where the boat would be alternately hauling itself up the side of a massive fifty-foot wave and hurtling down the other side of it, in pitch darkness, in blood-freezing cold, in iceberg country with a broken radar. For the moment, I was only having to deal with the first kind. (And to tell the truth, after dealing with the second kind I started thinking I would have to come up with another name for the first!)

But for the present we were slapping along through sullen seas, our frustrated brains grappling with the unsettling and illogical fact that we were still holding on to seventh place in spite of our excruciatingly slow progress. The only bit of excitement was sighting the Spanish coast. (Well, you have to make do with whatever thrills you can get in quiet weather at sea, believe me!) This happened at about 0200 when I went on watch, and I also spotted *Nuclear Electric* in the distance. The yachts were strung out neatly with about twenty energy-sapping miles between them. We slipped down to ninth place, then up again to sixth, pulling away from *Nuclear Electric* and *Ocean Rover*, which perhaps makes it sound like we were having a fierce battle out there on the seas. In reality, the only battle we were having was keeping going. As we passed the coast of Portugal, things started to liven up a bit with swell washing over the deck and Sean and Sid wearing silly wigs. We had also moved up to fifth position, with *3Com* just ahead and *Group 4* twenty-seven miles in front.

At 0700 we were passing the Berlengas Islands, a set of small islands off the coast of Portugal. The sea temperature was hotting up at about sixty-six degrees, and tempers also started to hot up on board when the spinnaker got wrapped around the forestay in the first of several problems we were destined to have with our spinnakers throughout the race. We eventually managed to recover the tapes when we were about 750 miles from the Canaries, and then managed to close up some of the distance between us and *Group 4* and *Motorola*. At 1400 we were all engaged in repairing the torn sail, and Clevor Trever the boat's professor started complaining of blisters. He was going to have to get used to this, however, because it wasn't the first time we were going to find ourselves congregated round the table stitching and sewing frantically. The only relief in the situation was provided by Sean, who kept us all entertained with his magic ball!

Eventually the wind picked up and we found ourselves in excellent downwind sailing conditions. Richard, Lars and Neil took turns at the helm with the heavy spinnaker up. We covered 269 miles from noon to noon, which was a record for a twenty-four-hour spell! Neil clocked the top speed of 18.5 knots and we duly moved up to fourth place.

But on the 3rd trouble came a-knocking again. At about 0600 we damaged our spinnaker again, really through over-enthusiastic use during the good wind spell. A major repair was required and we were tied into a repair shift all day. In spite of all this, however, we managed to move up to third place by 1900, just as we approached the Canaries. It was Pete Calvin's birthday (of whom more later!).

The spinnaker repair was a huge task; we worked all through the day on deck and carried on work below deck at night. Yet we still managed to maintain third place and gained on *Group 4* until we were only eleven miles behind, with *Toshiba* another eighteen miles in front. I often wonder what our final race performance would have been like if we had had indestructible spinnakers, but unfortunately they haven't been invented. For the present we carried on using our promo spinnaker as we sailed past the Canaries. At 0800 the measured sea temperature had risen to seventy degrees.

On the 7th I went on watch at 1800, but when the watch ended I was co-opted onto the spinnaker working party and decided to work on through until the start of the 0200 watch on the 8th! There wasn't much wind and very little sailing action. On top of this it had become very hot and our position had slipped to sixth. The only good thing was that the repairs were nearly finished, although we now discovered that the other spinnaker also needed some small repairs. We passed north of the Cape Verde Islands, where conditions were tricky for tacking, but we managed to maintain a good position through skilful use of the wind.

Now, I think I should mention at this stage that, at various times during this account, you could be forgiven for thinking that you had accidentally picked up a copy of *Oedipus Rex*, the blood-soaked tragedy of maternal incest and patricide, instead of my jolly sailing adventure. This will probably happen whenever I write something like "Sid on Mother again," as, in fact, I am doing now. (There. Don't pretend you didn't just sneak a confirmatory look at the cover. I *saw* you!) Well, whenever you find a comment like that, please rest assured that we did not have any of the crew's mothers with us on board, and that, even if we had, incestuous tendencies would have been nigh impossible under the cramped circumstances, and at any rate I am sure that any attempts would have been firmly stamped on by the authorities, i.e. Richard. (But having said that, who watches the watchmen?)

No, the significance of the word "Mother" in this context is that it is conventional shorthand for "Mother watch" (not to be confused with *Watch with Mother*, which is a different proposition entirely!) Mother watch is the affectionate term for the basket of duties which…well…which a mother might indulgently perform for her children if they were engaged in steering a sailing boat around the world. These children need feeding and looking after as they go about their perilous play, and basically someone has to be doing the "housekeeping" while the actual business of sailing the boat is going on. So, whoever is on Mother watch does the cooking and cleaning, and no doubt if there were any supermarkets at sea, he or she would do the shopping.

Quite a lot of the time, it was I who played Mother. I think there were two reasons for this. The first was that I was really "along for the ride". That is not to say that I was not extremely fit, ready, able and willing to throw myself into whatever task was required of me; what I am trying to say is that I wasn't doing it because I was a sailing enthusiast (and I'm still not!) I was merely doing it for the challenge, and was happy to be along on the boat whether I was being Mother, or working the winches, or helming, or going out and risking life and limb to retrieve a stray halyard.

But the second reason why I ended up doing "Mother" a lot of the time was simply that I had the strongest stomach! Whatever the weather, however much the boat was pitching about, my iron stomach always made sure that I could be relied upon to produce the goods while everybody else was losing theirs over the side! The only other person whose stomach appeared to be made out of the same material as mine was Sean.

Anyway, now you know what "being on Mother" means, and I won't be receiving quite so many letters from Disgusted of Surbiton. Or at least, not for that reason.

At last the repairs to the spinnaker were finished. We had continued to make good progress in spite of our disadvantage in sail power, and had remained in sixth place (which is actually better than it sounds, because the boats were fairly well bunched together at the time). We crossed into the tropics, and I sent a fax to Zena. When Richard saw what I was doing, he said something unrepeatably rude about her, which made me very annoyed. (OK then, I will repeat it: "She doesn't sweat much for a fat bird!") I never let these things upset me, however, as I know that the laws of karma are very powerful. Sure enough, later that evening Richard mysteriously found a rat in his bed. What a happy coincidence!

At 0600 came the moment of truth. This was when we were finally going to put all our spinnaker work to the test! Tentatively, like virgins putting their faith in a Durex for the first time, we hoisted the medium spinnaker and held our collective breath. The sail billowed and filled and hoisted and held together! Jubilation all round, and even the flying fish got in on the act. Suddenly there were hundreds of them, skipping along with us on the road to Mandalay...or something like that. Our new spinnaker didn't make any difference to our position, however. We continued to make good progress although we remained in sixth place.

We were approaching the Cape Verde Islands, which approximately represented halfway for the first leg. The medium spinnaker was still holding out, and I sent a fax to Kate as Sirius and Orion rose clear on the horizon. At 1100 we found ourselves passing my island in the Cape Verde group – Sao Nikolau!

Then at 0220, disaster struck again. With Trevor at the helm, the medium spinnaker blew again. Now we would have to begin the repairs all over again. So as we passed the Cape Verde Islands we found ourselves once more spinnakerless, and I found myself on a Mother watch from Hell! The temperature had risen dramatically, and it was as hot as a sauna in the galley. I was up all day, as it was all hands to the sewing needles! Once again we made good progress in spite of the lack of sail power, and moved up to third place as we passed down the African coast.

I was now having problems sleeping – the start of a problem that would recur throughout the voyage, usually when the heat was getting too much. I was up at 0600, and spent one and three-quarter hours helming in the fierce morning sun and getting very sunburnt. We were still making very good progress, holding our third place, gaining on Mr Nasty (our pet name for Simon Walker, the skipper of the *Toshiba* boat!) and pulling away from the rest of the fleet. The spinnaker repairs continued desperately in the rising heat, and at 1100 the sea temperature was pushing up to eighty degrees.

On the 13th, I was still unable to sleep in the enervating heat. The result was that I was totally exhausted but couldn't do anything to alleviate my fatigue. At 0200 I was on watch with the Genoa sail up. The weather was unpredictable with occasional squalls, and our speed was frustratingly slow. When I came off watch my bunk quickly saturated with sweat and I couldn't sleep again. Instead I climbed back above deck and was very glad I did, because I got drenched by a blissful rainstorm. I don't think I have ever been so glad to feel rain!

We were still in third place and holding our own as confirmed by the 1100 results, with *Save the Whale* (our pet name for the Save the Children boat) catching up. Then at about 1800 they overhauled us. We were experiencing more squalls in this notorious Doldrums region, and the weather was very difficult to predict on radar. The result was another watch from Hell at 2200! The only relief came from a tropical shower followed by a salt water shower on the foredeck. From about 0600 to 1200 we got some good weather, but in spite of my taking the helm for about half an hour, we managed to lose out to *Save the Whale*! I had a fax exchange with Zena and everything seemed to be going fine back at the ranch, for which I was very thankful. At about 2100 on the 16th the sea temperature had gone up to about eighty-nine degrees F as we slipped into the Doldrums. Once again we made very slow progress and we also slipped back down to fifth place. Rather appropriately, an ill bird took up occupation on the deck, just as we were feeling sick as parrots! We were desperately trawling the reports trying to find some weather, but couldn't even find any information, let alone any wind! Just for fun, we hoisted the medium spinnaker and the Genoa. They looked very pretty, just dangling there in the hot, syrupy air! At 2100 we were still fifth, and the wind freshened and built at last to about 9 knots, blowing away the sauna conditions of the late afternoon and leaving a silky dark night with crystal skies. In these pleasant conditions, I helmed for two hours, my first taste of helming at night – though certainly not my last!

Later that evening we were flying the Genoa and staysail and moving steadily down the rhumb line. At 0100 I took the helm again for another hour. Soon we were back in the chase again, and at 0600 the results were announced during the chat show confirming that we were on course and going well. We were still flying our Genoa and staysail and still hanging in fifth place. At 1200 we changed to No 1 headsail and enjoyed a further spell of good sailing. Ian was still desperately searching for weather and sea info while on Mother. I took a rare opportunity to create my own weather conditions with a very welcome shower. I also managed to get some washing through the mangle. I have always been quite fastidious about cleanliness, and I think that for me the length of the spells we had to endure without washing were one of the severest trials we faced!

On the 18th we were conscious that we were approaching the equator, those of us who had never been across it before with trepidation and those that had with gleeful anticipation. That unmistakable "rite of passage" feeling was in the air! There were also about 1,700 miles to go to Rio, which would probably take us about seven to eight days. At 2300 we were steaming along and approaching the equator fast. At midnight there were only 5.9 miles to go, and then suddenly at 1255 we were in the southern hemisphere – never to return to the north until the following year (if at all – perhaps my old friend the Southern Ocean would have other ideas!) We managed to gain on everybody, while a friendly Bombay bird, who obviously had nothing better to do, tagged along, following our boat and no doubt hoping for any spare food we might throw overboard. He quickly came to realise that we were not as generous as your average pleasure boat (I mean, did we look like a pleasure boat?) King Neptune was obviously having an extended lie-in because we were still untroubled by the slightest bit of challenging weather. But never mind, all that was about to change where we were going!

Some mischievous soul whose name escapes me sent a fax off to Race HQ with a request that they replace Richard (Merriweather, our skipper for those of you who haven't quite caught up with me yet) with Will Sutherland. This request was turned down with typical Race HQ po-facedness. God we were such children, couldn't we just get on with racing instead of making silly jokes all the time? The point of this particular piece of seaman's wit being that, in the first-ever race the crew of Will's boat had got so pissed off with his leadership style that they had demanded a replacement, and that was how Richard got his first opportunity in round-the-world yachting!

During this spell I was at the helm for about an hour, and achieved speeds up to 10.5 knots, which was not at all bad considering the conditions. I received a fax from Kate about the proposed rendezvous in Wellington after the first Southern Ocean leg – I tried to focus on it but it still seemed like a long way away. I sent a report fax to CU West End (I imagine nowadays all this is done by e-mail!) and was at the helm again at 1630, getting more good speeds: four readings of 10.8 knots was again pretty good, but we were actually on course as well, which made things pretty miraculous in Richard's sarcastic eyes. A large number of dolphins suddenly appeared, and we wondered if they were trying to tell us something. It seemed that they were, because at about 1900 Neptune (Richard!) turned over in his bed and threw the contents of the galley in as many different directions as there were on our compass. It was great if you liked the idea of raw rice mixed with chocolate cheesecake, flour, broken biscuits and McDougall's beef stew, but sadly none of us did.

At 0300 we were approaching the Arquipelago de Fernando de Noronha at a speed of 11.1 knots, then at 0615 it was very wet on the foredeck, and we had to put a first reef in the mainsail (NB: in the context of this sort of sailing, "putting a reef in" a sail means bringing it down a certain distance on the mast, so that it catches less wind when the wind is stronger than is comfortable).

I was at the helm again, and was getting more and more pleased with my progress, even though Richard seemed determined to force my results down with a generous helping of sour grapes. I was getting used to him by now, however, and I had realised several days into our first leg that he wasn't exactly one of life's optimistic little sunbeams. (One particular indicator of his temperament was our infamous swearing bet, mentioned elsewhere in this account.) In this session, I achieved two readings of 11.4 knots, and two readings of "subdued grunt" on Richard's enthusiometer (not the most sensitive of instruments). We had taken to flying our gib in order to give us better ability to read the wind (particularly in view of the difficulties we were having in getting accurate, or even any, weather information. At 1600 we had covered 4,200 miles with 1,110 to go, but by 0100 the night had turned very quiet. When the latest results came out at 0150 *Group 4* had slowed down – for once! We flew the medium spinnaker for a while but fell back on No 1 and staysail by 0700. I was on Mother all day but wasn't feeling too well, so tried to get some sleep but couldn't until the afternoon – but then I managed seven hours of blissful oblivion.

At 0100 we were working along well at 9–10 knots with the heavy spinnaker up, and suddenly at about 0400, we realised that we were getting into traffic as we sighted a couple of boats off the starboard bow: a sure sign that we were getting near to port. This prompted a sweep on the likely arrival time in Rio, and I drew 1900 on 25th October. At 1000 we ran into more traffic in the form of a Norwegian merchant ship bound for Baltimore with wood products, and exchanged greetings. At 1250 the sea temperature had soared to eighty degrees F, and when the results were announced we were fifth, lying thirteen miles behind *Save The Whale*. We were still flying the medium spinnaker at midnight on a starry night, when we realised that the traffic wasn't all man-made: the port watch sighted a whale off the starboard side, arcing majestically out of the water with slow, lazy grace in the glittering half-light.

At 0200 we were sailing well on a flat sea with a clear, bright moon. Then, disaster struck again at 0430. We were flying the medium spinnaker, when it came down with Neil at the helm, shredding completely down the port clew. We had to resort to Genoa staysail and full main, but in spite of this we were managing good speeds again.

I was very hot in my bunk and couldn't sleep, so I got up again at 1000 and joined in the spinnaker repairs on deck. Once more, we were having to juggle resources, setting up teams for long sessions of laborious stitching and having to peal between the promotional and heavy spinnakers.

On the 23rd at 0200 we found ourselves twenty-eight miles off the Arquipelago dos Abrolhos. We were very close to *Save the Whale* and at 0600 we glimpsed their starboard light on our port beam. We kept gaining on them throughout the morning and at 1200 our hard work was rewarded with an equal fourth position. We continued to vie with them for fourth place and to gain on the leaders in spite of having to devote a large part of our time to sail trimming and repairs.

We spotted a large number of whales giving spectacular displays. They were almost as energetic as the dolphins had been on leaving Southampton. At 0600 the wind picked up. We promoted the promotional spinnaker to heavy, and jibed three times. *Save the Whale* were flying their medium spinnaker, and we found ourselves in a breathtaking spell of match racing, jockeying with them for fourth place in 22 knots of true wind! This was the sort of exhilaration that real sailors live for, but spells of it were all too few in our long trek round the world's oceans. I helmed for one hour during this spell with a top speed of 11.6 knots, and I came off watch soaking wet from my final stint working on the foredeck. And then we received two unmistakable signs that left us in no doubt that we were approaching human habitation, and nearing the end of our first leg. The first was the romantic warm glow suffusing the air from the lights of the Brazilian coastal towns; the second was the less romantic warm stench suffusing the air from the sewage output of those same towns.

We were still battling with *Save the Whale* for fourth place, tacking regularly to try and get the best out of the wind. Then, abruptly, our bubble burst. At 2125 I was on port watch, when we started to slow down, and eventually came to a standstill. We had got caught up in the nets of a Brazilian fishing fleet! All hands were called on deck, our sails were lowered, and suddenly we all felt very tired. It was more than the normal fatigue that we were all fairly constantly feeling. It was an additional, hopeless feeling that, even when things are going along well, and after you have coped with various emergencies in the form of burst spinnakers and so on, something comes along to literally take the wind out of your sails. I think there was also the feeling that burst sails were a fair risk that you ran when trying to calculate to get the most out of the weather, but that getting caught in fishing nets was just random and gratuitous. It wasn't anything to do with the race, it was just an external factor that had come along with the express purpose of sinking your ambitions, a bit like a block of ice dropping out of the sky and smashing through your foredeck. 2230 found Neil and Bransom floundering around in a dinghy trying to cut loose from the netting, like an episode of *Last of the Summer Wine* that some misguided director had belatedly decided to rescue from the cutting room floor, but luckily by 2300 we were underway again. As time went on, however, it became clear that we hadn't managed to cut completely loose. In the end the fishermen arrived and cut through the nets, but then we still had a busy night until about 0200 untangling ourselves from the remnants. But after all was done, we were, quite miraculously, still in fifth place, which made us all feel a lot better!

Then at 0700 we found ourselves at a standstill again for a more familiar reason – there wasn't any wind! We were completely becalmed. Just to cap it all, we realised that we weren't getting any information on what little wind there was anyway because our Windex system seemed to have broken down. We began to feel that maybe we should all go back to bed and admit that it just wasn't our day! Ian went up the mast to fix the Windex bulb and check that other things were working properly. Richard, predictably, was very fed up and sarcastic. Specifically, with the boat limping along at between speeds of zero and 1.5 knots, he said to me, "You might as well helm, Nick. It's not going to make a lot of difference!"

At 1400 things picked up again, and it looked as though we might storm into port after all. At 1500 our progress was getting better all the time and we reached speeds of 8.5 knots. News came across that *Group 4* had finished at 1452. In our part of the world, however, the wind was still very unpredictable and we didn't pass Cabo Frio until midnight. *3Com* and *Motorola* were very close to us at two and four miles. At 0900 Sean appeared live on *Live & Kicking*, the race radio chat show, when we still had about ten km to go with a speed of about 3 knots. It was a very frustrating end to a leg where we felt we had acquitted ourselves well in the face of adversity. We eventually dribbled into port in fifth place. I tried to ring Mervyn and Mary (Kate's parents) but couldn't get through.

Ah well. Life has its consolations. Rio beckoned, with its endless wells of ice-cold lager and other stimulants. At that time, the Southern Ocean seemed a very long way off.

But really, all the time, it was just around the corner.

# I Heard It Through the Grapevine

BRANDIES FOR breakfast. That's the way things were going. In Lloret de Mar I had resolved not to get into the state where I was drinking continuously again, and for someone of my alcoholic appetite, that meant sticking to beer. So, had I stopped to think about it, I would have had to acknowledge that I wasn't doing very well, even by my own standards.

But such was the force with which I hit land that I had to cushion myself in the only way I knew how. Months of training had prepared me brilliantly for life at sea. You could keep me on the boat for weeks and not let me smell a drop of alcohol (except for champagne on special occasions like Christmas, or crossing the equator), and I would weather whatever storms the elements and the enforced cramped living conditions threw at me.

But let me put in at port and suddenly I was all at sea, if you'll pardon the expression. And if you will pardon another (for it seems the best way to describe it) I had no anchor. No daily tasks, either connected with making the boat go faster, or with the daily chores of subsistence at sea, to keep me occupied and to stop me thinking about other things.

I think of my state of mind at that time as being a bit like the solar system, with several heavy objects of varying weights revolving round a central object. When the objects are evenly dispersed around the system, the effects more or less cancel out, and the system is stable. But allow all the objects to congregate on one side, and the system becomes unbalanced.

When at sea, all the worries were randomly dispersed around me. But when we were on land, they all swung round into an alignment, pulling me off-centre, sending my system haywire. There was Kate and the girls. There was Zena and our insurance business. And swinging ever closer in its slow, stately and inexorable orbit was a huge planet: the one I tried most of all to ignore, but whose influence nonetheless it was impossible to escape.

One might think of this planet as Jupiter, being the largest planet. But Jupiter is traditionally the bringer of joy, and is forever branded with Holst's famous characterisation. Who could fail to be filled with hope and serenity on hearing his swelling melody? No. The planet that threatened me in this schema was Neptune. It was also a large planet, but it exerted a much colder, harsher influence. Its domain was the sea, and its effect on me was becoming stronger, the closer we came to the Southern Ocean.

Hence you find me sitting in the bar at breakfast, sprinkling brandy on my cornflakes and refusing to get up from the table until Richard, Sean and I have finished the bottle.

We were due to drive out to the airport that morning to meet Richard's and Sean's wives, Rafi and Shirley, who were visiting them during the Rio stopover. But on ringing the airport, we found that the flight had been severely delayed. They would not now arrive until after lunch.

So what else was there to do, with the morning stretching ahead of us like a becalmed sea, lunch nothing but a distant mirage on the horizon? Why drink, of course. If in doubt, get pissed. Although, in fact, we were never even in doubt.

So a second bottle of brandy went the way that all good bottles of brandy must eventually go, and having thus successfully beguiled the time we set off for lunch at the Yacht Club.

The Yacht Club in Rio is an exclusive bubble of moneyed comfort. You are not allowed in unless you are (a) a member wearing clothes and jewellery totalling in value at least £10,000 or (b) a visiting crew member of a boat which is of the requisite level of interest in the world of sailing. BT Global Challenge boats automatically qualify under (b).

The restaurant is on the ground floor, looking out over the swimming pool. The linen napkins are so crisp that they crackle as you unfold them. There is a pervading murmur of well-bred conversation and the genteel clinking of heavy china, crystal and cutlery. You certainly couldn't hear a pin drop. Not because of the noise, but because, if you were so unfortunate as to drop one, a waiter would materialise from nowhere and catch it before it hit the ground.

We were shown to a table by the window, and sat reading our menus. And then a throbbing started in my head. At first I thought it might be one of my hypertension headaches, but then I realised that the throbbing was more musical than painful. A familiar bass line was pushing up through my fuzzled brain and blossoming into song as the silky smooth voice of Marvin Gaye swooped down to join it:

> "Oo-ooh, I bet you're wond'rin' how I knew
> 'Bout your plans to make me blue
> With some other guy you knew before
> Between the two of us guys you know I love you more
> It took me by surprise I must say
> When I found out yesterday
> Don't ya know that I heard it through the grapevine..."

I simply had to get up and dance. I looked across at a table where a family was seated—obviously a very wealthy father, with a beautiful Latin wife whose slow-burning fuse crackled and popped beneath the icy veneer she was wearing for the benefit of the Yacht Club. Opposite her sat her daughter, with a much faster-burning fuse, and a concomitantly more glacial exterior.

I rose to my feet, and managed to slip both of them a wink and a smile. They glanced at each other, then back at me, questioning. What was I going to do? The husband and father was engrossed in the menu. Marvin's music continued its pulse in my head. It was Levi's ad time!

Like an old pro who had been strutting the night clubs ever since Spandex had been invented, I unbuttoned my shirt and displayed my pecs to their best advantage. My jeans followed, and I was standing in the middle of the smartest restaurant in town wearing just my swimming trunks.

I think the Latin ladies were expecting the "Full Monty". But I am afraid I disappointed them. I turned to the window, climbed up on the ledge and dived out into the pool below.

The water was beautifully cool, and, as I hit it, the throbbing music in my head ceased. I surfaced and swam gently to the edge. I had done the whole thing in a kind of half-trance. I knew what I had done, but thinking back on it there didn't seem to have been any volition involved. I simply felt that I had been dancing to an irresistible tune, like somebody in a carnival ecstasy.

I climbed out of the pool, returned to the restaurant and sat down at the table again, obviously dripping wet. By covert signs, my companions managed to convey to me the fact that the Commodore of the club was sitting at the far end of the room. And that if looks could kill instantly, he would have readily traded in his eyes for a pair that dealt out a slow, lingering death instead.

So I said to my friends, "I'd better get dressed then," picked up my clothes and went and got changed in the gents. Logically, I do not understand why I did not simply put my clothes back on in the restaurant. I mean, it couldn't have caused more offence than taking them off had done. But in any event it gave me a bit of thinking space. I had surprised myself by what I had done. Indeed, I had not even thought about what I had been doing until after I had done it.

So I gathered my clothes from their various locations around the room, in an atmosphere of astonished silence. Then I wandered off to the gents, leaving a dripping trail behind me on the plush carpet.

When I emerged, I went straight up to the Commodore's table and sat down opposite him. He stopped eating with a forkful of food halfway to his mouth, and raised an eyebrow in enquiry.

I stammered slightly. My mind was frantically casting about for a logical explanation, although there didn't seem to be one. Then, suddenly, it occurred to me in a flash of what seemed like genius that this man was a sportsman. He wouldn't be Commodore of a sailing club otherwise.

"I'm sorry," I said. "I, er, did that for a bet."

The Commodore's eyes registered no forgiveness whatsoever.

"Look," I said, "I'll buy you a drink afterwards, OK?"

At last, the Commodore's eyes twinkled a little. But as soon as they did, he looked down at his food in order to hide the fact. Turning his attention to his meal once more, he murmured softly:

"You *may* buy me a drink later. But *not* in here."

Thus chastened, and thus absolved, I thanked him and returned to my seat.

We never did meet up again for that drink.

Now, I'm sorry about the continuity here, I really am. But I'm afraid at this point my inner narrative refuses to dovetail neatly with any other events that took place in Rio. As I look back and try to recall those events, my mind feels like an old Super 8 film that has been burned in places and cut and chopped and spliced and plastered with scant regard for the original chronology. I can almost hear the spool of my memories unwind, leaving the loose end of the film ticking aimlessly against the sides of my skull until the projectionist comes along and switches off the motor. It's at times like this that I fall back on my natural presentational props: my inexhaustible supply of one-liners and shaggy dog stories.

So now I'm going to tell you the one about the three Italians, two Argentineans, the mad Dutchman, the British fugitive and a (not so shaggy) dog.

Sitting tight? OK, here goes.

"One of these days, we all gonna go home and get some sleep."

So ran one of my mumbling inner mantras at intervals during the whole of the race, on both land and sea. At the time it was just part of my inner landscape: the environment which my consciousness inhabited. But now I see it as a kind of prayer: an incense offered up to the sea god: strangely akin to "not my will, Lord, but Thine," in that there is no specification of what kind of sleep we are talking about here. It might simply be the grateful sleep that comes after hard and strenuous exercise. Or it might be something more sinister. It might be the sort of sleep Hamlet was on about. The sort you find at the bottom of the world, at the bottom of the Southern Ocean. Whichever you wish, O Lord, whatever you want. You choose.

I remember when personal music systems first came on the market. You would plug in your earphones, and you would immediately be transported into a film. An uneventful, film, certainly. A sort of Andy Warhol "slice of life" film, or, at best, a tale of brave Ulysses after the manner of Joyce. But a film nonetheless. You might be taking the dog for a walk, or going to the dry cleaners, but you were doing it to a soundtrack, the rhythm of your footsteps clicking along to the Norman Bates beat of "Psycho Killer," or dancing an Arabesque to the crazy Camus logic of "Killing An Arab":

> *"I can turn and walk away, or I can fire the gun,*
> *Staring at the sea, staring at the sun,*
> *Whatever I do it amounts to the same:*
> *Absolutely nothing…"*

Nowadays, *ichabod*! The glory is gone! We are familiar with the experience, and now if you listen to a personal stereo you just feel like you're listening to a personal stereo. No film, no personal glamour, no starring role. I am not Prince Hamlet, nor was meant to be; am an attendant lord. One that will do to swell a progress, start a scene or two...

Or something like that.

Similarly, we now have the daily experience of seeing people apparently declaiming their inner soundtracks in the streets. Mumbling to themselves, shouting to themselves, prophesying to the wind, much as Cassandra must have done, or the oracle at Delphi. Glossolalia revisited. Then we realise that this is not speaking in tongues. It is not the revival of the ancient magic that we are witnessing, but the celebration of the new. It is one side of a mobile phone conversation that we are hearing, the user fearing the effects of radiation and wearing a hands-free earphone kit, so that he appears to stand naked before his god, the hotline of prayer singing in the wind. Once upon a time, we will tell our grandchildren, telephone supplicants would stand in red metal cages to conduct their echoing conversations. They would punctuate their speech with thumps of their meaty hands on the windows of the booth; they would stare out unseeing at the featureless urban landscape, mouths frozen in mid-word rictus as they waited for their interlocutor to finish speaking; they would twist and turn and saw the air with their free hands as they threw themselves energetically into their reply.

Finally, they would slam down the receiver and slump disconsolately over the empty telephone directory holders before making a theatrical exit for the benefit of their appreciative audience gathered in the street. Why was it that only such conversations appeared to take place in red telephone kiosks? Nowadays a typical mobile phone conversation is more likely to be a domesticated husband phoning home to his wife to check what sort of breakfast cereal she wants him to buy on his way home from the office.

But I digress. I was talking about how the magic had gone out of personal stereos, and I was about to say that in Rio I had no need of a stereo for my inner soundtrack. Furthermore, as I was shortly to find out, I had no need of a mobile telephone. My glossolaliac talents were latent within me, and ready to come to my aid in my hour of need with no assistance from modern technology.

My mantra was humming crazily in my head as I stumbled through the hardly-remembered streets of Rio one hazy morning, following in the wake of the rumbling *Jagganath* of the dawn. It was just rolling over the horizon, strewing its foul-smelling flowers in its wake: decaying vegetables, pools of nameless liquid, carcasses of fish. The rotten and rotting detritus of the night before. As I stumbled on my way, I passed by a high-fenced yard. I stopped at the gate and looked in.

There was a dog there. A dog of terrifying proportions. We looked at each other silently, acknowledging one another. I knew, and he knew, and we both knew that the other knew, that we would meet again. I don't know how I knew but I knew.

> *"...keep the dog far hence, that's friend to men*
> *Or with his nails he'll dig it up again..."*

"See you later," I thought.

✍

There are certain groups of words which invariably warn you that you are about to hear something offensive. I suspect these differ greatly for different people. But one of my particular warning signs is: "I'm not racist, but..."

These words always seek to excuse something that is to follow which would, were it not for those words, be construed as racist.

Well, I'm not racist but...

Now everybody reading this will immediately understand, as they may already have done from the title of this section, that I am about to say something racist. Well, I have to run that risk. But I must say in advance that I do not regard as racist everything that people call racist.

I mean, perhaps I should start by saying that I *am* racist. Or at least as much so as anybody else is, since I do not believe that we can purge from our minds all prejudices that arise on all sorts of grounds, including those most obvious discriminators of race, creed, colour and sex. In fact, the very fact that racism is an issue ensures that we cannot come to the concept with an open mind. The very consciousness of racism means that we are aware that certain prejudices exist, and we have to decide whether we agree with them or not, and therefore set our own prejudices in turn.

I think it is more useful to accept that I can only say that I am as far away from racial prejudice as I can make myself. But if you include in racism the suggestion that certain nationalities tend to have certain national characteristics, then I am afraid I must subscribe to that view.

This idea was planted in my mind firmly by a friend of mine who is a teacher of English as a foreign language. At one time he happened to be teaching two classes. One class consisted entirely of Italian men. The other consisted entirely of Swiss.

As an interesting exercise, he decided to ask each class the same question. I don't think at this time that he had any idea of exposing national characteristics at all. He simply wanted to generate interesting conversation for his lessons. But the answers he received nevertheless had the effect of establishing national characteristics directly according to popular stereotypes.

The question he decided to ask was: "Suppose you had a friend. What would that friend have to do in order for you to break off the friendship?"

An innocuous enough question, you might think. But the two classes closed battle ranks as surely as if you had rallied them behind their respective national flags and urinated on them (the flags, I mean).

The Italians, with typical, as I now feel justified in saying, Mediterranean hot-bloodedness, immediately and independently came out with replies showing strong family loyalty and Catholic chivalry towards the sex of the Holy Mother:

"If he attack my mother, I could never speak with him again!"

"If he insult my wife, that would be the end!"

"If he rape my sister, then I could not be his friend!"

"If he ask a lady friend of mine on a date, and stand her up...I spit on him!"

The Swiss, however, were different right from the start. They considered the question very quietly as a group, and started talking among themselves in a very rational manner. Finally, a spokesman appeared to have been elected by common consent, who solemnly delivered the following reply:

"If I invited him to my house, and he was late, then I would break off the friendship."

Slightly stunned, my friend unconsciously started to take the side of the unfortunate guest. What if he had been taken ill, or had had an accident on the way and had to be taken to hospital? Or if there was a truly unavoidable traffic delay? Surely these would be valid excuses for tardiness?

The rational huddle formed again. And a minute later, the spokesman intoned:

"Well, maybe. But he wouldn't get a second chance. If it happened again, that would be it!"

Having said all that, I do wonder with hindsight whether the national characteristics of the Italians in this episode might have had more to do with my imagination and paranoid state than anything else.

I have said elsewhere that none of my intensive training satisfactorily prepared me for life on land, with its unlimited access to alcohol, and unlimited time in which to brood upon the looming terrors ahead of me at the bottom of the world. As soon as I got into Rio, I was doomed to slide down into the same pit from which I had so painfully climbed after Lloret de Mar.

And as I descended through the circles of the alcoholic equivalent of Dante's Inferno, I passed many people whom I observed with a similar detachment to that of the poet. From the time we landed until just before we set off again for the second leg, I was cocooned in a swathe of alcohol-soaked cotton wool. Nothing seemed real, or important, or, as you will see, capable of posing me any threat or danger.

Let me begin with the Mad Dutchman.

His real name, so far as I can remember, was Pieter. He was the barman at one of our favourite haunts in Buzios. And he had a manner of speaking, or manner of laughing (I cannot say which, since the two functions were, in his case, almost completely inseparable), which was, at least to my haunted mind, sinister. My memory of him is that he never talked without laughing, or laughed without talking. Whenever he said something, he would punctuate his speech with gales of hissing laughter that sussurated in my ears like the imagined chaotic music of the Southern Ocean.

I quickly formed the idea that the Mad Dutchman was out to get me. In my worst phases I would refuse to go to the toilet because I was afraid he was in there waiting for me. My waking hours were spent in a shadowy flight from a series of imagined perils. Flitting back and forth between places of safety, flimsily constructed by my fevered mind.

Medical students go through years of terror as they study pathology. Their textbooks are crammed with the horrors of a perilous world. So many diseases, so many conditions and syndromes: so many symptoms, signs and markers, peppered over a sea of existence as deep and wide as the Southern Ocean. As the Marquis de Sade wrote: "…we reveal ourselves as oases of horror in a desert of boredom". Thus, to the bored medical student, his own life only becomes interesting in the sudden imagined glare of the X-ray backlight, or the watchful cyclops eye of the endoscope.

A swelling of the fingertips. Pruritis, pins and needles. A pain in the lower leg. Lumps and lesions, loss of acuity of vision. Sudden pains in the chest, arms and head. What can they all mean? Surely they are not all imagined? Something's bound to get you, out of all those pathogens and that host of eponymous conditions that sounds more like a menagerie of exotic family pets than a catalogue of serious diseases. Baker's cyst. Cushing's syndrome. Kernig's sign. Surely they are all too homely to have any harmful effect?

Just as the medical student's mind recognises chimeras among the familiar pages of its daily reading, so mine began to find monsters in its daily currency of alcohol abuse. Through the haze of medical learning, the clangour of possible diseases sounds its muffled warning, striving to be heard above the voice of scientific reason, the rational, even-tempered murmur of differential diagnosis. So, in my mind, the spectres of paranoia waved their threadbare arms and wailed like men born into an Eduard Munch painting, even while I sat and contemplated the very ordinary surroundings of a Buzios bar, and what I was going to have for my next drink.

And whenever I managed to get some sleep it would be punctuated by the howling of wind and waves. Sea sounds, weather sounds, sucking and swelling sounds. Whipping sounds and singing sounds as invisible fingers and bows plucked and rasped at the rigging, wresting terrible music from its tensions and strains. Thudding sounds and thrumming sounds as fists of wind pummelled and pounded frantically on the swollen sails.

And all these sounds, these wheeling, circling, plundering sounds, would merge one with another into mirthless laughter and meaningless speech. Elements which in turn would resolve themselves into the gasping, laughing voice of Pieter, the Mad Dutchman. The man who talks while he laughs, and laughs as if his neck has a hole in the back of it. A hole through which the black humour of the universe blows in force 12 hurricanes, devastating all in its path.

One night during this phase, Vicki arranged a "celebrity visit" to a local bar. We were all due to meet one of Rio's most famous ex-pats, Ronnie Biggs. Strangely enough, paranoid though I was about perfectly normal people such as Pieter, when confronted with the idea of meeting a known fugitive from British justice I went completely the other way. For the whole of that week, meeting Ronnie became a passion with me. I spent hours in my hotel room trying on my different outfits, practising slurred witty one-liners through the neck of the whisky bottle, consuming its contents hungrily the while.

And then finally the big day arrived! And, with classic Bacchanalian hubris, I lay down on the bed and fell asleep. When I woke, it was midnight. I shook off the alcoholic weeds that entangled me in the bedclothes, completely forgot my earlier attention to my appearance and my irrational fear of Pieter, ran out of the hotel and sprinted down the road to the bar. As I had feared, not only was there no sign of Ronnie, but all my fellow crew had disappeared as well. To have missed this party seemed to me a great misfortune at the time, and I stumbled through the night from bar to bar, cursing my drinking whilst drinking ever more, and vowing to myself that I would stop drinking—or stop drinking shorts at any rate.

It was at this point that the Argentineans entered my life. I came upon them in a quiet corner of an early morning bar, two beautiful and vivacious young women on holiday (well, if truth be known, one beautiful and one not so). They were staying at our hotel with their husbands, who had left them for the evening to go out on a night-clubbing binge. They were obviously feeling very much at a loose end, and we got talking. I think more in an effort to get back at their deserting husbands than anything else, they suggested going for a drive with me down the coast later that day. I readily agreed, as their company was very congenial, and we agreed to meet in our hotel foyer at ten that morning.

So it was that I set off for the day with two married Argentinean beauties, while their husbands slept off their night's excesses in the hotel. It was a very enjoyable trip, although the significant thing about it was that it was completely uneventful. I say "significant," because absolutely nothing of a scandalous nature happened. We spent the day sunbathing, swimming and, of course, drinking, to say nothing of smoking a kind of Argentinean herbal "peace pipe" concoction! We had a brilliant time, and returned in the early evening. Although it looked strange for me to be in that situation, and ulterior motives were no doubt imputed to me, I can solemnly state that nothing untoward happened. I know, because it is one of the few days in Rio when I can account for every hour!

Darkness was settling on the land, like a heavy hand upon a shoulder, as we returned. We went to the bar to have a final drink before dinner. Slowly, and characteristically imperceptibly, my paranoia began to return. This had left me during the distractions of the day, but here in the claustrophobic atmosphere of the hotel bar it began, like its dark companion outside, to press its heavy hands down on my own shoulders. There were three Italian men sitting at a table in the corner, and they were throwing menacing glances every now and again over to our table. They were straight out of a spaghetti western, one fat, one thin, and one impossibly good-looking, but with an edge of danger to his features, like a newly stropped razor blade. They were probably called Sergio, Mario and Luigi. Well, if you're going to go in for stereotypes, you might as well do it wholeheartedly.

As I have said, my paranoia was returning. The ghost of Pieter had been replaced with three much more menacing apparitions. I told myself that I was just imagining it, as I had done so many times before. And, as before, I didn't believe me.

Every time I tried to reason with myself, my inner voice answered facetiously, like a cheeky parrot sitting heavily on my shoulder:

"Just because you're paranoid doesn't mean they're not out to get you!"

And the perspicuity of this parrot became obvious as the evening wore on.

I parted from the Argentineans, and joined Sean, Richard, Shirley and Rafi for dinner. When we had finished our meal we returned to the bar, but I must have passed into one of my alcoholic trances, because the next thing I remember I was sitting on my own. The bar was about half full and it felt like about two in the morning. And as I became aware, I realised that the stage had been set for my big performance, the big showdown. It was high noon.

A number of people were up on the dance floor, and the three Italians were watching from the bar, where they were leaning with insouciant, slovenly grace. Among the dancers, I recognised my Argentinean companions from earlier that day. Once again, their husbands were not in evidence, and they were dancing seductively with a pack of men who looked as though they would have started howling if the music had stopped for any length of time.

The situation had a charged, explosive energy about it, which was almost palpable. As so often happened on this adventure, my inner soundtrack started playing a tune. This time it was the Eagles, from "Heartache Tonight":

*"Some people like to stay out late*
*Some folks can't hold out that long*
*But nobody wants to go home now*
*There's too much goin' on.*

*Somebody's gonna hurt someone*
*Before the night is through*

57

*Somebody's gonna come undone*
*There's nothing we can do."*

The Italians weren't just watching now. They were getting involved. This wasn't spectator sport; this was audience participation. They were cat-calling to the Argentinean girls, and making lewd comments in Italian and Spanish. The girls sensed that things were getting out of hand, and went and sat down at their table with their drinks. The disorderly pack of idiot dancers carried on cavorting on the floor. They pretended to ignore the girls, but nobody could have missed the sidelong glances of lascivious longing that slid across the floor to their corner.

But the Italians wouldn't leave them alone. Further offensive verbal assaults were made, and the girls were beginning to look quite nervous. The handsome Italian, the one I thought of as "Razorface", pushed himself, leering, away from the bar. Then he faced the girls and ground his hips slowly a few times, looking over his shoulder for the approval of his compatriots, who cheered and applauded enthusiastically.

The girls looked away, disgusted. It was the usual female no-win situation. To look at all encouraging is to invite trouble, but to look away is merely to play hard to get. "Flash yer gash and show us yer tits" probably has its equivalent in every language on earth, but there are very few effective retorts in any tongue. "There are two types of woman," runs the subtext. "Insatiable sluts or frigid bitches. Which are you?"

One of the girls caught my eye. It wasn't a pleading look. It was just a long-suffering, "what can you do?"-type look.

Well, I didn't know what I could do. But I did it all the same. Like going for a dive out of the Yacht Club window, I was running on autopilot. Something just took over. In a dangerous situation in one of the Indiana Jones films somebody asks Jones fearfully, "What

do we do now?" He replies, "I don't know, I'm making this up as I go along." That was exactly how I felt.

I rose from my seat, and walked to the bar, as steadily as I was able. As I walked, I affected a nonchalant manner, placing my hands in my pockets. My right hand encountered my sailor's clasp knife and my fingers closed around it comfortably. The way ahead was suddenly becoming clearer.

I walked deliberately to the bar, straight between the fat and thin Italians. I leaned on the bar easily and made my own space, so that they had to move away from me slightly on either side. I looked slowly at each of the three faces in turn. I felt a bit like Alan Ladd in *Shane*. You know, in the scene where he walks into the local saloon, right through the middle of Jack Palance's henchmen and asks for a soda pop.

As it was, I ordered another double Jack Daniels, and downed it in one. Then I turned to face the Italians.

They looked as though they were about to break out into sardonic Sicilian laughter at this display of *High Noon* bravado. But before they could do so, I slipped my clasp knife out of my pocket. I opened its blade, and calmly tested its sharpness by drawing it across the back of my hand until bright little beads of blood sweated up to the surface. Then I laid it carefully on the bar and lifted my eyes once more to their faces.

They weren't laughing. They were looking at me with frozen wonder. I could almost see their mangled machismos shrinking to bundles of limp spaghetti behind their eyes. Now was the time when their insulted manhood would either rally its forces and kick the shit out of me, or crawl away and cower in the corner. I am reasonably fit, and was superbly so at that time. But I don't have any secret weapons—no black belts or anything like that. Fighting and violence are simply not in my nature.

Had I been more sober, or less dazzled by the hazy headlights of whatever awaited me in the Southern Ocean, I think I would have been more circumspect. I do think I would have intervened, but I would have done it in a more reasonable manner. "Now, now boys, let's just calm down and have a drink together" sort of thing.

Instead, I looked at them coolly, and spoke. I didn't think about what I was saying. It was almost glossolalia, as if the words were planted in my head and I was the mechanical speaker, the organ of delivery:

"I'm from British Intelligence. And I'm here to take Ronnie Biggs home."

They looked from one to the other, wild-eyed and swallowing. Nobody said anything.

"That OK with you guys?"

Suddenly, Razorface blurted out:

"Y-yes. That's great. It's a great idea. That's exactly what I think should happen to him."

They were all nodding vigorously, and started offering their opinions on Ronnie Biggs and British justice. As soon as they decently could, they slunk away. For my part, I had another drink and wandered out into the night. I had an obscure feeling that I had an appointment. But I couldn't for the life of me remember what or where it was.

I must have lost consciousness again as I traversed the streets. When I became aware again, it was very dark. The darkest hour, right before the dawn. I was standing before a gate. This must be where my appointment is, I reasoned.

I stepped through the gate and approached the rear of the house. There was a flight of stairs, which I began to climb stealthily. It went up quite steeply, veering to the right and then onwards to the top. And as I climbed the last few steps my eyes drew level with a pair of glowing moons on this most moonless of nights. I realised with a shiver that they couldn't be moons after all. They were not glowing with reflected light, but with an inner luminosity.

I drew my head back, and realised that I was staring into the eyes of the dog. In the dark, its outline appeared to resemble that of a small horse. I fingered my throat unconsciously, knowing instinctively that that was the area it would attack first of all. But as I did so, I realised that I knew, deep within me, an amazing fact.

This dog was not going to attack me. It would have attacked almost anybody else. But it wasn't going to attack me. I was only here to meet it, for some reason I did not yet know. For the moment, we breathed the same air, felt the same balmy night caressing our skin, and gazed through the moonlike windows into each other's souls.

Then I turned my back on him and descended the stairs. And as I walked unscathed from his territory, I thought that we had something in common. He had just seen me off with the minimum of force. Just as I had seen off the Italians earlier that evening.

Me and my dog. The minimum force merchants. I smiled as I faced the dawn and the misty rain and picked my way through the streets back to the hotel.

Back in my hotel room, my sense of well-being evaporated as the morning mist. I was as tired as a pig but I knew I wasn't going to be able to sleep. The Italians were now out to get me, along with the Dutchman. They were even now plotting to come and drag me from my room. And what about this sleep thing? Who said that humans could have the luxury of sleep whenever they needed it? What about if I had lost the power of sleep? What if I could never sleep again? What if I had so upset the chemical balance of my brain that I was doomed from now on always to stay awake? What if I had committed the ultimate sin, and was forever banned from Eden?

I wrapped myself in a blanket and hid in the wardrobe, moving as little as possible, making as little noise as possible. But eventually I began to tremble. This couldn't carry on. Trembling made too much noise. I had to stop it. And the only thing that would do that was a drink.

I wandered down to the bar in my blanket, and ordered another of my habitual brandies for breakfast. Except, as I now realised, it was nearly lunchtime. I sat down, and glanced at the person at the next table. I almost wept for joy as I recognised Sean.

I confided my latest paranoid state to him. And for once he didn't tell me to snap out of it. Instead, he said there might be something in my paranoia after all. Because two things had happened during my absence.

First, the Italians had been thrown out of the hotel, for a misdemeanour unspecified. But Sean thought it had something to do with me, that perhaps the hotel management had noticed my altercation with them and decided to side with me. Naturally, this made me feel more paranoid than ever. They would really be out to get me now!

But that feeling was as nothing compared to that which his second remark engendered:

"Oh, and your Argentinean friends. Their car was badly damaged last night. The police are crawling all over it carrying out an investigation right now."

# Rio de Janeiro to Wellington

THE SECOND leg ran from 19th November to 31st December 1996
− a mere forty-two days at sea in some of the worst conditions that
we encountered.

We were going to leave Rio in fifth place. That was obviously
not good enough. The boat and team were in sad need of a show of
support and loyalty to boost their performance. That is why Sid, Sean
and I decided on a last-minute visit to the hairdresser's.

My BT Challenge tattoo back in Lloret de Mar had been my first
attempt at sympathetic magic, my first outward show that I was
absolutely committed to this insane exercise. I think that is why it
had such a ballistic effect on Kate when she saw it. I was branded. I
was property. The Challenge had taken over my existence and there
was no way she was ever going to break its power.

This latest voodoo venture was to be more spectacular but, thank
God, less permanent. We had identified one of the local barbers' shops
as being the best place to do the job. The idea was that you went in
as a besuited insurance broker or drink-crazed nutter (I had gone
from one to the other in the space of a few weeks) and asked for
your usual Number 2. At the end, the barber would look at you with
a knowing smile and say, "Anything for the weekend, sir?"

At this point, you would have an internal struggle. Should you accept the offer implicit in the barber's insouciance, or should you primly refuse? In this case, we were definitely going to go for the weekend of pleasure. Yes. Damn our precious British reserve. We were going to go all the way!

So that's what we did. We sat patiently and had our hair cut, all three of us in a row. Mine was finished first (well, I had a bit of a head start, if you'll pardon the pun) and the barber stepped back a pace, the better to observe my features.

"Anything for the weekend, sir?"

It was make or break. "Y-Yes, please, actually," I stammered, wondering as I did so at the way we British throw the word "actually" around although it doesn't actually mean anything.

The barber smiled around the room as if to say, "Yes! I've got one!"

"Yes, sir. And which colours would you prefer?"

"Er, blue and yellow stripes, please."

A quarter of an hour later, we all staggered out into the blazing Rio sunlight, resplendent in our blue and yellow stripes. And I should perhaps clarify at this point that I am talking about hairstyles, blue and yellow being the Commercial Union colours. You see, in Rio, football is the religion. The only thing you could possibly consider doing to celebrate the weekend in Rio would be to get branded with your team's colours. If you were one of those strange perverts for whom football did not form a major element in your weekend's entertainment then what were you doing in the barber's? There were plenty of chemists' shops for people like you!

We made our way to the boat, where our new livery had the required impact. The CU team were certainly going to stand out from the crowd on the evening news reports of the fleet departure!

So, on 19th November 1996, we set sail on our second leg. Everything up until now had been an outing on the local park boating pond. We were heading for my Nemesis, the Southern Ocean. The worst place in the world was waiting for us, just round Cape Horn.

Passing that staging post would open all the horrors that the physical ocean had in store, and unlock all the private fears that each of us held in the depths of the seas heaving at the bottoms of our minds.

As we pulled away and broke into the open sea, the contrasts with the Southampton leave-taking came home to me with numbing force. There were no sounds of "Daddy, Daddy, Daddy!" ringing in my ears, and although there were sad farewells to Vicki, Michelle (girlfriend of *Motorola* skipper) and Kim (*BT* co-ordinator), these were nothing to saying goodbye to Kate and the girls.

All the events of the past few days of the stopover folded into my memory like a collapsed concertina: the Prince Michael presentation; the Buzios trip; Ronnie Biggs and the Italians; Sean and Shirley renewing their marriage vows. Good times. Crazy times. And maybe the last times? All now fading like the dregs of a lurid hangover. But no! No negative thinking! The last good times we would see for forty-two days. And then, after Wellington and Sydney, there was another tough Southern Ocean leg to take us to Cape Town.

It was a miserable start: cold, rainy and overcast, without even the blessing of a good wind to give us a bit of an adrenaline rush. We were all given a miniature of whisky at the send-off which brought a little warmth and cheer, but also accentuated how long we were going to have to do without such comforts.

We put up the spinnaker and Genoa in order to make what we could of the wind. But it was slow, restless going. Our first dolphin popped up alongside as if to say, "Want a race?" but we were obviously not going anywhere very fast, so he gave up and went about his own business. For our part, most of us trooped down to the galley where a "Days to Go" chart had been prepared. We stuck it on the wall and looked at it glumly, nobody speaking. Each of us was silently realising that we had forty-two days to go, in cramped and miserable conditions, with what was likely to be the worst weather in the world for company. The Southern Ocean was, for each in his or her own way, the equivalent of Room 101. It meant something slightly different to each of us, and we stood there and contemplated our individual inner fears.

Two days out to sea, we had dropped to fourth place, but our spirits had lifted dramatically. The sky was clear and, although we weren't exactly on the road to Mandalay, a school of flying fish struggled bravely to create that illusion off our port bow. I got off watch at 1200 and had a couple of hours' excellent sleep, with my dreams far from the Southern Ocean. In fact, to hear the way we had all brightened up, you would have been forgiven for thinking that we had called the whole thing off. We were just going to have a few days sailing down to the Cape, and then come back again for more fun and games in Rio. The sun was shining and the weather was warm. I remember thinking that I could get to like sailing if it was like that all the time!

We were skipping along at a good rate, with seven other boats in view. It felt like a real race with some wind in the sails and some competition in sight, and my body was ready to perform again. The race is not always to the swift, nor the fight to the strong, but that's certainly the way you want to bet. And when I feel on top of things, it takes a lot to stop me putting all my money on myself! The only blot on the horizon came with Neil going down with a mystery illness. Now that would be a fine thing – an epidemic breaking out on board with the Southern Ocean just around the corner!

It was Sophie's birthday, so I sent a fax to Kate, hoping she would have received the present I had sent back from Rio with Roger. Then I went up on watch.

> *"You just call out my name*
> *And you know wherever I am*
> *I'll come running*
> *To see you again.*

*Winter, spring, summer or fall*
*All you gotta do is call*
*And I'll be there, yes I will*
*You've got a friend."*

I came off watch at midnight to the strains of Carole King, Sean's choice of music. Given the circumstances, I might have thought that the lyrics would have made me feel melancholy, but they didn't. It had been a near-perfect day's sailing, and the song just made me feel confident that there was a family back on the other side of the world who loved me and were thinking of me. At that moment, love seemed stronger that anything the Southern Ocean might have in store. Time would tell.

I was back on watch at 0200, when the unfamiliar blanket of the southern sky was stretched above us. I felt dislocated, knocked out of place, as though I had been transported to another planet. The sky was full of brilliant stars, but the northern skymarks that I had unconsciously grown up with had been swept away and replaced with these foreign interlopers. My mind grappled frantically for a recognisable constellation, but all it could find was the Southern Cross, familiar from astronomical photographs, and sighted now in real life for the first time.

I was very disquieted by this, and couldn't immediately pinpoint the reason. Certainly the sky was an unfamiliar sight, but why should that upset me? Then I realised with a shock that I was counting the stars in the Southern Cross over and over again. It was the number of them that was disconcerting me.

I am not superstitious. But growing up in the northern hemisphere it is difficult to get away from the power of the number 7. It is everybody's lucky number. And why? Well, look at the night sky. The dominant shape is the Plough, with the four stars of its body and the three of its handle boldly etched on the sky, and on our consciousnesses, for millennia. Similarly with Orion, the mighty hunter who stands resplendent on our northern horizons. Although there are more stars in Orion's makeup, seven is the number you count, the number Seven. The magic number. It was only now that it was absent that I could see how important it was. It seemed like an omen. Suddenly it hit me that this wasn't a game. I really was here, thousands of miles from home in the worst place in the world.

At 0500 I was up and on Mother watch. All the watches had their good and bad points. Mother watch meant cooking breakfast, lunch and dinner for all the other watches, but it had the final overpowering benefit of six hours unbroken sleep afterwards — assuming all went well on board. But this time the watch was made almost unbearable by a crushing headache, which I surmised must have been due to the pressure (or perhaps the relief) of coming off an unbroken twenty-four-hour period of watch routine. The high point of the day was when I managed to get my first shower of the leg, which was absolutely fantastic. For a time the freshness and vigour it inspired in me dispelled the headache. But I was certainly ready for my sleep when it came.

At 0600 I was up again and back on watch after a luxurious sleep. Once again it was very sunny and the sailing was exhilarating. I was feeling very fit, my sleep having banished the remaining shreds of my headache. I was operating primary winch for most of the time, with Bransom and Neil on the helm. We were sailing under medium spinnaker, running before a decent wind.

I was feeling great, when I spotted an albatross. It was an awe-inspiring sight. A four-foot body, and the famous fifteen-foot wing span. But, as sailors, we couldn't help but be a little spooked. The albatross being the bad-luck bird of those who took to the waves, through years of tradition culminating in Coleridge's epic. But then I remembered that the sin of Coleridge's wedding guest had been to shoot the albatross. It was that action which had brought ill-fortune

to the boat, not the simple sighting of the bird, and I felt unaccountably relieved.

The next moment, there was a heart-wrenching scream, more like that of a human child than a bird, and the albatross jerked violently in the air. Its wings crumpled like dirty linen, and it fell with a deadening clump onto the deck. Unable to believe my eyes, I turned to see Richard in the stern, lowering a crossbow from his eye.

"I've always wanted to do that," he grinned, as he went back down below.

And for those among you who ever doubted it, those last two paragraphs are a complete fabrication. Complete lies. Take no notice, it's just what anybody who knows me will tell you passes for my sense of humour! The albatross, to the best of my knowledge, is living to this day, happily following boats around in the Southern Ocean.

I went off watch again at 1200 and had another great sleep. When I went back on watch, we were in the middle of the shower belt. This was an eerie feeling – it was a little like being in the Doldrums on our way over to Rio, but tinged with menace. In the Doldrums we had been becalmed in the baking sun, and we were close to home. There was no danger, no promise of anything more threatening than a comfortable bed, good food and as much alcohol as we could drink (which in my case had proved dangerous enough!) But here we were cold and wet, and there was lightning away in the west, flickering silently. I remembered reading somewhere that there are about 100 lightning flashes every second somewhere in the world – the atmosphere is continually discharging to Earth. In the distance the lightning looked so harmless, so detached, like a school science experiment. I began to laugh inwardly with a fragile confidence. All this Southern Ocean stuff had been a hype. There was no real danger. We had been fed this big bogey man image to make sure we weren't fazed by it when we met it. Sure it would be tough, but we could handle it.

And yet…

A Portuguese Man o' War floated past, a gigantic bloated carpet of jelly on the flaccid surface of the sea. My mind flitted back to childhood, examining jellyfish on Chesil Beach in Portland with a kind of fascinated horror. But there was something about seeing the Man o' War here, with the lightning in the background that particularly set my memory off. What could it be?

Then it came to me. My mind ticked back to my previous thought about the school science experiment. Of course! How could I have forgotten? A science lesson many years before. I must have been about ten. A funny experience. A bit of a joke, really. Certainly we had all laughed uproariously at the time…

The science master, Mr Haddock, had been a bit absent-minded. He was well-known for making statements that flatly contradicted what was said in the textbooks. He seemed to live in a different world which obeyed completely different laws of science from those that the rest of us were familiar with. Still, his "fuzzy logic" had the beneficial effect of making most of us read more assiduously than we might otherwise have done, just so that we could revel in his confusion when we revealed Science's truth to him.

Anyway, one day we were having a demonstration of a Wimshurst machine. One of those things where you wind the handle and it produces a discharge of electricity between two metal balls. Mr Haddock successfully demonstrated this to us, and then, like some demented TV magician, asked for a volunteer from the audience.

My friend Jonathan was either foolhardy or brave enough to accept the challenge. Mr Haddock smiled, and explained that he was going to teach us about insulation. He invited Jonathan to stand on a rubber mat, to insulate him from the Earth. The Earth, explained Mr Haddock, acted like a sink for electricity, and would always take the shortest path down the plug hole. If you stood on a non-conducting material like rubber, then the electricity couldn't get to the Earth, and you were safe. The danger came, he said, when you made your body available as the shortest path for some electricity to the Earth.

Mr Haddock then set out to demonstrate this unusually accurate exposition of scientific theory. He wound up the Wimshurst machine, and we all laughed as Jonathan's hair rose on end.

"Now, you see," droned Mr Haddock above the crackling of the machine, "Bartlett is safe because the rubber is stopping the electricity in his body from travelling down to the Earth. Now, in this situation, the worst thing you could do would be to touch Bartlett on the shoulder…"

There was a crack like a gunshot, and a blue flash, and poor Mr Haddock was thrown back against the fume cupboard. His head snapped back against the glass, which cracked but mercifully did not break, being reinforced with wire mesh. He had gone very grey, and his mouth was opening and shutting like a specimen of his namesake, stranded on the deck of a fishing boat.

We all started laughing hysterically. That may seem heartless, but we were only ten, and we didn't understand the true nature of the danger. In any event, I think the laughter was in large part a nervous reaction to the situation. But mainly it was just the latest manifestation of Mr Haddock's craziness. Our laughter was renewed amongst us as we recounted the incident to each other in breathless tones.

"Did you see…?"

"…he actually said that the worst thing you could do was to touch him…"

"…and then he…"

"…patted him on the shoulder…ha ha ha ha ha ha!"

And in the meantime poor Mr Haddock had slipped to the floor. Suddenly it was as if a cold blanket of air had slipped into the room and was spreading amongst us like dry ice. All at once, we seemed to realise that the situation was serious. Somebody dashed out of the room, and rushed to find the headmaster. Then we remembered that the head himself was away that day, and that Mr Haddock had in fact been deputising for him. Eventually, we unearthed the foppish Mr Brunton from his English class. He went trotting down the corridor, his elaborately coifed hair flapping on his thinning pate.

He called an ambulance, loosened Mr Haddock's clothing and gave him mouth-to-mouth resuscitation, but Mr Haddock just lay there, very still and grey. Eventually the ambulance came and took him away.

Mr Haddock survived, but the shock had been worse than might have been expected for him because of his weak heart. He was off school for the rest of the term, and the following day the head was still away.

So we were all given the following day off. Which is why I was able to go to the beach and see the jellyfish.

I was woken from my reverie by Sean punching me on the shoulder. "Wake up, Nick. Wind's picking up."

By 1400 we had the medium spinnaker up, but the wind continued to rise so we changed to Genoa and staysail. By 1700 we had a very scary and hectic watch on our hands, and we hadn't even rounded the horn into the Southern Ocean yet. I was quickly re-appraising my earlier confidence. It was obviously one of those irrational bursts of optimism that human beings get from time to time. As adults we tell our children "everything is going to be all right", while fighting down our greater knowledge of the world, by which we know it to be a lie. What we would say if we were honest would be:

"Everything may well be all right for the time being, but there is no guarantee of that, and in the end everything will not be all right. Or at least it may be all right if you subscribe to this or that belief in the afterlife, or it may be all right if instead you can reconcile yourself to returning to a dissociated mass of inanimate material at the end of it all, but it really all depends on your frame of reference." Or something like that.

But we can't tell our children that. They wouldn't understand. Well, how could they, when we don't even understand? So we tell our children "everything is going to be all right". And, at times of stress, that is what we tell ourselves as well.

Anyway, we were about to get a taste of what the Southern Ocean was going to be like, and we hadn't even reached it yet.

My main problem was turning out to be fatigue. But I had excellent residual fitness, and I knew this would carry me through. I have always been lucky in that my stomach just doesn't respond to unpredictable motion. No matter how rough it gets, I don't get sick. It's what they call an iron stomach on the boats, and I was about the only crew member to possess this invaluable piece of equipment.

In the gradually worsening conditions, it was necessary to make several sail changes. This is an unfortunate fact of sailing life. When the conditions are worst, the boat, sails and rigging need proportionately more care and attention. And yet you are in a worse position to provide it because of being cold and wet and tired and (in most people's cases) seasick! And because of sickness, most of the crew don't eat properly, further reducing their strength. That night, only Sean and I managed to eat dinner.

But then again, adversity usually brings out the best in people. I am a great football fan, and it has often struck me that, when a player gets the red card, his side, left with only ten men, usually does unexpectedly well. The commentators all despair of the team's chances, but the truth is that the remaining men play their hearts out, and the opposing side relaxes because they think they have already won the game. Very often this leads to an "unexpected" result.

Golf is also one of my great hobbies. And it is fascinating to see how often players win tournaments against the odds, or lose them because they think they are so far ahead that they have already won them. In all of human sporting endeavour it seems to me, adversity is to be welcomed as a stimulus. And on the foredeck of the Commercial Union that night we certainly had enough to keep us happy!

We were changing sails to one setting and then back again when it didn't work, then reefing the mainsail and changing again. I was working with Ian as his number two and admired his bravery and tenacity in battling through while he was obviously quite ill. He had to stop several times to vomit. So he was hanking on the headsail one minute, and honking over the side the next! One thing you learn very quickly on a boat in conditions like that is an almost instinctive knowledge of where to stand when you have a seasick companion. Upwind is definitely the place to be!

At one point I was hauling on the headsail halyard and I got boxed in by the sail and the weather. I couldn't manoeuvre out of the situation quickly enough and lost my balance. The next thing I knew I was sliding down the deck in a torrent of water. I fetched up at the bow with my head hanging over the edge, but felt no fear. In the back of my mind there was always the knowledge that I had safely clipped on my harness. I had obviously conquered my fear since our first day out of Southampton. Later when I was changing sails again with Bransom, this happened several more times, and I began to view it as just part of the job. I actually came to enjoy it after a while. It was like riding the water splash at the fair! During this watch I worked very well with him. He was standing at the mast and holding on to me while I coiled the headsail halyard on the mast winch.

I was really enjoying myself by now. As one of the only people who hadn't voided his stomach I volunteered for every job available. Eventually I was identified as the ideal person to work below decks on packing the sails. I was assigned this job with Trevor (who also had to run to the heads to be sick on several occasions). I was sitting on a large fender in the sail locker, and it felt like I had reverted to my childhood and was sitting on a Space Hopper, but one over which I had absolutely no control. Every now and again I would be thrown into the air and smack my head on the underside of the deck and land back down on the Hopper again.

It is amazing to look back on it, but I was in fact gaining genuine enjoyment from the situation. I felt able to keep up cheerful conversation and keep myself and others motivated. Come to think of it, I must have been a real pain!

By the 25th we had moved up to sixth position, and we were very close to *Nuclear Electric* and *Toshiba*. We split the watches down into one hour for each pair – half an hour on deck and half an hour below. At 1800 there was a large number of boats "parking" off Rio de la Plata, Argentina, everybody husbanding their energies for crossing the place where the Atlantic and Southern Oceans meet. A fax arrived from my sister-in-law, Margaret, who is a nun in a closed order. It was a great surprise to me to realise that even they were following our progress. And in my confused religious state of that time, it was also somehow comforting to receive this message at the gateway to the Southern Ocean. I could just about see Dante's warning, inscribed above the gates of Hell:

"Abandon hope all ye who enter here"!

The weather had mellowed, and somebody had put on CDs of Cat Stevens ("Morning Has Broken") and Laura Figgi. The sun sat on the surface of the sea for a long moment, as if waiting to ensure that it had an appreciative audience. Then, like a plump prima donna playing to the audience, it did its stuff. Shimmering colours bled across the ocean in reckless profusion. And as the moon rose, the colours were transfused with pastel tints. The moon was full and the sky turned a deep crimson. It was one of the most beautiful sights I had ever seen in my life.

There was a lone bird bobbing on the surface of the sea. Suddenly Richard remembered that another boat had won the prize for the most beautiful photograph on the first leg with just such a sunset as this. Although not as striking, that sunset did have the advantage that a bird had decided to choose that psychological moment to take off into it, providing the final picture postcard element.

So Richard decided to throw a jam jar at the bird, in order to persuade it to take off as required. But the bird was obviously enjoying the spectacle as much as we were, and refused to move. We did speculate about getting a stunning shot of a bird and a jam jar bobbing along together looking at the sunset, but we didn't think it would have quite the same impact!

The 26th dawned bright and clear. Apart, that is, from Richard's mood! We had slipped back to eleventh place, and my initial feelings on leaving Rio that fifth wasn't good enough for us seemed very wide of the mark now.

I was reading Michael Crichton's thriller, *Sphere*, and thoroughly enjoying it. It was one of those books that stuck to your fingers, and so reading it on a boat where you were continually interrupted with requests to go on watch probably was not a good idea. It was also creepy, and things like that often send me hyper – I find I just can't sleep. Once again, in an environment where it was often difficult to sleep, and where you needed every hour you could get, it was probably a bad book to be reading. Especially when you were nearly 6,000 miles from your destination! Perhaps my tiredness contributed to my lack of co-ordination later that evening. I cocked up a spinnaker drop, and Richard was very sarcastic. (We tend to use polite euphemisms on board ship quite a lot. When somebody is "sarcastic," it means that they are closer to absolutely livid!)

By 0100 in the morning, the water temperature had fallen dramatically. The wind had also risen and we were surfing along, gaining respectable speed with the use of our heavy spinnaker. Seas were heavy, but we were making good going with them, when suddenly all those of us on deck were startled by a sound like a small explosion. The boat seemed to check itself in its headlong rush down yet another mountain of water, and there was a considerable drop in the noise level on deck, although this still remained chaotically high.

Our stomachs filled with lead as we realised what had happened: our heavy spinnaker, the best tool we had for taking the fullest possible advantage of high wind, had blown. Not only did this mean that we would lose time in potentially fast conditions, but it also meant that we would have to spend laborious hours down below in the "sewing club". We were still in eleventh place, so we had really been running to stand still, and this period would be a true test of our characters and our ability to work together. It's all very well being a team when things are going well. It's whether you can hack it when everything's going down the pan that matters.

Trevor and I were the first to start up humorous banter, merely in an effort to stay sane. It's always been something I'm quite good at − keeping a flow of high spirits going when there is very little to be high-spirited about. But it's my view that the only chance you have of making something out of a bad situation comes if you stay on top of it. You might very well fail in your objective to get something good out of it. But one thing is certain: that you won't get anything good out of it if you give in to it.

Claire used the time well by putting a little bit of extra effort into the cooking, and produced what we all agreed at the time was a gourmet meal. This did quite a bit to lift our spirits, although whether, if analysed on land, the same meal would have earned the description "gourmet" is very debatable. It would have been fitting to carry on the "gourmet" effort into the next day for the sake of Bransom, our token American on board, as it was the 28th − Thanksgiving Day. Unfortunately, however, there was not a turkey in sight. Bransom was not given any special treatment either − he was simply woken at 1.45 in the morning as usual, and told to go on deck and steer. Later on, his Thanksgiving Dinner consisted of boil-in-the-bag golden vegetable dumplings with pasta spirals and "plastic" peach delight!

I worked straight through three watches with Eileen to repair the spinnaker, which of course meant no sleep, but the smell of Madeleine cooking fresh bread and rolls kept me going—that and the addition of Margot's last tot of brandy to my industrial strength coffee. At 3.30 in the morning I was able to go to bed. It was a toss-up whether I would be hyper all night and unable to sleep, or whether the various substances, the coffee, the alcohol, the warm fresh bread and the melatonin and L-dopamine which were no doubt rushing around in my blood in large quantities, could come to some sort of peace deal in a smoke-filled back room of my consciousness and allow me to get some sleep. Luckily they reached a deal. The next thing I knew I was being woken at 6.15 in the morning with a fax from Zena back at home at work. She had just sacked somebody, and, knowing her, felt terrible about it. I felt for her and wished I had been there to lend support.

Richard was very pleased with our work on the sail, and put me straight up on the helm with number 1 staysail and full mainsail. Unfortunately, this setting needed premature revision when the wind suddenly rose unexpectedly. I was detailed to make the necessary sail change and got soaked on the foredeck.

We had improved our position to eighth as we passed that troublesome outpost of the British Empire – the Falkland Islands. We passed to the east of them, although I had to take Richard's word for it, as they were not visible. I was on Mother watch, so decided to stay up all day. That meant I could go to bed at 1700, and enjoy an almost unheard-of sleep of twelve hours through to 5.15 the next morning!

This was the day before we would enter the Southern Ocean. And on this day, so close to confronting my greatest fear, things started to go wrong for me. I was washed down the deck during a sail change and injured my ribs. Luckily, or perhaps I should give the credit to good training, I was clipped on, and avoided being washed overboard. But still, it was not a good omen. I spent the rest of the day downstairs repairing sails, but the next day I was back up on watch at 0600.

Conditions were very difficult on the foredeck and Bransom, as usual, was fussing around worrying about everything, like the fact that the port head and generator didn't seem to be working properly. There were only ten gallons of water left, so there would have to be water rationing soon. But he seemed to be worse than usual. Looking back, I think it was probably because I wasn't the only one who was apprehensive about meeting the Southern Ocean. As so often on this adventure, lines of Eliot's poetry came to mind. This time expressing the final irreducible fact, that we are all alone when we come to face our demons:

> *"I have heard the key*
> *Turn in the door once and turn once only*
> *We think of the key, each in his prison*
> *Thinking of the key, each confirms a prison*
> *Only at nightfall, aethereal rumours*
> *Revive for a moment a broken Coriolanus"* [1]

And, as Eliot quotes in his own note to the poem at this point:

> "My external sensations are no less private to myself than are my thoughts or my feelings. In either case my experience falls within my own circle, a circle closed on the outside; and, with all its elements alike, every sphere is opaque to the others which surround it.... In brief, regarded as an existence which appears in a soul, the whole world for each is peculiar and private to that soul."[2]

Donne's words also came to me: *"No man is an island, entire of itself..."* What rubbish, I thought. We are all islands. The best we can do is send distress signals to each other.

---

1 T S Eliot, *The Waste Land, Part V: What The Thunder Said*.
2 F H Bradley, *Appearance and Reality*

So, in a nutshell, although Bransom and I and everybody else were all in the same boat, we weren't. Bransom's worries even annoyed Richard, who openly accused him of worrying too much. It was a rare burst of bad humour for him as well, so presumably even this hardened leader and sailor was going through his own inner turmoil, although I suspected that this had more to do with the race positions than with any danger that might be awaiting us round the corner.

So it was that I helmed us round the Horn, while sharing shifts with Bransom in high anxiety mode. The seas were heavy, but it was an anti-climax for me after all the build-up. We actually rounded the Horn at 11.55, but in the end I couldn't even see it!

Before getting down to the serious business awaiting us in the Southern Ocean, Sean and I had a little traditional business to see to: having our ears pierced like true old-fashioned Clipper sailors. As soon as Margot had finished wielding her needle and cork, and inserted a neat gold ring in my right lobe, I went back up on deck. Looking out into the fine twilight mist, more of Eliot's lines came to me:

> *"Phlebas the Phoenician, a fortnight dead,*
> *Forgot the cry of gulls, and the deep sea swell*
> *And the profit and loss.*
> > *A current under sea*
> *Picked his bones in whispers. As he rose and fell*
> *He passed the stages of his age and youth*
> *Entering the whirlpool.*
> > *Gentile or Jew*
> *O you who turn the wheel and look to windward,*
> *Consider Phlebas, who was once handsome and tall as you."*

That poem kept coming back to me! And with good reason. It might have been written about me. Or at least to warn me. What

had I done here on this adventure if not leave my business, forgetting "the profit and loss"? And what was I doing in my inner landscape but "passing the stages of my age and youth"? Was I not also, in physical reality," entering the whirlpool? And was I not regularly in the position of "turning the wheel and looking to windward"?

Consider Phlebas, who was once handsome and tall as you…

And then I realised. It was just a warning. Like the albatross. "Consider Phlebas…". Yes, I thought, consider him, and make sure you don't end up like him! That is to say, make sure you are clipped on at all times on deck, and don't end up at the bottom of the ocean donating your new golden earring as payment for your burial!

I lightened my spirits by recalling Wendy Cope's take on *The Waste Land*. She once did a very good job of reducing the whole ponderous poem to five limericks. The relevant one ran:

> *"A sailor called Phlebas forgot*
> *The ocean, his business, the lot.*
> *Which was no great surprise,*
> *As he'd met his demise*
> *And been left in the ocean to rot!"[3]*

We were now sailing through heavy seas, and I was helming with Neil while Bransom was on Mother watch. We were making good progress in spite of difficult conditions in lumpy seas. Once again I was washed down the deck and partially through the tow rail. I was getting used to this by now. I was into the habit of making sure I was clipped on now, and this saved me once again.

Our good progress meant that we improved our position from tenth to eighth by the afternoon. At this stage Richard decided to introduce a little healthy internal competition to see who could manage the

---

3 Wendy Cope, *Waste Land Limericks*, from *Making Cocoa for Kingsley Amis.*

best helming speed. This had an immediate effect, and our position improved once again to seventh. Richard's mood lightened so much that he fashioned a "Deputy Dawg" hat out of a sailing cap and a pair of gloves for ears, and wore it for the rest of the day. It was difficult to carry on taking him seriously (as if I ever had!)

Richard had also introduced a simple system to help us acclimatise to the numerous disruptive time zone changes that the crew had to cope with on their progress round the world. This meant that at 1400 we changed over to GMT minus four hours. It was probably while I was momentarily distracted trying to work out what time it was that I was washed down the deck again during a sail change. This time it was more serious, and I was forced to stop being so blasé about the process. I ended up on analgesics with an extremely badly bruised back. This had immediate repercussions the next time I was helming. It was a dry morning on a flat sea, so there was not a lot of effort required on my part compared with some of the conditions we had experienced. But I didn't perform well because of my injury. As I have said, people can be very "sarcastic" on a racing boat at times like this. This time it was Bransom who had a dig at me, and unfortunately I wasn't in the mood for it. I retorted that he didn't help with his continuous whining and worrying. I told him that his transatlantic drone was seriously getting on my nerves, and a lot worse. We became very heated, and this was the first time (but not the last!) that I really lost my temper on the boat. Eventually we were brought down to earth by Richard doing his "diplomatic team leader" rôle.

I calmed down, but the weather did the opposite. By the afternoon we were ploughing through rough seas and Lars, who was on Mother watch, spilled the vegetables he had been cooking for our evening delectation all over the galley. This was a fairly normal occurrence, but for some reason I found it very funny this time but he certainly didn't find it funny. For the second time that day, I found myself at odds with one of my fellow crew.

The following day was Sid's birthday. I was on Mother watch, and Madeleine, who is a qualified masseuse, gave me a very stress-relieving massage on the galley table. (For my injured back, I hasten to add!) It did wonders for me physically, and I think also helped my mental state as well. I managed to have a fantastic sleep in the morning, and when I awoke, Madeleine had turned her talents to cookery and produced a chocolate cake for Sid. Sean, the biggest kid on the boat, provided the balloons and fun foam!

I managed to relax for an hour or so, and finished Roald Dahl's *Diaries of Uncle Oswald*. I enjoyed it immensely, although being in the middle of forty-two days at sea wasn't the best time to read it. It is a very funny book, but it's all about Oswald's sexual adventures and just made me hungry for things that weren't on the menu! Basically it's a series of stories about a modern-day Don Giovanni (who coincidentally has a particular fondness for Mozart's operas) whose adventures are considerably complicated by factors such as pheromonic drugs and other Dahlian sexual devices.

After this, I was up on deck helming again, although conditions had worsened to a storm. I was finding it very difficult. My back was just beginning to flare up again after all the pampering it had received earlier on, when I was suddenly thrown from the helm by a wave which whipped the boat up violently in the water. My back went once more into an excruciating spasm, although I could hardly feel it because the pain was drowned out by a new one in my side. This pain was about the worst I had ever experienced, and it seemed impossible that it could get any worse. And then I tried to breathe. And realised how wrong I had been.

Margot, the crew's qualified nurse, tucked me up in bed with a hot water bottle and analgesics. These did the job very well, and thankfully helped me to sleep as well. This was a real bonus, as I doubt if I would have been able to sleep naturally. Firstly because of the pain, and secondly because of feeling guilty that I was lying up in bed while the rest of the crew were battling the difficult seas.

The next day, I was able to get up and walk around. We were truly in the thick of the Southern Ocean now, with unpleasantly cold temperatures and broken heaters. (First rule of being on a boat miles from anywhere: everything works fine until you need it!) We spotted some killer whales off the port bow, and they made a very impressive sight. These were the sort of animals I had only seen in captivity before, but seeing them cavorting with their ponderously slow leaps in the unchained wild was majestic. Just the fact of seeing them in their natural habitat eclipsed any clever tricks I had seen their domesticated relatives get up to at the zoo!

The cold and wet conditions were definitely getting to everybody, and we were all very grumpy. Even I had had the humorous stuffing knocked out of me by the injury to my ribs. It was just too painful to laugh! We changed the clocks to GMT minus 5, and realised we had got exactly halfway. 3600 miles gone, 3600 to go. At about this time Neil managed to get the heaters working again and immediately became everybody's hero. If he had decided to cash in all the gratitude we offered him when he got to Wellington then he would probably have died of alcoholic poisoning!

The next day was the 12th. For some reason Sean decided this was a good day to produce "Death By Chocolate" for pudding, but under the conditions it turned out not to be such a good idea. A big wave hit the boat at just the wrong moment and covered him and the whole galley in various types of chocolate. However, it looked very tasty, and it was all we could do to keep ourselves from licking the walls clean!

I wrote a fax to Kate to tell her about my ribs. My immediate diagnosis while lying on the deck – that two had been broken – had been all but confirmed. In the afternoon there were winds of 45 knots while I was on deck with Bransom and conditions were wild and wet. My ribs were complaining seriously and I was forced back down below to take over Mother watch with Madeleine. Clocks were changed again to GMT − 6, and I agreed with Madeleine to go back on watch at 2200.

When I went back on watch I was back riding shotgun with Bransom at the helm. The ribs were giving me a seriously hard time but I stuck it out until 0200 on Friday the 13th, which has always been an unlucky day for me. Well, after all, Kate was born on Friday 13th May! (This is a long-standing joke between Kate and me and I know she won't get upset at my mentioning it here. Ouch!) I went below and stoked up on more painkillers. When I got up at 0600 the pain was a lot better, but as the morning wore on I realised it was just the effects of the drugs. It was time for a crisis meeting. I wasn't performing at full potential, and I was preventing myself from healing by trying to. It wasn't good for me or the race effort.

So I had a summit with Richard as skipper, Neil as watchleader and Margot as nurse, the result being that I was to rest for five days and then have a reassessment. But I couldn't simply go and lie down on my bunk. I determined that I would at least help people out on Mother watch as much as I could. So I helped Sean on Mother for the morning, and then had a blissful four and a half hours sleep until 17.30. In the evening I relaxed with Sean and Richard in the galley, until the day's results came through at 2100. We had improved to eighth position behind *Pause To Remember*, who were sailing about two miles off to port. So the crew was obviously doing fine without me! The next day this impression was confirmed when we moved up further to seventh place. At 1647 we rounded the waypoint. We were close to *Nuclear Electric* and closing on the rest of the fleet in bright, sunny weather with a north-westerly wind. Some more killer whales even showed up to cheer us on our way.

In the evening, I was allowed a glass of port (purely medishinal purposhes!) which helped me gain another slice of healthy sleep. At

0730 I was up again and playing Mother's little helper, although I also had to go up on deck to fix the main winch, which was one of my assigned responsibilities. Then I plunged back down below to deal with the nasty downside of being Mother's help – cleaning the piss out of the shower trays! Somebody had even left a rubber frog for me which I found extremely funny. Not!

The next day was the turning point. I was able to come off the analgesics, but still stayed on Mother watch with Madeleine to bring my back and ribs back into the rigours of boat life gently. The musculature seemed to have healed although there was still some tenderness in the ribs themselves, but all in all the amazing regenerative processes of the human body seemed to have done what they were supposed to do. In the afternoon I was doing what I do best – engaging in humorous banter and cracking awful one-liners on a radio chat show with Sean. It must have been something to do with my state of mind after my injuries, but I was more "sarcastic" than is my wont, and apparently upset a lot of people on the other boats—especially Sid's girlfriend Anna, who was crewing on *Pause To Remember*.

Towards the end of the afternoon we entered huge seas, and it was very difficult down below (so I hate to think what it was like up above!) There were pots, pans, medical kit, CDs and personal possession of all kinds flying around like a scene from *Poltergeist*. As usual my system was shaken but not stirred and I managed a reasonable sleep, dreaming of going back on full watch duties in the morning.

I rose at 0430 and made breakfast, and then was up on deck at 0600 giving my back and ribs their first real test. There were various sail changes and main reefs to be managed and I got through them without incident. And then things really looked as though they were improving when I got a fax from Kate saying she was still trying to organise to come and meet me in Wellington. Things like that are extraordinarily comforting in that sort of situation. You feel that, with a goal like that to work towards in a few days' time, it doesn't matter what's going to come in between – you'll get through it somehow.

And then a mishap to Sean made me feel a little better. Not that I was glad that he was hurt, just that it showed me that anybody could have an accident, even somebody as strong and hearty as Sean. He was working on the foredeck, and a heavy hank swung and hit him just below the right eye. There was a huge swelling, but he was very lucky that the eye itself was OK. Margot's first aid kit came out again, and Sean suffered Richard's merciless ribbing (well, at least he wasn't "sarcastic"!)

The 18th was a horrible day. It made me think again about that idea of getting through anything in between if I knew I was going to meet Kate in Wellington. There were 50 knots of wind across the deck, and mountainous seas all around. Down below was a chaotic nightmare, and depressing news started coming from outside as well. *Concert*, one of the other boats who had incidentally been doing very well, had lost their mast in the horrendous conditions. I felt extremely sorry for them, as this was effectively the end of their race. In pure racing terms, of course, this meant that there was one less competitor for us, but life at sea is far too riddled with superstition for anybody to indulge in even a moment's *Schadenfreude* at such news. The philosophy is much more "poor buggers, there but for the grace of God go we". A huge amount of effort, anguish and heartbreaking emotion goes into mounting such an expedition, not to mention a considerable amount of personal money.

The same thing happened to the British Steel boat back in 92/93, in almost exactly the same position, when British Steel themselves were the race sponsors and the event was known as the British Steel Challenge. Immediately we all became hyper about safety and ran around the boat in the atrocious conditions checking all the rigging. It was a good job we did (as I said, there but for the grace of God...) because we soon found a problem with the port lower aft mast support.

We basically rigged up some support wires and crossed every digit in sight. The severity of the situation didn't sink in until much later. At the time we were all too busy just getting on with it, and when you're in the thick of it, that's all you really can do.

There were numerous sail changes and reefs to be made, and the extreme exertion brought my ribs back out of their hibernation. I was severely exhausted and in dire need of sleep by 1800. The only slight comfort was that we were hanging in there at seventh place and would improve because of the Pyrrhic victory over the hapless *Concert*. *Motorola*, as the nearest boat to *Concert*, halted their race to lend assistance. In the end they transferred fuel to them so they could motor to the Chatham Isles for repairs.

The following day we learned that *Time And Tide* also had to put into the Chatham Isles with an injured crew member. We also heard on the grapevine that other boats had also discovered rigging problems. It began to dawn on us that *Concert* had simply been the unlucky one to get hit first. We were all in disgrace, it was just that *Concert* had been the one who had to take the rap. *Heath Insured* fell back a long way, and we made serious inroads on *Motorola*'s and *Global*'s territory – all because of rigging problems.

But there was humour even in the midst of all this drama. *Nuclear Electric* picked up another craft that was in the area, *Amelia*, on the chat show. It turned out that this was an American woman in a thirty-seven-foot boat going around the world on her own! It made us all feel very small. But at least we could comfort ourselves with the fact the way we were doing it was at least partly sane!

The next day was cold and grey, but a lot calmer. At 1200 Ian went up the mast to check the rigging, and we changed our clocks to GMT − 9 in the afternoon as the sun broke out and bathed us all in warmth. It was quite unbelievable after all the carnage of the night before. And, to cap our new-found feeling of wellbeing, we had moved up to sixth place.

On the 21st a gale was forecast, so at 0100 we reefed the main and hoisted the staysail. Everyone was more apprehensive than with a normal gale warning because we knew that Hurricane Fergus wasn't far away! By 0800 the gale still hadn't hit, and Margot was filming a BBC session on deck with the on-board video. At 1300 Tim received a major soaking near the hatch. He was making such a habit of this that we started calling him Rigsby (Leonard Rossiter in *Rising Damp*!) By midnight there was still no gale in sight, but Richard suddenly and mysteriously wanted to test the boat's boltcutters. He wouldn't tell us why and we were all speculating what the reason could possibly be. We thought that either he knew something we didn't, or the strain of it all was finally getting to him.

On the 22nd we realised how lucky we had been to get an extra day's reprieve. The 21st had been the classic lull before the storm and now we were really in for it. Storm conditions hit us early in the morning and we had to hoist the storm jib and staysail and put three reefs in the mainsail. From 0600 to 1200 we had extremely heavy seas, and winds were reaching 50 knots across the deck again. I received faxes from my brother John and his wife Mary, and also from Kate and the girls and these managed to cheer me up for a short time. But the conditions were so threatening that I couldn't let my mind stray too far for too long.

The next day there were loads more Christmas messages. This was a major boost to me at the time, and I don't think that the people who sent them ever realised how much they were appreciated. So I'm telling them now! Ian went up the mast to sort out our rigging problems so far as possible, and he was the hero of the day as he was also leading the bowman challenge at the time. Just as we were finishing our operations, *Toshiba* reported problems with their rigging. So, once again, we were ahead of the game.

All of a sudden it was Christmas Eve, and I hadn't even noticed it creeping up on me. It was very eerie and strange to be sitting where

I was, yet knowing that back home in England everybody was getting excited about the following day's festivities. Faxes were flying all over the place. I sent one to Kate and the girls, and numerous others arrived for the whole crew, including greetings from Regent and CU West End.

I was on early watch from 0600 to 1200, and we had an excellent spell of sailing on a south-westerly course, averaging 10.40 knots. This was just what we needed. Madeleine made some decorations for the galley and the chart table, although I must say they did look very out of place given the circumstances! We were still lying sixth but making good progress, with excellent helming during the night watches. We were right on course and motoring along at an average of 10.50 knots.

Christmas Day arrived at last, and Madeleine insisted on staying up until 0300 making a stollen cake for breakfast! I sent a fax to Kate and the girls to say that at 0600 when I was up on watch, Santa still hadn't been to visit! The fax was returned almost immediately, and it was strangely cheering to be in such intimate contact with them – however remotely.

The morning saw us continuing our good sailing, although in fact we lost out to *Pause To Remember*, who managed to edge seven miles ahead because of an unlucky (for us) adverse current. The Christmas meal perhaps doesn't sound like much by landlubbers' standards, but it was a feast to us at the time: curry dip, tuna nibbles, vacuum-packed chicken in sauce, cranberry sauce, dried mixed vegetables and sweetcorn and boiled potatoes, with Christmas cake (courtesy of Madeleine) and chocolates to follow. The big surprise was champagne and brandy, provided by Richard. (We weren't so much surprised by the existence of these luxuries, as by the fact that Richard had managed to preserve them unopened for thirty-six days!)

Bransom and Neil actually volunteered to helm while the rest of us enjoyed ourselves, professing not to have much Christmas spirit in them anyway (Bah! Humbug!) Well, their loss was our considerable gain. CU had recorded Christmas messages on tape and sent them out to us, and Sean caught the whole proceedings on video, including a Christmas ditty I had somehow managed to find time to compose. Some of the rhymes and metres were very strained, and I thought about tidying it up into a more polished offering for presentation here now that I have the leisure. But in the end I thought I would leave it as it is. After all, it gives you an authentic taste of what passes for humour after a month at sea!

## Christmas Day Ditty – 2nd Leg Blues

*Christmas is coming and Richard's getting fat*
*Please put nineteen grand into Chay Blyth's hat*
*If you haven't got the money then a mast will do*
*If you're Concert and haven't got one*
*Then God\* bless you.*

*Christmas day on board CU*
*Means only one thing, and that's beef stew*
*But if you find you've bitten off more than you can chew*
*Then let's take a seasonal look at the motley crew.*

*Richard the skipper is renowned for his belching*
*And a little-known secret is the quality of his felching.*
*He thinks the girls find him sexy when he gets a little randy*
*But they leave him with his mast up and a fizzy hand shandy!*

*Then come the watch leaders, Tim and Neil*
*And who can separate them for their sex appeal?*
*Neil wants to learn the art of sailing a soling*
*But the only problem is that he can't tie a bowline.*

He should listen to Tim who certainly looks set
that's because he spends most of his time getting wet.
Lars's forte is in the galley
where he combines his talents for mixed veg and banana flummery.
We find them a bore
but he insists that we eat them from the floor.

Bransom the yank has made it plain that he doesn't like curry
so why does he still continue to worry.
Perhaps that's because he can't find the right meal
you know the one we asked Ocean Rover to steal.

Now we come to Sean who's a dab hand in the galley
what a shame about his eye but I'm sure he is learning
as he is about to give up his career on boats
and return to London's Burning.

Then there's Ian, Mr Tall, who's our number one bowman.
I'm sorry, Sid, but for you he's a bad omen
When he's up on deck I must award him the banner
And when he's down below he could well be bedding Anna!

Talking of Sid, alias David Shanks
He's made a career out of playing with hanks.
His only problem is when Richard says, "Helm it!"
That's when he's better off below banging on his helmet!

Next comes Clevor Trever the professor with the mostest
Who spent his time in Rio with a blind blonde hostess
Who's allegedly hung like Errol Flynn
but you had better ask the blind (blonde) woman in Rio who says it's
    the size of a pin!

Then we have my two flat mates, Margot and Madeleine who always
    want rumpy pumpy
although I won't touch one of them because she is always grumpy.
As for the other one she's known for her trim
but I promise not to tell Nick that's she's now living in sin.

Well what about Eileen (Elaine)
who drinks everything but Pony?
it's a shame that we have got to wait until Wellington
to get trashed with Tony.

Last but not least we have the lovely Claire
who makes a habit of washing her hair
She sits at the fax at the end of her wick
that's because she's continually being sick.

Well the ending is tricky
what we really need is Vicki.
We could rely on her to fabricate the story
and then communicate it to Chay who will have all the guts and take
    all the glory.

It's left to Chay to wish us a happy Yuletide as the ghost of Christmas
past and to pay us the money for a new flaming mast!

But the final word must go to Nick whose renowned for his Christmas
wit but I know the crew think he's really a shit, I mean hit!

*Belief in God is common in sailing circles, and He is generally believed
to have been made incarnate at about this time of year in the person of
Chay Blyth. No form of ritual execution has yet succeeded, despite many
attempts.

When all the revelry had died down, the same thought seemed to strike all of us at once. What the Hell were we all doing here on Christmas Day, thousands of miles from anywhere, in one of the most dangerous and uncomfortable places on the globe? Many of us asked the question—some out loud to our companions, some to ourselves. But, no matter how many times and in however many ways the question was posed, none of us could give an answer. Shaking our heads in bafflement, we set about our tasks once again.

On the 26th I was back with good old Mother, and made some excellent (though I say it myself) bread. After all our good work we slipped back to eighth, losing out to *Pause To Remember* and *Nuclear Electric*. We were all feeling disappointed, particularly after the relative highs of the previous days, but at 0600 we had overhauled *Nuclear Electric* once again and were gaining on *Pause To Remember*. This was exciting stuff. We all felt that we gained a true sense of what the excitement was all about at times like these, when we were in tangible competition with other boats. But of course, for so much of the time, all the boats were separated from each other by comparatively large distances. At 1000 there were 666 miles to go to reach land. By 1800 we had overhauled *Pause To Remember* again, to everybody's immense relief. We changed our clocks once more to GMT − 10.

On the night of the 27th, the temperature started to climb again. I felt great, and got out of my sleeping bag for the first time in four weeks. Nevertheless, I couldn't get to sleep. I lay awake listening to the blessed sounds of my family's voices on the Christmas tape. Then I played one of my favourite CDs − *The Lamb Lies Down On Broadway* by Genesis, from the Peter Gabriel era.

At 0600 I was back on watch and our clocks went back to GMT − 11. We were sailing directly along a correct course, but the wind was only light. At 1100 we tried the light spinnaker, but there wasn't enough wind for it to take. I was bowman − Ian had been rested after his magnificent spell – but I certainly carried on with excellent, not to say inspired, sail changes!

Our instruments showed that we would arrive in Wellington about a month later if the wind carried on as it did! It was just like arriving in Rio, but here we still had over 500 miles to go. So much for Windy Wellington. To come 8,247 miles and then hit a snag like this was very frustrating. Our instruments were showing an ETA of 7th January. "Which year?" somebody quipped. It might even have been me.

For hours we were literally just slopping along. At one point we were travelling one mile in one hour! We lost out once again to *Pause To Remember*, sending us back to 7th place. Hurricane Fergus was apparently still around – where was he when we needed him? At midnight we jumped a day to GMT – 12.

On the 30th we were in sixth place with only 321 miles to go. We were leading *Pause To Remember* again and had five miles' grace. At 0600 we were able to hoist a racing rig again: number 1, staysail and full main. *Pause To Remember* was gaining slightly, and our radar showed that she was now 4.9 miles behind. At 0700 we came to where east meets west. One minute we were as far west as we could be, and the next we were as far east as we could be. Very confusing!

We tuned in to the chat show and learned that *Group 4* had arrived already. So in my usual irreverent fashion, I logged on to the show (hosted by Heath Insured) and pretended to be the *Group 4* skipper. I reported our position as horizontal – in the bar at the Wellington Yacht Club!

As we approached Wellington we were at last able to get in some good speeds, clocking 10.9 knots at one stage. Our final worry was making it into port before the New Year. We had already spent Christmas at sea, and we didn't want to see 1996 out on board as well! In the end we made it just in time, at 2245. There was a huge party on the quay in Wellington. And, I have to admit, I had a few drinks!

# WELLINGTON STOPOVER

SO, THERE I was, putting into Wellington, half the Southern Ocean behind me, half of it ahead, still yawning at me like the maws of doom. Also behind me was the extraordinary personal mayhem of Rio—the internal psychological violence and physiological vandalism, the broken busted wreck of a life torn willingly from its moorings, dragging its anchor round the world with a crew of neuroses, anxieties and self-doubts and a leaden cargo of death wishes.

Now that wreck had limped into Wellington looking for further damage.

At this stage in writing up my adventures, it seems fitting to pause and reflect on the history of this book. When I landed in Wellington I felt the need to take my bearings, to draw up a schedule of dilapidations, to quantify the damage and see what could be done to get things halfway seaworthy before resuming the voyage. Similarly, at this stage in my account I feel the need to say a few words about my approach to the narrative.

When I first decided to write this book I was sitting in the middle of the Southern Ocean in the worst weather I have ever experienced, expecting to get drowned any second. I think to a large degree making the decision to write the book was as much an attempt at life affirmation as anything else. I mean, when you are facing possible death, it certainly helps to be able to focus on a rosy future beyond the current horizon where you will have the leisure to do things like write and publish books. And that becomes even more true when, because of the immediate and incessant violence of the surroundings, *possible* death appears to your fevered imagination much closer to *probable* death.

At that time, I suppose that I was simply thinking of writing up my log. Just telling the story like it was. But as time has gone on, I have come to the conclusion that the only way to tell it like it was is not to tell it like it was. I mean, if I ask you, the reader, the seeker after truth, if that is what you really want, you will probably say yes without thinking about it. But then, if you do think about it, you will realise that the answer must surely be no. Do you seriously demand a back-breaking record of every second we spent languishing in the Doldrums? Would you like me to serve up details of every reconstituted McDougall's meal that we consumed? Having been through them all in real life, I certainly would prefer not to go through any of them physically again, and mentally my appetite for them isn't that great either. I don't want to go through any more of them than is necessary to give you an idea of how it was.

In any event, even if you wanted that sort of account and I wanted to give it to you, it wouldn't be possible. I have read accounts of adventures where the authors have claimed to be true to life because they have not used any "time compression". Well, if that's what you particularly look for in a narrative, I'm afraid that I can't even begin to comprehend how to give it to you. I would have to write a book that took ten months to read while you gave it your undivided attention both day and night. I mean, seriously: if I'm going to write about a ten-month adventure in a book that takes a few hours to read then it stands to reason: some sort of compression has gone on somewhere!

But suppose that was what I wanted to do, to let you have a faithful blow-by blow account of the experience of what it was like to be jogging along on this little sailing trip, skipping gaily over the water like a stone, I still couldn't do it. Whatever I do, it will only be a tale from my angle, from my point of view. And I have to tell you, if you haven't worked it out by now, my point of view was pretty distorted, deranged and dislocated, torn, tattered and torched, fractured, fragmented and frankly flambéed, to say the least.

So that is what this book is like. It is as fragmented as my own recollection of events. That means that while at sea you will only get as much of my experience as my untidily-written, water-damaged log will allow me to reconstruct. And, necessarily, you will only get filtered detail relating to the most interesting events, and you will only get it written up with the kindly benefit of hindsight and the rosy glow of experience gained from the luxury of observing one's actions from the distance of history. The reality is that ocean-going race teams cannot afford the luxury of dedicated scribes who will sit in the galley recording a balanced account of events as they happen. They can only afford full-time crew members, who in their spare time tend to be slightly more tired than the average runner at the end of a weekend double hill-marathon. Such people are often less than willing to forfeit a proportion of their precious sleeping time to committing details of the last watch's most dramatic moments to paper for posterity.

So that's the problem with telling the story of the seafaring bits. There are long stretches where nothing happens – but you don't want to hear about them. And then during the exciting bits that you do want to hear about I was so busy dealing with the situation that the last thing on my mind was siting down and writing about it.

But the problems associated with the landfaring bits are, if anything, even greater—or they certainly are in my case. That is because, whenever I set foot on land, I would stop having to deal with a sea of water, whose effects were largely external, and would start having to cope with a sea of alcohol, whose waves hammered mercilessly on my psychological coastline, eroding all semblance of reality.

So, inevitably, people are going to ask, "Are the things you wrote about in that book true?" And I'm going to have to say, "Yes," or,

"No," or, "Sometimes," or, "Maybe," or, "It depends on your point of view," or, "It depends on your definition of truth."

I mean, look at it this way. The legal system is presumably supposed to be a system for getting at the truth. People have arguments about things – about who gets the assets in a divorce case, about who is responsible for damage in a negligence case, about who caused a serious road accident. And yet talk to each party in a case that goes into a court, and they will appear absolutely convinced of the validity of their argument. The wife complains that her husband was unfaithful, but he complains that the atmosphere at home was so hostile that he could only find comfort elsewhere. The shipping contractor is blamed for losing a cargo when it falls off the ship into the sea, but claims that the responsibility for seeing that it was secured belonged to some other agency. One driver says it was the other's fault because he was drunk, while the second driver says the first was speeding in a stolen car. And then a witness appears on the scene and points out that neither appeared to have noticed that the traffic lights at the junction weren't working. And so it goes on. Every story has at least two angles and probably a lot more, and that is what happens in a supposedly sensible legal system. How much more is the potential for confusion when we're just talking about trying to remember what happened during a series of drunken outings? As Pontius Pilate famously remarked before shaking his head in perplexity and symbolically washing his hands, "What is truth?" To which his interlocutor, equally famously, made no reply. I rest my case.

For those of you who demand and must have an answer, yes, this story is true. Absolutely and incontrovertibly true. But, if the notion is not too paradoxical for you, I have to qualify that by saying that it is *my version* of the truth. Because it is my version, it can be absolutely true in a way that absolute truth cannot. And, since I do not even attempt to claim any monopoly on the truth, it is also incontrovertible. My vision of the truth is big enough to allow anybody else to come along and set up an alternative version – as long as I retain my right to tell it my way.

Or perhaps there's another way of looking at it, and that is that I am telling that part of the truth which I can see. Distorted though it is through the bottom of a brandy-stained glass and a crazy-paving paranoia, the lineaments are there. Other people who were there may be able to provide other pieces of the picture, to build up a more complete record…but in the end what the hell? All I'm trying to do is tell my story. And it's while I'm doing this that I realise what a heroic – and futile – occupation historians are engaged in when trying to find out, say, what happened to the Princes in the Tower, or who the Man in the Iron Mask was, or even the true facts about the last days of Princess Diana.

But please understand that I regard myself as having discharged my sacred duty, even though I have willingly mixed up the geographical locations of certain events and otherwise taken liberty with trivial facts such as names of both places and people. Sometimes this has resulted from my complete inability to remember accurately, and sometimes from a well-meaning desire to protect the guilty.

So we hit Wellington, and, as usual, some heavy drinking and high jinks went on. But mainly this stopover was marked by peace and serenity, with Kate coming over to visit me, and Richard absorbed in the process of working out his own complex life. So this seems like a good opportunity to fill in a bit of history, and give a bit of background to the whole chaotic mess of relationships that entangled the crews of the various boats whenever we made landfall. The story takes us all the way back to Southampton, before we even set sail…

I had just got back from a training sail with some other crew members and Andy Hindley, who eventually skippered *Save the Children* (the boat affectionately known as "*Kids*"). Sid was there and so was Pete Calvin of *Nuclear Electric* ("*Nuke*"), one of the notorious Calvin brothers and a habitual sparring partner of mine. We had made straight for our favourite Tapas bar and had settled in for a cosy all-day drinking session. But you know how these things are, one drink after another gets a bit monotonous and you start looking for ways to liven things up. In this case I had brought one of my own games to the party which I had picked up on a football trip to Magaluf just before the training sail: "snorting" Tequila!

This was an idea (admittedly a very bad one) that I had picked up from the Warrington Rugby League side, who had happened to be in Magaluf at the same time as us. We got involved in quite a few of their wind-ups, leg-pulls, take-offs, rag-legs, pull-ons, push-ups and take-downs, one of which had been this extraordinary habit of Tequila-snorting. Now, I don't know a lot about the physiology involved, but I imagine that the main reason why people snort cocaine, for example, rather than sprinkling it on their popcorn and eating it is that it is more efficiently absorbed through the nasal membranes. And if that is true of cocaine then it is presumably true of alcohol. Such logic, or something very like it, presumably passed through my mind the first time it was proposed to me. But then again, perhaps not. In fact it's probably more likely that it just seemed like a mad thing to do and so I did it. So far as I can remember (and that is not very well, but then that's part of the point, isn't it?) it did an extremely efficient job of getting the alcohol into my bloodstream, and simply accelerated what for me is a normal process. For me it was just an efficient (if uncomfortable) way of getting the job done. But there was one rugby player who tried it and came off very badly. I had never fully understood the meaning of being "pole-axed" before, but this guy demonstrated it very neatly for me. Following his "snort", his eyes simply glazed over. It was just as if someone had switched off the current. The pupils dilated, the eyes themselves fixed momentarily on a distant point and then went slack and rolled upwards. Then he keeled over and fell off his chair. Nobody seemed to take any notice and as far as I know he's lying there to this day.

Anyway, back to Southampton, where I was hell-bent for some reason on going all out to kill myself. "Snorting" seemed as good a way as any. I don't know whether I was worried about the race, or about how work would carry on while I was away, or how they would get on at home without me, but I was taking the alcoholic ostrich approach and burying my head in the blood and sand (well, actually snakebites, but it wouldn't have gone with the ostrich). After getting thoroughly poisoned with the "bites" I started showing Sid how to do the snorting trick. You get a straw, insert one end into the drink, the other end into one of your nostrils, close off the other nostril and inhale sharply. I did one to show him how it worked, then he had a go. He sat back to savour the effect and…blood started gushing from his nose. The same thing happened with a lot of other people. Whether it was something to do with the state of mind, or the level of blood alcohol, my nose held out while everybody else's seemed to start haemorrhaging.

Eventually, however, the inevitable happened. I keeled over and was duly carried back to the boat by Andy. When we met again the next morning, he took me aside for a solemn chat. He took me into the galley, shut the door and sat me down.

"Nick," he said.

"Andy," I replied, trying to suppress the grin on my face and failing miserably. (It is an almost pathological condition with me – I simply can't take anything seriously.)

"Do you know what you were doing last night?"

"Not after passing out in the Tapas bar, no. It's a complete blank."

"Well, I'll tell you. Now remember, I've seen a lot of sailors, and I know what I'm talking about. So listen very carefully: I'm telling you right now just as sure as you're sat there grinning at me, you're not going to make it even to the start of this race. You've got a big red switch in your head with 'self-destruct' written all over it in large letters, and you've got it continually jammed in the 'on' position. You were up half the night visiting the toilet, and whenever you took a walk you were supplementing it with ear-splitting renditions of Gary Glitter songs." Here he started giving his own versions in a sarcastic parody of me parodying the sequinned one: "Rock and rooooo-oll, rock and roll. D'you wanna be in my gang, my gang, my gang, d'you wanna be in my gang, oh yeah! I love, you love, you love me too love, I love you love meeee! Do you wanna touch, Do you wanna touch, do you wanna touch me there?" He stopped and gazed at me wide-eyed, as if to ask whether I was registering how mad my behaviour had been.

"Well, Andy, that's perfectly reasonable. We all have our moments after a night on the town…"

"Well Dave didn't think it was very funny. He came that close…" he held up a pinched thumb and forefinger "…that close to laying you out. The only reason he didn't is that he knows you quite well and understands that you're not doing it to be annoying. Unfortunately it's just the way you are."

I winced. True, this was a bit of a sore point with me. The Calvin brothers (Dave, Pete and Mike) were notorious good-time boys for whom I had enormous respect. Mike was a journalist with the *Daily Telegraph* at the time and had just won the Sports Writer of the Year Award. As things turned out Dave eventually pulled out of the going on the race. I really hated the idea of upsetting people like this, but there didn't seem to be anything I could do about it. It was just in my nature.

But I really am at a loss to explain it. I suppose I simply have a Jekyll and Hyde character. Anyone who knows me will tell you that I am a completely non-confrontational person in normal life. Friendly, always ready with a joke, mild-mannered to the point of self-effacement. And yet, I suppose, once I have filled up with enough heavy fuel then I build up such a momentum that I just don't notice when a situation is turning nasty. I carry on worrying at a joke long after people have ceased to find it funny. For example, I remember upsetting two other skippers during the run-up to the race (apart from, of course, our own dear leader Richard Merriweather, whom I used to upset routinely just as a daily exercise to make sure I wasn't losing my touch). Once was while we were in Freddie's Bar in Plymouth after a qualifying sail. We had got back from the race, the course of which had been the equivalent of the annual Fastnet race, and settled in to our usual drinking pattern. I got talking to Richard Tudor, whom I didn't know at the time but who ended up as the *Nuclear Electric* skipper, and my wind-up instincts began to kick in pretty well immediately. I could tell that here was someone who was going to rise to my bait – although that makes it sound more calculating than it was. As I say, the process was much closer to instinct than anything else. I started by asking him what sort of qualities you needed to be a captain, and when the quality of leadership was mentioned I latched onto it like a lamprey:

"Yes, Richard, that's what I thought. But, forgive me, how does that allow you to qualify? I mean, don't get me wrong – you seem like a nice enough guy – but a leader? I mean, particularly with women. You have to remember there are quite a lot of women in the crews, and surely you need at least a dash of sex appeal to go into the mix…"

And so on. You get the idea. He got more and more heated, responding to each of my points as if he was taking it all completely seriously, but I was just carried away with the joy of the wind-up. I swear I didn't realise it at the time, but I was told later that he had been on the point of laying me out, and it was only the intervention of two of his crew, Pete Calvin and Mark Johnstone that saved me. They stepped in behind the scenes and explained that I was OK, but that I just couldn't help doing this kind of thing, which was (and is) absolutely true.

A similar incident occurred in Southampton with Mark Lodge. He knew he had been appointed *Motorola* skipper and was obviously chuffed about it. Once again, I got my pins out to burst his bubble.

I pointed out that he had crewed on the last race under Richard, our skipper, and asked how he could therefore hope to beat us. I even went so far as to suggest that he shouldn't have been there at all. Once again, my talent for touching the right nerve produced a heated reaction, and I can honestly say that it is the only time I have seen him lose his cool.

As far as the little chat with Andy Hindley went, however, I think I can safely say I had the last laugh. The record shows that I confounded his prediction in fine style: not only did I make it to the start of the race, but we were the only core crew to complete every leg of the race! I saw him recently down in Southampton while we were both there watching the start of the latest race. He was on a boat putting out into the Solent; I was on a gin & Jag vessel close behind. As we passed them I gave him a wave:

"Hi Andy! I'm still here!"

At about the same time, however, there was another incident that really did set me thinking about whether I should continue to be involved with the race. Perhaps it was all blown out of proportion, but at the time it really did set me back on my heels. I think it is the only time I ever seriously thought about withdrawing, in spite of all the rational arguments against taking part and the frank hostility to the idea that I faced at home. It all hinged on an incident of urination.

Surely I am not the only person who has urinated in strange places? Have we not all been caught short and been forced into an embarrassing situation, or done something silly in the middle of the night when not fully *compos mentis*? I know a very good friend of mine who went out for a meal with a lady to whom he was very attracted, and they ended up going back to her place and having a fantastic night's lovemaking before falling contentedly asleep. Imagine his embarrassment when he found himself waking up on her landing and realising that he was sending a merrily splashing yellow waterfall down her beautiful

Axminster stair carpet. He worked out afterwards that he had unconsciously navigated to the equivalent spot relative to the bed where the toilet stood in his own house – but that was little consolation either to her or him! Another friend tells me that he once awoke in the middle of the night after a heavy drinking session and found that he was literally *paralytic*! He was simply too drunk to move, and the reason he had woken up was that he urgently needed to empty his bladder. There was nothing for it but to let rip there and then, lying in his bed. The only consolation was that he had drunk so much that his urine was practically pure water anyway. And my own dear departed father got so keyed up about finding our house and being on time when visiting us once, that he had no choice but to wet himself in the car. Kate very kindly washed his clothes during the visit and had them ready in time for him when he left!

I have heard other stories where people have mistaken a wardrobe, a waste paper basket and a dog's bed (occupied, unfortunately, by a large and noisy dog) for a urinal while half-asleep and confused in the middle of the night in a strange house. But all this anecdotal wriggling is simply to try and alleviate my embarrassment at my own misdemeanour, about to be set down here for the first time ever (in my knowledge at any rate).

It must have been about February or March, when we had all been assigned to our final crews. We had just got back to Southampton from either the training or the qualifying sail. The idea was that we would all stay on our boats with our crews in order to get used to each other's nasty habits and foster some sort of team spirit and "bonding". However, Sean and I were bonding so well together on our own that we decided to book into a hotel for the night. There was no élitist motive to this; we simply felt like spending a night in a comfortable hotel instead of on the boat. I understand some of the crew were annoyed about this, but although the expectation was that everybody would stay on the boats, it certainly wasn't a three-line whip. Anyway, the upshot was that we booked into the De Vere. But then, true to form, we got so steamed in Southampton anyway that we never managed to find the way back to the hotel and ended up in the boat anyway! I woke up in a hyper state in the middle of the night and vaguely remember going to the galley for some reason, forgetting why I was there, and just pulling down my zip and urinating all over the place. Then, for some inexplicable reason, I decided I wanted to go and stay in the hotel after all. I went haring off at top speed through the town and eventually reached the hotel at about four in the morning.

The next morning I woke up and remembered nothing (the details above only came back to me after I had made a concerted effort to remember). I had a chat with Sean and then went back to the boat, in all innocence, to pick up some gear. When I got there I found a note on the galley door, signed by most of the crew, basically saying, "Nick, get your f★★★ing act together!" (Their swear word, not mine!) "Do you realise what you did last night? You've been down here in the middle of the night pissing in the galley." A lot of the censure came from Lars, who was complaining that I had urinated in his boots! The note ended with an ultimatum to get into the galley, clear it up, and, above all, sort myself out.

I was truly upset, because at that stage I could not remember a thing about the previous night. I duly went in and penitently cleaned the galley from top to bottom, flashes of the offending activity slowly coming back to mind in the meantime. Then I left the boat guiltily, with my tail very much between my legs. I had to admit to myself that I had got completely out of my head, and as I gradually pieced together all the fragments I realised how much I must have upset my crewmates.

As I was milling aimlessly round Southampton, seriously questioning whether I should pull out of the race, I ran across Vicki who also seemed to be at a loose end. We repaired to the Tapas bar and I had a serious heart-to-heart with her. I started out by saying that I was going to write personally to each of the crew, apologising and telling them I was withdrawing from the race. But she was absolutely amazing. There was no way she would even hear of me doing such a stupid thing. She put it all in perspective and told me that if that was the worst thing that happened throughout the whole adventure then I would be very lucky. Certainly an apology was in order, but running away from the situation was completely the wrong thing to do.

She was absolutely right. I owe my whole fantastic adventure to her because without that chat I could easily have given up and thrown in the towel. When I got back to the office I sent a personal letter to everybody who had signed the note, apologising and explaining everything. I told them all about how their note had made me think seriously about what I was doing; how I had been on the point of giving up but Vicki had got me over it; how I was more than ever determined now to carry on. Most people accepted the situation and, to their great and eternal credit, wrote me back some very encouraging and supportive letters in reply.

It was only later that I realised how right Vicki had been about putting things in perspective. Lots of these hiccoughs were going to happen to everybody and we just couldn't waste time getting worked up about them all. For instance, once I was sleeping in with Claire, and she kicked me out for snoring. I had to go and sleep in the sail locker, which was extremely uncomfortable. Claire went whinging to Richard about it, but he told her in no uncertain terms to shut up and get on with it, because if she couldn't put up with that then she ought to be at home tucked up in bed with her teddy. It is literally true: worse things *do* happen at sea! Getting screwed up about things is par for the course and it happens to everybody.

I suppose the last watershed before leaving was the Grosvenor House Leaving Ball. I got completely blotto with Sean and Eileen's partner Tony. In the end Sean had to give me a fireman's lift into the taxi.

Mabel, who was a big driving force at the time for CU, and who was eventually the person who managed to settle Kate down and get her to come to terms with my taking part in the race, came back home with us with her husband and stayed the night. She looked after me until I woke up the next morning in a right state.

I think it is fair to say that my state of mind was caused by several factors. First, attending the Leaving Ball had, I think, finally brought it home to me that I was in this up to my neck and there was no going back now. Although it is true that it didn't seem to affect the others as much, I realise now that very few of them had the same pressures on them as I had. Most of them were single, or at a quiet point in their lives where they had some time to take off and do something: "sabbatical sailors" is how I like to think of them. Whereas I was taking on this hazardous thing with a very full home and business life on my plate at the same time. For the many journalists among the crews, in fact, the whole thing was very much grist to their mill and could almost be seen as part of their work. And the other factor was that a lot of people just skipped on and off for a leg or two just for the experience, whereas I could see little point in getting involved unless I was going to do the whole thing.

In fact, I do wonder whether this tendency for people to sign up for only one or two legs is cheapening the event and making it more like an adventure holiday than anything else. The original ideal of dedicated crews fighting it out for ten months while struggling first to build and then maintain coherence in their team has gone largely by the board. But then again, I suppose this was inevitable as the race began to gain a higher profile and became more and more commercial. The organisers have to strike a balance between making the race accessible to a wide enough range of people while maintaining a respectable level of difficulty.

One thing I know for sure is that Sean would have stayed the course with me had he remained fit. It was my one greatest sadness throughout the experience that a friend whom I had come to rely on as being completely true and dependable should have suffered a serious injury that took him out of the race after the second leg. I will always remember the time just before leaving when I just broke down and cried with the strain of it all and he and Shirley were there to lend me their broad shoulders. He let me know that I wasn't alone; that there were about 200 other people going through similar feelings and that he was one of them. That day I learned that Sean was someone I could rely on: someone whom, without being melodramatic, I could trust with my life.

One of the greatest times I had with Sean before leaving was the naming ceremony at St Katharine's Dock. We sailed up the Thames into London, past Tower Bridge and into the dock, where the LWT TV team were waiting to interview us – live! The plan was that they would interview Sean and have a basic discussion with him about naming the boat and so on, which they did. But then at the end of the interview Sean said, "And before we go, we would just like to show you what true commitment to the race is really all about…" upon which I stood up, turned my back to the camera, whipped my trousers down, bent over and displayed to the gawping London audience a fine pair of examples of the tattooist's art. I had already had "BT Global Challenge 1996-1997 Round The World Yacht Race" tattooed on my right buttock some months previously in Lloret de Mar, and a few days before the broadcast I had completed the job with the addition of a fine BT horn player logo, resplendent in true blue and red livery.

The clip was shown on early and late evening news, which was the first Kate had seen of the new version. She was devastated. She had always looked on the first tattoo as my being "branded". I was possessed by the spirit of the race and she basically understood that she wasn't going to get me back until it was over. This second tattoo was simply confirmation of that state of affairs. The impact on our friends and neighbours was predictably huge. Most people knew me as a sedate, middle-class insurance broker who wore smart suits to work and who certainly didn't have any tattoos on his buttocks, and, even if he did, he kept them to himself and didn't bare them on national television!

The last little bit of fun that we had before setting off was the "Man O Man!" competition. This was a kind of spoof Miss World-type contest to find the hunkiest man among the crews. Much like the Miss World contestants have to show themselves proficient in wearing evening dress and swimsuits and in making polite small talk with the compère, the Man O Man! contestants had to show their prowess in being able to drink beer (a) in large quantities and (b) at high speed, remove a woman's bra one-handed in the shortest possible time and…the final test of skill…compose the ultimate chat-up line!

Vicki thought I was going to go all out and win, but I couldn't take it seriously. (And anyway, I don't think we were meant to! If we were then it all begins to look rather sad!) So I decided to lose deliberately by coming up with a true foot-in-mouth line that would hand the competition to the man I really thought should win (and who in fact did in the end): Paul Hathaway, a deaf crew member from *Time and Tide*. So I put a lot of thought into coming up with the following lines:

Do you work for DHL? I thought I saw you checking out my package.

I may not be the best looking guy in here, but I'm the only one talking to you.

I'm an ornithologist and I'm looking for a Big Breasted Bed Thrasher. Have you seen one around?

I'm fighting the urge to make you the happiest woman on earth tonight.

Oh, I'm sorry, I thought it was a Braille name tag.

Is that a ladder in your stockings or is it the stairway to heaven?

You may not be the best looking girl here, but beauty is only a light switch away.

Are those real?

If it's true that we are what we eat, then you could be me by the morning.

You know, if I were you, I'd have intercourse with me.

Those clothes would look great in a crumpled heap on my bedroom floor.

Do you believe in love at first sight or should I walk past again?

Hi, I'm Mr Right. Somebody said you were looking for me. Can I buy you a drink or would you rather just have the money?

But eventually I settled on:

"Facially you're really attractive, but if you lost a couple of stone you'd be even better!"

I had in fact already tried this out on Suze after our modelling stint together – so I knew about the deadly effect it could have on women. Needless to say, she recognised it and thought it should have won!

So that brief history gives you some idea of the context in which my stopover adventures should be seen, and perhaps provides a flavour of the mayhem that was in store whenever the BT Global Challenge crews hit town!

One of the first things that happened in Wellington was that I had a drink with Pete Calvin. But the only thing is that it is impossible to have *a* drink with Pete Calvin. It's like the alcoholic's dearest wish – to be able to go into a pub on the way home and "have a drink". The truth being that if the alcoholic does succumb to the temptation, he won't get home probably for days.

What I'm saying is that this guy simply doesn't deal in singles. If you have a drink with Pete Calvin then you are more than likely signing up for a marathon session.

So it was that we found ourselves in a bar in the marina area, probably Shed 7, although I was in no state to be able to swear to it. It was a typically riotous night. The Paris St Germain football team was there for some reason and had reverted to childhood and was playing "Pin the Tail on the Donkey" but with the subtle twist of using Richard as the donkey! At one point there was a particularly attractive lady who went to the bar and ordered a baguette. When the barmaid asked her what she would like in it, Pete, who had been salivating at the other end of the bar, whipped his dick out and laid it on the bar shouting, "Make a sandwich out of that!" His suggestion was coolly ignored. Shortly afterwards I asked him if he wanted another drink. He was obviously disappointed at the lack of success of his "Man O Man" chat-up line, to say nothing of being completely off his tits, and said, quite sensibly, "No I've got to go now," and suited the action to the word. (Incidentally, there were stories later that night of him stripping off and dancing naked along *Group 4*'s boom, which made me feel no end better about my "pissing in the galley" incident.) But again I cannot swear to the location and now I think about it, it seems more likely that this happened in Southampton before the race!) Wherever it was, I stuck it into him mercilessly the next morning, in my highly talented and typically annoying fashion. Yet again, I just knew how to wind him up.

His brother Mike was doing an interview for the local newspaper, and so I said to him, "I'm afraid your Nancy boy brother couldn't hack it last night and left early"! Mike knew that this would be a major bone of contention with Pete, so he quietly took the notes and then went to consult with Pete about it. Naturally enough, Pete was not happy, and he came straight back to me with a challenge: a session at our adopted NZ pub, the Malthouse.

Now, this name strikes fear into hardened drinkers throughout Wellington. There are thirty-five different real ales lined up on the bar, one less than there are holes in a double round of golf. For this reason, local drinking lore has it that only one person has ever managed to go "two rounds" with the Malthouse in a twenty-four-hour stretch. If you think about it, it is just about manageable. You would have to pace yourself really carefully, aiming to consume a pint about every twenty minutes, but you would have to watch out for the strong beers: although some were normal strength, there were a few par 6, 7 and 8s on the course!

This was the Olympian challenge that Pete threw down to me. And, being an adventurous sort of guy, I was very happy to accept. We never got around to it, however and, like the drink with the Commodore in Rio, this is one that still remains in the future. If I may be allowed a little bit of pre-match speculation, I think the format of the match would favour my style. I am very much an autopilot drinker, and can sink beer virtually indefinitely. The only things that throw spanners into my works are the "silly drinks", as my father used to call them. He always said I'd be fine as long as I stuck to beer and stayed off the shorts – and that has been my experience in life. If I just drink beer, then I may get drunk but that is all I get. Whereas if I drink spirits I end up getting "hyper" like I did in Rio and all sorts of psychological chimeras start plopping out of the woodwork. I get bad hangover headaches and suffer badly from dehydration, but my experience is that if I just keep drinking then I never reach that stage. Anyway, Pete, if we ever meet up again in NZ, I'll be ready!

Some might say that I have an alcoholic lifestyle, but I don't think that is true. Certainly, I do drink heavily, but I am always in control and never let it wreck my work schedule. I'm always there in the morning when I'm supposed to be, and my drinking habits have never caused friction with my partner, Zena. Kate (my assistant at work rather than my wife) has been with me since we were at Wimpey together and she knows me inside out. She knows just how to describe my escapades and how to deal with anyone who might want to contact me. For example, there was one day when I was meeting a friend for lunch at one-thirty. We went out, started drinking, reminiscing and getting heavily involved, and then I was meeting Sean in the evening, so there was a seamless transition from the afternoon's drinking activities into the evening's. Kate (my wife, K1) had rung through at about two about some crisis at home, and I understand the conversation with Kate (my assistant, K2) went something like this:

K1:  So where is he then?

K2:  He's out at a meeting.

K1:  Yes, but what is he really doing?

K2:  Well, he's started early.

End of conversation. Both Kate's knew exactly what the other was saying – complete understanding!

The last time I got into a real state with drinking "silly drinks" was when I was coming back from a Whitley Bay football trip in 1999. My mother had just died and I felt terrible. It was a case of absinthe for elevenses – and at every other time of the day as well! I don't know why I latched onto absinthe – I'd never drunk it before and haven't since – but that day I literally drank the hotel dry of the stuff. That night I was carried back by the boys, put in the shower fully clothed and left to sober up. I woke up four hours later, went out and met the boys again and carried on. I was in a terrible state, in the old hallucination mode, with paranoia oozing from my pores as I walked the streets, flinching from people who I knew were out to get me. A gardener starting up a chainsaw to cut a down a tree was out to get me; a guy with dark glasses getting into a car was going to run me down; and I couldn't go to the toilet alone because there were people in there waiting to jump me. Not surprisingly, with all that to contend with, I arrived back in London a day late. And I haven't drunk stupid drinks since. I certainly wasn't taking drugs, unless someone was spiking my drinks. But I know that the sort of drinks I was drinking were plenty fuel enough to set my turbo-charged imagination alight, because they've done it before on so many occasions.

I was, of course, looking forward to Kate coming out to visit me. I really needed Kate as a stabilising influence – she would give me a bit of breathing space. When I am away from Kate, I drift. I have no anchor, no base. When she eventually did arrive, we organised a fantastic trip to the South Island along with Richard and Raff. It felt a bit like being in a 1960s' time warp hippy commune, because of all the flowers, faded jeans and cheesecloth shirts that people seemed to insist on wearing, but it gave us all a tranquil feeling of peace and love which is just what we needed. Even though we were right in the middle of it, the Southern Ocean seemed a million miles away.

Shortly after Kate left, I landed in another two of my "difficult" situations. The first was merely humorous, but the second was potentially dangerous. The first occurred when I went into a bar that was frequented by a lot of the crews. At the time I was sharing an apartment with Sid and Anna, and was sitting there chatting with them. While we were talking, a girl from another crew came in. I knew her slightly from our training sessions. She had obviously liked me then, but she was very young, so I never really thought about her affections as being serious – I looked on them as something more akin to a teenage schoolgirl crush than anything else. She came in, obviously a bit drunk, and slid by me, playfully removing my CU Wellington stopover hat. Later in the evening I went to the toilet and realised that she had never given it back, but thought what the hell, I'll get it back from her some time. I went back to the bar, and saw across the dance floor another girl who I thought at the time was one of her friends. Now this lady was really very attractive and I was certainly not averse to spending some time with her. So I used the other girl's disappearance as a pretext for going over and talking to her and we got on really well. One thing led to another, and I ended up walking her back to her hotel at three in the morning. We said goodbye and presumed we'd bump into each other again, but that was emphatically that.

Then I climbed the stairs to my apartment. I unlocked the front door and then opened my bedroom door. Immediately I felt as though somebody had dropped me into an episode of *Fawlty Towers*. In fact, I behaved very much as Basil might have done. I shut the door again, and walked in a kind of daze to the toilet. While I was washing my hands, I was thinking to myself, "It can't be. It's impossible. When I go back in everything will be back to normal." But when I did go back in, it wasn't. I have this memory of standing there opening and shutting my mouth just like Basil does, and saying nothing but, "But …", and "Where…?" and "How…?", and in the back of my mind I could see a very disturbing image of Kate, waving her finger at me in a fairly good imitation of Sybil.

In my bed, smiling in her sleep, was the cap-stealing girl from the bar, wearing, as far as I could deduce from the fact that I could see her clothes strewn all over my floor, little else besides my stopover hat. Stupidly, the first thought that came into my head was, "Oh, good, at least I've got that back again." My second, and much more sensible thought was, "How am I going to explain this to Sybil… I mean Kate!" In the end I crawled into bed very quietly beside her, trying not to disturb her. When we woke up the next morning I simply said goodbye and got her out of the door as fast as I could!

Her friend kept in touch with me though, and the night before we left she enticed me out for a meal in breach of curfew. The evening started off pleasantly enough, but pretty soon alarm bells started to ring. First of all, she started to tell me about this little problem she had: she desperately wanted to have children, but her husband was infertile. But apart from that she was fed up with him anyway, and she was set on me. She wanted me to jump ship, settle in NZ and let her make me happy! By this time I was looking for the way out, and then she started talking about her husband again: what a heavy training schedule he had and how he was never at home and always out with the team.

At this my blood froze. She had mentioned his name, and some pieces started to click into place in my head. I managed to get out:

"Wh-which team is that?"

"Why, the ********, of course!" and she mentioned a very famous Rugby Union team indeed. "Good God," I thought, "how do I manage to get into these situations?" I waved for the bill, paid, and got a cab to take us back to her hotel where I said a hasty goodbye. We never saw each other again.

In a sense one of the main problems of being in Wellington was the fact that there is a very strong sailing consciousness, and when people knew that we were connected with the race we were treated like gods, we could do no wrong. Everything was free, every door was opened, and a more than usual degree of bad behaviour was condoned. It was a bit like what Keith Richards says about being born under the star sign Sagittarius: "half man, half horse, with a licence to shit in the street!"

And I suppose I am a similar contradiction, half-sane, sedate, family man; half-tattooed nutter with a death wish and a talent for attracting troublesome women. But unfortunately with a licence only to try and clean the shit up before I step in it.

# Wellington to Sydney

WE SET off at 1025 on Sunday from Queen's Wharf with a great big hole in the boat. Fortunately, it didn't sink and in fact it started moving a lot faster, because we were a good deal lighter! Sorry, Sean, but you've got to laugh, haven't you? It's the only way to deal with the sadness of having to leave you behind after forging such an excellent relationship with you, both on and off board. So yes, there was a great big hole in the boat where you used to be, and because of the size of the hole, or at least the body that had previously filled it, the boat was a lot more manoeuvrable! Well, that's what Richard said, anyway!

But seriously, leaving Sean behind was in a sense almost worse than leaving the family back in Southampton. That might sound a bit disloyal to the family, but it isn't meant to be. When I left them, I was launching off into the unknown. I knew that I was leaving everything behind, but there was obviously no way that any of the family could physically be going with me. Sean, on the other hand, had been my number 1 companion thus far through the race. We had been through some close approximations to Hell together, and had come out the other side laughing. His good humour and down-to-earth attitude had seen me through many a dark moment, both aboard ship and on shore. And now I would be facing the rest of the voyage without him. There was no way anyone was ever going to replace him.

But there was no way out of the situation. Sean had damaged his back very badly in Wellington and there was no help for it. Any participation in strenuous activity was out of the question. We fervently hoped that he might be able to join the race again in Sydney but we would have to wait and see. This was to be a short leg, and if Sean were able to recover quickly then we would hopefully be able to look forward to a joyful reunion later. But in the meantime the crew, and particularly me personally, would have to find a way of getting on without him.

He had been my closest team mate even though we were on different watches. We got on so well socially that the relationship transcended the artificial on-board teams and divisions and we built up a close relationship both on and off the boat. In fact, I often wonder what might have become of me on the many occasions when I went AWOL from my head on shore. Sean just seemed to understand my need to get as far away from earth by drinking as much rocket fuel as possible, and he was always there to help following yet another tricky landing. As far as being on the boat was concerned, he operated in a similar way to me. Like me, and unlike everybody else, he never became seasick, and it was often the case during the worst weather that we were the only people who were fully functional. In the end I did manage to form a fairly good relationship with Alan who joined the crew in Sean's place, but it was never quite as natural.

So it was that once again I was setting out from port with mixed emotions. Just like back at Southampton, I was very nervous, with a gaping hole in the pit of my stomach that felt as though all the rats that had ever ended up in Richard's bed had been gnawing away at it. In reality, I was getting to know most of these rats very well. The only new one was the one that represented leaving Sean behind, but the others were now like old friends: the one that stood for Kate and the girls; the one that stood for Zena and our business back home; and, of course, the big, black, fat one that stood for all the horrors that still lay ahead in the other great Southern Ocean leg. I mean, on a purely selfish level, there wasn't much point in worrying about those two smaller rats if I couldn't deal with that other big one.

Shortly after setting out on this leg at 1300 we found ourselves in third place and going well. Sean accompanied us out of port on a New Zealand naval vessel, and Mabel from the CU team was following on behind in a separate launch. We passed the Barrett Reef Buoy in unpleasant conditions and went beating up Cook's Straight in a foul tide accompanied by rain, very choppy seas and, as usual, the obligatory dolphins.

I went on watch at 1800, very tired after a full day's activity on the primary winches. This is a very strenuous job, and a difficult one to get straight back into after an extended period on shore. It's the sort of thing you'd rather work up to by means of a few lighter jobs, but having said that, somebody has to do it straight off and it might as well have been me as anyone else. Throughout the day there had been numerous sail changes and a lot of reefing to be done, with the result that I went to bed at 2200 completely burnt out! My next watch was from 0200 to 0600, which would have been fine had I been back into the rhythm of life at sea, but as it was I fell asleep on watch which was very embarrassing. I made a mental note not to let this happen again. Luckily Richard was asleep in his bunk at the time, or I would never have heard the last of it!

They say the darkest hour is right before the dawn, and so it proved today. Sunrise came very late after a long spell of impenetrable darkness. Then I was on Mother at 0600. I cooked up the usual porridge, then served up the easiest lunch I could think of – frankfurters and peaches. Then I was able to unwind with a great sleep, which usually tended to be the case after a watch with Mother.

At 1300 we passed the Cape Farewell Spit of the South Island where I had spent a lot of time with Kate, Richard and Raff during the Wellington stopover. In a fit of nostalgia, which always seems strongest when future challenges and danger loom, I sent her off a fax just to let the family know I was thinking of them. We were sailing well in bright sunshine and, although we had slipped to sixth place, we were only six miles behind the leaders. We were just giving ourselves a qualified pat on the back, when we noticed that we had a problem with the upper diagonals. We thought this was simply a minor glitch, and Ian went up the mast to check it out. It was only then that we realised how close we had been sailing to disaster.

It appeared upon examination of the rigging that Ian had forgotten to put split pins in to secure the diagonals to the mast when we had been carrying out our maintenance in port. Ian obviously rectified the situation there and then, putting new pins in immediately. When he came down we discussed the situation and soon realised that we could have easily lost the top section of the mast. Needless to say, Ian was very upset, but looking back on it I feel that it was probably a case for tighter controls on maintenance. After all, anybody can make a mistake and forget to do something. That is exactly why aeroplane crews receive that well-known instruction from the captain just before take off – "Doors to automatic and cross check". It is of course most unlikely that anybody would forget to put the cabin doors into the correct state for take off, but if this did happen, the results would obviously be disastrous. Thus the crew are told to cross check, so that in the unlikely event that somebody has forgotten, disaster can be headed off. I personally think there was a case for all the crucial maintenance jobs on our boat being double-checked by another member of crew who had not been involved in the original maintenance task. Looking back with the benefit of hindsight, it is easy to say that such a system would certainly have saved us heart-stopping moments like that one!

*Ocean Rover* and *3Com* were now in sight, and we formed quite an attractive procession of boats as twilight fell, and *Orion* came striding over the horizon. I dropped into an excellent four-hour sleep. It was a heavy night for all watches, with most of the crew being sick in lumpy seas. As usual, I was the exception to the rule. When I came on watch at 0600 I found the galley flooded and also discovered that we had had a minor explosion with the cooker. Richard, as you would expect, was extremely concerned because the sailor's worst enemy isn't the sea, or the weather, or icebergs, but fire (and we had even left our resident fireman behind in Wellington with a bad back!) As long as you've got a boat, you can do something to combat the other hazards. But fire is the thing that is most likely to destroy your boat itself. And without that, you're sunk (sorry!).

(Since that time, I have seen a television documentary called *MIR Mortals* about one of the last crews to inhabit the MIR space station. Now OK, if we'd had a fire on board it would have been serious. But communication technology would have probably saved our lives even though we would have found ourselves out of the race. But on the MIR station they actually had an incident where an oxygen canister caught fire! I dread to think what would have happened to them if they hadn't succeeded in extinguishing it.)

In the case of our cooker there appeared to have been a build-up of gas, which had then ignited, and there is no doubt that it could have been a very serious incident. But I felt strangely detached from the situation, as if viewing it from a distance. In spite of all my misgivings about the Southern Ocean and all the perils that lay there, I think I always had at the base of my being a conviction that I was going to be all right. Whatever happened, I was going to get through this adventure and enjoy telling everybody about it afterwards!

Of course, there is always the possibility that this sanguinity that I felt on the voyage at times of stress is merely my psychological defence mechanism. It may be that it just kicks in at times when necessary to keep me from panicking. But whatever the explanation of my reaction, the practicalities of the situation were that there was no time to stand still and speculate about the cooker. There was a far more immediate problem with the galley, which was completely flooded because of problems with some of the hatches. Water was pouring through at an alarming rate, but we didn't even realise how bad the situation was at the time. Only when we had pumped the galley dry and taken stock of the situation did we realise that we had just had two extremely dangerous situations in one night.

The morning of the 11th dawned with a reduced wind and some sunshine. At noon we put the clocks back in accordance with Richard's system for keeping pace with the time zones. We were eleven miles behind the leaders, chasing *Motorola* in ninth place, who were 2.6 miles ahead. Not much else happened that day, although late in the afternoon I had to pump both bilges with Neil because the deck pump wasn't working. It was a beautiful evening again, with a whole train of boats strung out close together like bright beads on a necklace. *Nuclear Electric* and *Toshiba* were in sight. We had dropped to tenth during the day, but at this stage we overtook *Motorola* to move into ninth place again. Most of the crew were still ill in the lumpy seas. Paradoxically, it was usually the case that lumpy seas would cause more seasickness than heavy seas, because heavy seas, although much worse, tend to be more predictably so! The other factor in sea motion is of course the swell. The swell is like the underlying motion of the sea on its own, whereas the "sea" is superimposed on this by the weather conditions. At certain frequencies, the two motions superimpose unfavourably to produce more unpredictable motion, and at others they superimpose favourably to produce more predictable motion. Lumpy seas consist of about thirty- to forty-foot waves (quite lumpy enough for most people!) whereas heavy seas are about sixty- to seventy-foot.

We had a 2nd reef in the main and No 1 yankee up (and that doesn't mean we'd stuck Bransom up on the mast – it's another name for the headsail). I was on watch from 0200 till 0600, and we were trucking along nicely with some good speeds. By the time I went off watch it was a crisp, bright morning, and I went off to bed and had an excellent sleep. At noon I was up again, and found Neil at the helm, still motoring on towards Sydney. He was debating whether to put a spinnaker up, and eventually we hoisted the heavy, but then took it down again almost straight away. The winds were behaving very unpredictably and before long we had decided to put it up again! We raised it and lowered it at intervals throughout the day and all in all had a very busy time of it. At 1700 we were still struggling with the variable winds.

My next watch was 0600 next morning, when I came on deck to find *Motorola* hard on our tail, with *Nuclear Electric*, *Concert* and *Toshiba* all in hot pursuit. We were going well and giving as good as we got until a problem developed with a batten on the mainsail (one of the supports). We had to replace this and obviously lost time as a result. This put us back to eighth, which was frustrating enough – but then in the afternoon the wind died and left us limping along at a very low rate of knots. It is at times like these that you find yourself having a bit more leisure to take in your surroundings, and I sighted a pretty big shark. So big, in fact, that at first I thought it might be a whale – then I spotted the tell-tale dorsal fin slicing through the water.

On the 14th I woke to huge disappointment: no Valentine's cards! Never mind, I'm sure it was only because of the difficulty of finding a nearby shop. Although you'd have thought that if anybody had been really passionate they'd have managed to make one themselves. Well, maybe it was just that they were too worried about being identified in the cramped conditions. Or, of course, it could be that after the long spells that we had at sea with strictly rationed washing facilities, nobody found anybody else very attractive any more!

We hoisted the promo spinnaker, and soon we were running really well down the rhumb line in eighth place. But yet again we found a defect in our preparation that took the edge off our performance.

This time we found that a batten was missing from the top car on the main, so we had to remedy that and put it back in. It was a pleasant, warm morning, and everybody was feeling great with the combined effects of the weather and the good results that were just coming in. They showed that we had made big gains and, although we were still in eighth position, we had closed the gap considerably. It was heart-warming to see the way that a little bit of good news together with the right conditions stimulated the team to greater efforts. There was a real atmosphere of intense concentration on watch between 1400 and 1800. At the time Bransom and Neil were on the helm, having proved themselves the two best at that time, and the rest of us were trimming away to coax every last bit of juice from the boat.

As the voyage went on there was a definite tendency to match people to whatever jobs they turned out to be best at. At the start, Richard was very keen to make sure we all enjoyed the trip as such. He was keen not to get too bogged down in the competition, subscribing to the philosophy that happy sailors are better sailors. (Having said that, this has always been the philosophy that businesses have applied to their workers – certainly ever since Bob Cratchett took Scrooge to the tribunal anyway. But I read recently that some people are now saying that happy workers aren't as good at working as sad bastards! You pays your money and you takes your choice, I suppose.) But then it got to the stage where we all started to feel a bit more serious about our chances, and certain people through previous experience were better at helming than others. And obviously if you start to get serious then you consciously allocate people to the jobs they are best at. But we were definitely not as rigid in this approach as, say, *Group 4*. Whether we would have done any better if we had adopted a more focused and "compartmentalised" approach from the start is impossible to say. But I do think that we wouldn't have all got as much fun out of it as we did, and we probably also would not have managed to keep our original core crew throughout the race

(we were, in fact, the only boat that managed to do this, and I am sure that it had something to do with the happy atmosphere on board.)

Later that day we were still flying the promo spinnaker and staysail, with Neil driving hard at the helm. Then, just when we were all getting fully into our rhythm and beginning to let ourselves go and enjoy some exhilarating racing, we were called back on deck because the promo had suddenly given up under the strain of Neil's relentless speeds and blown a hole. We hoisted the heavy instead. This continued into the 15th with a good watch and great speeds, with different people getting a chance to helm. We were about fifteen miles behind *Group 4* and doing well. My maximum speed was 12.1 knots, which is very respectable, even though I say it myself. I kept it going for an hour or so and then at 1800 I was back on watch with Neil on the helm, again achieving more good speeds. Then Bransom took over from 2200 to 0000 and continued the good work.

Bransom, apart from being quite good at the helm, had another skill in which he was simply unsurpassed. There was nobody on our boat (nor, I believe, on any other) who could hold a candle to him in his real area of expertise. He had learned this skill through years of dedicated study and practice, and he had diplomas and certificates from internationally recognised bodies acknowledging his prowess. Many institutions had asked him to give visiting lectures and even whole courses on the subject, and I have it on good authority that he had even been asked to represent his country internationally at the highest level in competition based on the use of his skill.

And this great skill for which Bransom was (and presumably still is) famous throughout the world? Worrying.

For Bransom was the greatest worrier the world has ever seen. He was never happy unless he was worrying about something, and preferably something trivial that nobody could do much about anyway. He always had a panic going about something or other, and at this stage it was provisions. We were running out of food, and it was part of Bransom's responsibility to ensure that we had adequate provisions laid in store for each leg of the journey. The result was that he was continually running around the boat, checking all the store cupboards, counting up the quantities of various provisions that we had, doing calculations based on the results and then going back and doing it all over again. He drove the rest of us to distraction.

I mean, what was the point? What was he going to do if, as appeared likely, we were running very low on provisions and might run out before we reached land? Nip off to the nearest supermarket? Arrange for the UN to drop us an aid package? If the worst came to the worst, we would have to set up a system of rationing. In the face of all the other privations we endured on a daily basis, rationing would hardly be the worst thing that could happen. In addition to this, he was getting on people's nerves in other ways as well. For instance, Tim ended up having a tantrum over Bransom's attitude to Mother watch. Apparently he felt that he was doing such a good job with his helming that he felt this gave him the right to drop out of certain of his other duties, e.g. attending to Mother. This was definitely a sore point with the rest of the crew, as most of them hated Mother. Once again, I was the exception here, as I was quite happy to do whatever jobs needed doing on the boat – and I recognised that my hardy stomach was very useful when it came to essential tasks like Mother. You certainly didn't want people feeling ill when they were dealing with the catering for the rest of the crew!

On the 15th we were running in sixth place, until we hit problems with adverse current. We battled on in the face of it, however, and managed to move into fifth place. I was having a terrible time with the heat as I usually did; it was getting very warm at nights and I was unable to sleep and had to come out on deck. At about 1630 on Sunday a buoy floated by with the single promising message of "drugs" written on it! I think we could have all done with some sort of stimulation, as we had run into another becalmed situation where nothing was happening. As happened on other occasions, frustration was mounting because we were in sight of port but couldn't do anything about getting us any nearer to the promised land. This time it was in fact worse, as we still had about 100 miles to go. All we could do was make the best of it, and the only good thing about the situation was that it was a balmy night, and everybody seemed to be in the mood for telling excellent stories. I remember having a long chat that evening with Trevor about life, the universe and everything, (never really having managed to get talking to him before then).

It was, of course, a big shame about the boat speed however. We dribbled along at precisely zero knots for about three hours before the wind picked up and when I came on watch again at about 0000 hours found we were in tenth place. At this stage, some underdog magic seemed to have afflicted the fleet and there was a huge switch around, with all the boats at the back suddenly gaining water and ending up at the front. Thus we had *Save the Children* and *Courtaulds*, who generally could be found bringing up the rear, taking pride of place at the head of the fleet. Eventually *Save the Children* came in six hours ahead of everybody else after lagging at the back of the fleet on the 16th, and having been thirty-six miles behind us at one stage. Truly, the lack of wind is a great leveller. What a nightmare for us though! We finished in thirteenth place (our worst position on any leg) but as this was the shortest leg it didn't have a major effect on our overall placing. We came in just twenty-five minutes ahead of *Time and Tide* (the disabled boat). Another frustrating angle was that *Group 4*, who were usually up there in the lead or thereabouts was with us in tenth place at one stage when a crucial wind forecast came through. For some reason (and this was not the only time this seemed to happen) they got hold of this intelligence before we did and were able to take advantage and move to a better part of the ocean (more southerly) and got the wind first. The result was that they eventually cruised in in second place.

Coming in thirteenth was, to be honest, a real dampener even though it was only a short leg. At such times, administrative tasks can almost seem like too much to bear – but they still have to be done. Thus we had to go through the normal registration procedures with passports and so on, but it was the last thing anybody felt like doing. Obviously, if you've got a high placing, you can't wait to get ashore, you're full of energy and you don't mind smiling through the bureaucracy and being nice to everybody. But in our state of mind we just couldn't be bothered putting up a good show. So much for Kipling's Triumph and Disaster, and treating the two impostors just the same! Richard was extremely upset at the time, and finished off about three-quarters of a bottle of brandy on the way in. When it came to the official duties, he was far too tired and emotional, so I had to take care of some of the formalities. What a reversal of the usual rôles!

The only bright spot for us was a bit of *Schadenfreude*: *Motorola* hit a rock on the way in and got hauled up in front of the harbour master along with Chay. Life isn't all bad! (Although Chay even got in on the act, as this was a wind-up!)

# Sydney Stopover

BEAR WITH me, please, while I go into a bit of Science here. I don't know a lot about it but, from what I can remember, there was this guy called Newton who discovered some natural laws that describe the way in which things move. There are three of these laws, and it is the first one that I keep coming back to again and again when I think about my life. So far as I can remember it, Newton's first law says that "any body will remain in its state of rest or of uniform motion in a straight line unless it is acted upon by a force".

Interestingly enough, the law makes no mention of motion in a circle. It does, however, imply it. Circular motion follows as a direct corollary of the law, because if something has a tendency to go in a straight line but there is a force constantly pulling it inwards, then it will go round in a circle. That's what happens with the Moon going round the Earth, and the Earth going round the Sun. But then, what happens if the central force disappears suddenly? Well, the circulating object will then be free to carry on in the straight line that nature decrees that it should follow in the absence of a force. In short, the object will go off at a tangent to the circle. It will fly off in a straight line and won't stop until something gets in its way or the sullen bonds of gravity drag it back into an orbit, or even bring it crashing into the ground.

People talk about "going off at a tangent" when they are, for instance, giving a presentation, or having a conversation, and they get carried away with a particular element of the subject and start talking about it to the exclusion of other, more relevant, topics. But for me this metaphor is entirely too violent, too tied up with the idea of a reckless hurtle into space, followed by a crunching return to Earth, to be used in such a mundane connection. I therefore reserve it for describing those times when I have been having a lunchtime drink in my local, or drinking with sailing colleagues in the Tapas Bar in Southampton, or making friends with a new bunch of rabid riot-raisers in one of the far-flung corners of the world, and I have suddenly and unmistakably felt a loosening of the bonds. I have felt the Sun at the centre of my orbit shrink away, slacken the reins, loosen the ties that bind me to the shadow circuit of the daily round, liberating me to go flying off – as I say – at a tangent, to land wherever my flight takes me.

I mention this here, because if ever there were a place that I might be expected to "go off at a tangent" that place was Sydney. Obviously, in Rio I went off at a spectacular tangent, but in a sense that took me and everybody else by surprise. By the time we hit Sydney, however, everybody knew me. And, by simple extrapolation from previous experience, everybody knew what was likely to happen.

Sydney must rival New York in its claim to being the ultimate twenty-four-hour city. It is a pulsating nexus where all the varied elements and strata of Australian culture meet and get into bed together. The place feels like nothing so much as a thermonuclear pressure cooker fuelled by wealth, sun, sea, drink, drugs, sex and the indomitable Australian spirit which is forever thirsty for new experience, new stimulation.

Where we were staying was right in the heart of the gay area. But there is something about the Australian approach to life that ensures that, even when they are being gay, they do it in a macho way. I don't know about you, but I think of being gay as a painful discovery usually arrived at only after long periods of self-examination and futile attempts to fit in to the normal scheme of things: half-hearted attempts to enjoy intimate relations with the opposite sex, trying to deny the feelings of attraction to the same sex, desperately trying to be a square peg in a round hole and gradually and painfully coming to the conclusion that you don't fit. In short, I've always thought that being gay was not something anyone ever chose to do – it was something you gradually found out about yourself.

But when I spent that time in the gay centre of Sydney my perceptions were turned on their heads. These people were full of a vibrant pride in themselves and their crazy way of life. It wasn't as if these Australian gays had gradually come to understand their orientation after clinging to a hollow wreck of heterosexuality for years. It was as if they had embraced that heterosexuality long ago, used it up and passed through it to what they regarded as a higher level of sexual enlightenment. Far from clinging to the wreck of their heterosexuality, they were the ones who had ridden it so close to the wind in the first place and steered it to founder on the rocks of their inherent machismo. In a peculiar way, the pressure cooker of Sydney life seemed to have compacted the Australian male psyche and pressed it into such a dense ball of testosterone that the transformation to gayness appeared more like an evolution than a mutation. The atmosphere was so charged with masculinity that male seemed to be the only option, the only thing to which to aspire, the only thing to admire. It was phallocentricity gone mad and collective Narcissism on a grand scale.

Now, as I have said, I have never felt any gay leanings whatsoever. Nevertheless, I am aware that I do hold quite an attraction for the gay observer. Sean realised this as well, and what's more he understood that within two hours of landing I was likely to have reached the sort of state of inebriation in which a Milky Bar Kid on Nembutal could have taken advantage of me. To make matters worse, it wasn't enough that we should be right in the middle of the gay area; we were also right in the middle of the run-up to what is probably the greatest festival of Gay culture on the planet: the Sydney Gay Mardi Gras!

As we disembarked, therefore, Sean met me and greeted me, and quietly pulled me to one side:

"Nick, we're going to start off drinking together. But I know you're on a mission to self-destruct. Inevitably, you're going to go off at a tangent. When you do, you'll need this."

He pressed a little bundle into my hand. When I opened it and examined it, I saw that it was a "Sydney survival kit". It consisted of a map of the city with our chosen drinking location (a twenty-four-hour pub) for the evening clearly marked in big, red, comforting letters; another sheet of paper with our hotel address printed in clear kindergarten script (it was the Holiday Inn in Oxford Street –roughly equivalent to being assigned to a knocking shop on the Earls Court Road); and a little pouch of emergency money. As it later turned out, Sean had read me exactly right and once again shown himself to be a great guy to have on your side. At the end of the ravages of the twelve hours that followed, his survival kit would turn out to be the one thing that saved me.

Sydney was where Sean finally had to admit that his back problem had brought his career as Mastman, and indeed his active involvement in the race, to an end. Until now, he had been hoping to recover and rejoin the boat, but it was not to be. So at this point I find myself reminiscing about how we first met and how I came to regard him as one of the people in this world to whom I would gladly entrust my life.

We first met at a Challenge Ball hosted by BT at the Grosvenor House Hotel in the run-up to the race start. He and his wife Shirley were sitting opposite Kate and me. The first thing I noticed through my usual drunken haze was that people kept coming up to him and asking for his autograph. At one point we had to ask for more napkins as Sean had signed them all, but at this stage I didn't know him from the Dalai Lama. I imagine that is one thing that brought us together: I was just interested in him because I liked what I could see of his character, not because I wanted him to sign a napkin that I would have doubtless promptly lost!

At the end of the meal I approached him and introduced myself, and said, "I'm afraid I've never watched *Rainbow*, so I've no idea who you are, Geoffrey!" This struck exactly the right note. He laughed one of his great, big, hearty laughs and we hit it off immediately.

His mild celebrity status came, I found out later, from a part he had played in the series about the fire service, *London's Burning*. Having been out with him on many occasions and seen how he is recognised, I realise how difficult fame must be to deal with for someone who is really well known. For instance, there was one occasion when we were out drinking and got talking, as you do, to a group of attractive girls.

Suddenly, Sean got up and went off to the toilet. When he didn't come back after about fifteen minutes I went to try and find him, but he was nowhere to be seen, and I didn't see him for the whole of the rest of the evening.

I called him the next day and asked what had happened. He told me that he had suddenly got cold feet talking to these beautiful girls. Even though everything was perfectly innocent, it would have taken only a flash of recognition and a snap from a handy camera to put him in a seemingly compromising situation on a front page, and a heap of explaining to do to Shirley. And once you get to know Sean and Shirley, you realise how upsetting such a thing could be to both of them – they are absolutely devoted to each other and will go to enormous lengths to protect each other from hurt.

Sean is anything but the stereotypical luvvie actor. He's a straight, down-to-earth guy who has time for everybody. He is genuine and generous almost to a fault, and knows how to enjoy himself. He has a very active social life, in spite of having to keep an eye open for paparazzi!

Our relationship developed quickly through the extensive schedule of social gatherings arranged by the race authorities as a warm-up to the main event. One such party took place at the offices of Commercial Union West End. The CU had adopted me as their selected crew member and had offered me a special gift for the race. After much thought I decided that I would ask for something for the whole crew. I settled on specially commissioned painted silk "Round the World" waistcoats, consisting of a full map of the race route starting at the front, going all the way round the back and out to the front again. As a thank-you for these handsome gifts, Sean and I offered to go to their offices to give a presentation to their staff about the race, and do a little fund-raising for the Save The Children, the official race charity, at the same time by selling autographed T-shirts, caps and so on. We didn't do any rehearsal for it, but after showing two race videos we naturally fell into a stand-up "Saint & Greavesie" style which was very well received. I always think that this shows how well and naturally our characters mesh. After the presentation, we all retired to the CU's adopted pub, The Golden Lion off Pall Mall, where we carried on promoting the drive to raise money for the race charity.

On another occasion, we were partying in the BT marquee at the Ocean Village, Southampton. The pressure of the race preparation and the thought of leaving my family and business alone to fend for themselves for ten months while I sailed through the world's fiercest oceans had taken its toll, and I suddenly broke down and became very emotional. Sean and Shirley consoled me, and Sean put his strong arms around me, gave me a hug and reassured me that it was a leap into the unknown for everybody, and I wasn't the only one who was going to ride the emotional roller coaster over the coming year.

Sean is and will remain a firm friend. He was sorely missed by the whole crew after he left the boat prematurely in Wellington. After he left, I switched watches for the final two legs and took over as Mastman. I'm afraid I felt like an interloper, vainly trying to fill the hole left by his departure. The rest of the watch did their very best to make me feel welcome, but I knew it wasn't the same.

So there I was, a super-fit, not bad-looking heterosexual guy with a tendency to self-anaesthetisation let loose in probably the most homosexual environment in the world. I felt like a marked man. It didn't help that the news coming through from back home was all about Michael Portillo's "gay encounters at university" confessions before running for his "safe Tory seat" in Kensington! I started the festivities by going off to a twenty-four-hour gay bar with Rob, a cameraman from the BBC. I was cavorting on the dance floor in my usual enthusiastic fashion and, fairly predictably, there was this one guy who seemed to have taken a liking to me that was more than superficial.

I started off with my usual bit of winding up by telling him that where I came from fudgepackers and shirtlifters like him would be rounded up, fenced off and a massive bomb dropped on them. As usual (he would probably have made a good BT Challenge skipper) he was about to lay me out and, again as usual, I was completely unaware of how far I had provoked him. This time Rob had his finger on the pulse and jumped in and saved me.

Sean and Vicki arrived soon after that. They had decided that they would find me at the most noxious and notorious den of iniquity in the city, and they were right. We sat down and had a chat and a drink, and I remember hearing little splinters of conversation from all around me, all to do with sex and from all the way across the culture and orientation spectrum. There was an obviously gay exchange between two guys discussing one of their friends (although I am sure they were talking about a man, they referred to him as "she"). They were from the top of the shitpile and sounded as though they had just come from the opera:

"Oh Roddy! Have you never rooted her? Well don't. I promise you, it's like fucking a bucket. The Greeks had a word for it – she suffers from what they called a *europrokton* - a europrocton – a "wide anus," implicitly one that has been rendered so by over-use…"

And again:

"Well I have to say that I've never actually humped a punchbag with a hole in it, but I tell you, the experience can't be far away from snoring the night away with Wayne…"

And then there was also a typically Australian heterosexual courting exchange that I overheard and witnessed at a nearby table:

"So then, Kylie, how about it?"

"Oh Reg, I'd love to, you know, but, you see I'm on me rag this week…"

Then her face lit up as a happy thought crossed her mind that had obviously never occurred to her before:

"Hey, but you can root me shitter if you want to…"

And so it went on. Talk of rimming and fellating and rooting and shafting and felching hummed around my head. I felt like St Augustine in the *Confessions*:

"To Cartage then I came, where a cauldron of unholy loves sang all about mine ears…"

And as I sat there meditating on my strange situation – sitting on the opposite side of the world from my natural habitat, and among people who came from the opposite side of the sexual world from me – I felt that feeling I have mentioned: the unmistakable slackening of the bonds as the sun shrank away below me…

The rest of the night reels between a blur and darkness. All I know for sure is that I was stumbling round an anonymous street at four in the morning. I eventually managed to get a taxi to stand still long enough for me to stagger over to it. When the driver asked, "Where d'you manna go to, mate?" I admit to being completely stumped. It was like sitting there in front of Magnus Magnusson when he's just popped you a particularly slippery question about an obscure work written by one of the minor courtiers of Queen Elizabeth I. My mind presented me with a perfect blank. He was just about to give up on me and drive away when a dim recollection came to me. Triumphantly,

I produced Sean's rescue kit. I showed him the map, and he looked dubious. But then I showed him the money, which was far too much for the fare and said,

"Look, you can have it all. I don't care. Just get me to the hotel."

Money talks. That clinched it. Twenty minutes later I fell out into the gutter outside the Holiday Inn. It wasn't the driver's fault – I just couldn't stand up – and in fact he got out and picked me up and saw me safely inside. Whether I got to my room on my own legs, on a stretcher or on a magic carpet I will never know.

While we were in Sydney a number of romantic dramas in the life of certain Challenge crew members were being played out behind the scenes. These dramas put the individuals concerned through the emotional mangle. So much so that most of the time they were fairly drunk, and obviously trying to find the answer to their questions at the bottom of a bottle.

I say this as somebody who got married at twenty-three. I think I was too young and I do freely admit it. I gave into peer pressure which said I should get married at the time, whereas I feel that I would have been better getting a few things out of my system first. I wasn't ready for the responsibility and commitment. But having said that, I do think that Kate and I have made an extremely good fist of it. We've stuck at it, and twenty years and five wonderful children later, we're still standing. I think if I am honest I have to say that I have been through some periods of regret during those twenty years. But when I look at my daughters and son and the way they are growing up, and when I see how talented they are becoming in their various chosen pursuits, I realise it has all been worth it. (Even if young Thomas' particular talent is depositing perishable items in places where they will cause the most annoyance, such as the tape slots of video machines and disc drawers of CD players!)

The day before we left Sydney, the gay Mardi Gras exploded onto the scene, and I am sorry to say that I can only remember two things about it. The first is the sight of all the heads turning as macho (and completely hetero) Neil, the watch leader, wandered down the street in tight-fitting shorts and a Spandex vest carrying a leather clip handbag (as men often do on the European continent). For an off-duty BT Challenge yachtsman this was fairly standard attire, but in this particular context it could only be termed provocative. If he had been raped and the case had come before court then a closet gay judge would no doubt have said that he was asking for it! He honestly didn't realise what a stir he was causing, with his dashing air of bravado (he is a keen motorcyclist who regularly participates in the Isle of Man TT and similar events).

My only other memory is of Pete Calvin performing a valuable service to the cause of keeping trash off the streets by locking Chay Blyth in a public mobile toilet, and of the man who started it all banging on the door and screaming, "Let me out!"

Unfortunately, he eventually did.

# 4TH LEG —

## *Sydney to Cape Town*

ONE THING you get to understand when you go on a round-the-world yacht race is that large bodies of water generally spell trouble. (Oh, sorry, that should have been spelt with a capital "T".) We had all been worried about facing the first Southern Ocean leg, which had certainly turned out horrendous enough for most people, and in one sense you might have thought that we were used to it by now: here we were facing a second stretch of similar size and threatened ferocity, and surely we knew what to expect? Surely we could just take it in our stride?

A logical enough argument, you might think. And so it looks on paper. But the truth was that we knew that, however bad the first Southern Ocean leg had been, it had had the potential to be much worse. The same was true of this leg: the taste that we had had of the first leg warned us that we were facing the potential for even greater problems. And, as it turned out, our fears were well grounded.

We had all been concerned about the first Southern Ocean leg, but that turned out to be a breeze compared with what was about to happen on this leg. And quite apart from the physical threats and dangers, in race terms this was the leg where the real tension built up, where it was all starting to come to the boil. As it turned out, this leg would make or break so many crews and so many people —

and even some unfortunate boats as well. It was the leg where every crew which harboured any real hopes of winning would have to do well. It was conquer or be conquered, dog eat dog, shark swallow shark, piranha strip piranha down to the bone.

And, to be honest, like many people before a big event, many of us were losing our cool.

For instance, during a training sail I got my right arm trapped between the forestay and Genoa sheet as we were going around on a tack. I suffered very painful but relatively minor rope burns and bruising, but it could have been so much worse. If the wind had been just a little stronger, or if I had just got a bit more tangled up than I did, I could have broken it. That would have been the end of my participation for that leg at least, and would have been the end of my dream of being one of the few crew on any boat who managed to stick with the race all the way through.

But the point was that normally it wouldn't have happened at all. The procedure for tacking was by now hard-wired into all our muscular memories. Like concert pianists who have practised so hard that they don't need the music any more, because not only is it now in their mental memories but also in their "finger" memories, all our movements were so practised that they had very little chance of going wrong. And like concert pianists, the only thing that caused a danger was "stage fright," the fear of the big occasion. So it was for me. The tension of building up for this important leg when so much was at stake had unbalanced my normally reliable motor control, and I had fumbled the sheet like a novice. Of course, this was bad enough, but it also showed me that a moment's inattention can have disastrous consequences. This time it could have been a broken arm. But out in the middle of the Southern Ocean things were inclined to be a lot more serious. Out there, such a lapse in concentration, for instance in forgetting to clip on to the rail when on deck, could exact a far higher penalty.

So that was how we were feeling the day before the off. Nervous for all sorts of reasons, with our very nervousness contributing to our nervousness in a spiralling, jittery vicious circle. In the event, what we needed was something interesting to divert our attention, a distraction to take our minds off the things that were in store for us in the vast, hostile Southern Ocean. And we certainly got it in the guise of the Gay Mardi Gras parade – which took place the day before we set sail again!

We had the dubious privilege of having ringside seats for this spectacle, situated as we were right in the middle of the gay area in Sydney's Oxford Street. We had, in the words of E M Forster, a room with a view – but Merchant and Ivory it wasn't! We had a stunning view of all that went on from our balcony. But then again, I suppose we weren't seeing anything like all that went on. We were just seeing the tip of the iceberg (careful now, you're supposed to be keeping your mind off that sort of thing!).

I mean, a Mardi Gras is one thing. But a *gay* Mardi Gras is something quite astounding. I suppose in the original sense of the word, all Mardi Gras are "gay". A gay Mardi Gras really consists of modern gaiety overlaid on old-time gaiety, or "double gaiety" (and if you're hetero, you're probably talking double jeopardy!) And another phrase comes to mind as well – "gay abandon". Certainly that is an extremely accurate way of describing the celebrations that went on that day. People when they are celebrating tend to lose all inhibitions. But, with the gay community, you are starting with very few inhibitions in the first place. The result seems, certainly to a hidebound hetero like me, to be complete abandonment of sanity!

Eventually 1st March dawned, and all of a sudden things looked grey again rather than gay. Once again I was setting off with very mixed emotions, knowing this time that I had lost Sean for the rest of the race. His back had not healed as it should have done, and there was no way he was going to be able to join us again—particularly on this leg, which promised to be the toughest of the tough and likely to aggravate any weakness in somebody who was not fully fit.

My compensation for losing Sean was Alan. He was drafted in to give some continuity over the next two legs. He was a BT engineer, and we quickly found out that he could fix anything from a dripping tap to a navigation system using only tin foil, old washing-up liquid bottles, paper clips, rubber bands, a pair of Richard's old knickers and anything else you might find in the average Blue Peter studio. Fairly predictably, he became known as Mr Fixit, and was a very useful man to have around, especially on a boat like ours where we seemed to have things breaking down and going wrong on a fairly regular basis! He was a great guy and we built up an excellent relationship. It was unfortunate for him that he was taking Sean's place because Sean was such a very hard act to follow, but in the circumstances he did brilliantly.

It had become a bit of a tradition that we tried to do something a little bit appropriately wacky at the start of each leg (like the blue-and-yellow died hair), but again, without Sean, a little bit of the madcap levity was missing. In the event all we could manage was Sid, Lars and myself wearing bush hats with those corks dangling from them, reputedly to keep off the flies (subliminal message: there are no flies on us!)

We got off to an excellent start, so much so that we were up there challenging *Group 4*, the habitual leaders, right from when we crossed the line. Unfortunately, however, we were challenging them a little *too* hard, and we were told that our start had been a somewhat over-enthusiastic: we had crossed the line early. To compound the felony, we got so carried away with our early performance that we collided with *Group 4* and suffered protests as a result. The collision incidentally also took a big chunk out of our hull, which although it was not a major problem didn't do us any good. We were penalised for the starting line infringement and had to do the sailing equivalent of Hail Marys or Mea Culpas, which was to execute a 720° turn. At the same time, Richard decided we should do another one just in case the protest for the collision was upheld (which it wasn't in the end). But even though this penalty was unnecessary in the event it was good tactics from Richard, born of his inshore soling experience where penalties like this are commonplace. The point is that it would have cost us greater loss of time to stop in full flow at a later time and do the penalty, whereas if we did it while we were already in "penalty mode" it was a lot easier. In the end, of course, the leg was due to last forty-two days, so the prejudice caused by these penalties was small in the scheme of things, and it was best to get them over with at the beginning so as not to interrupt later performance. It was far better to get it out of our minds and concentrate on the race, sure in the knowledge that we wouldn't be troubled again.

We had been in third place coming out of the heads and then dropped back due to the penalties and then also blew the medium spinnaker and had to put the heavy up. I was on Mother and made CCC and rice although there weren't a lot of takers for the food. Looking forward to my long sleep. Also sarcastically I was so looking forward to the southern ocean! Reminded of ribs injury, huge seas, large swell, all came flooding back.

At one stage we could see all thirteen other boats and were only two miles behind the leader. That day ended with us lying third overnight, but the early morning found us tossing and turning in funny seas with fickle winds again. Then we were hit with torrential rain, but without any drop in temperature. It was very hot, sticky and uncomfortable below and we felt like a pan of steamed vegetables. We tried to pick up the East Australia current but had no success.

The result was that during the 3rd we lost out big time to the other boats, slipping back to thirteenth place, seventeen miles behind the leaders. Lots of the crew were sick because of lumpy seas, and at one stage we had 45 knots coming over the deck. However this dropped and fluctuated as far as 6 knots, and it was the sheer unpredictability of the conditions that were doing for most people. Although I was as usual unaffected by the conditions so far as my stomach was concerned, I did, also as usual, find it difficult to sleep. Looking back on it, I do find my inability to sleep paradoxical, because it was definitely a symptom of worry. And yet, as I have mentioned elsewhere, I did have an overarching feeling throughout the whole voyage that – yes – things were going to turn out all right.

At 0600 I came on watch to the cheering news that we had now found what we had been looking for – the East Australia current. We had suddenly managed to pick up about 3 knots of current in our favour, resulting in about 10 knots of boat speed. A major pattern was developing among some of the crew members in which they would be sick for long periods of time. Alan and Jim had particular problems in this respect, and it obviously caused some difficulties with organisation of watches and general administrative matters. And that sort of thing tends to become a vicious circle; sick breeds sick, it is its own emetic. Thus at the time Bransom was Mother's helper and suffered from sickness, which was actually very rare for him. But I think it probably had something to do with cleaning the heads when they were very much in need of it.

Conditions down below were not very good either, and I remember Eileen, who was Mother at the time, suffering too. There was also a foul-looking cooking pot with leftover porridge in it that nobody had bothered to clean for days, which I think could have been very upsetting for whoever eventually had to deal with it (in this case, Eileen). The other factor was of course that people were not eating very much, which again caused insidious vicious circles. Thus, people feel ill, so they don't eat, which makes them weaker and less able to deal with life, particularly on a boat in heavy and unpredictable seas, where you have to be at the peak of mental and physical condition just to stand a reasonable chance of surviving, all of which ends up with people feeling even more sick and helpless.

Everyone was feeling so terrible that all we could think about was getting out. But, of course, there was no way out but forward. Eventually, like a convict, I put up a "days to go" calendar in the galley. I was the one to do it because I was the only one feeling well enough to think about anything else except the state of my innards, but I think I managed to catch the mood of the crew pretty well! When I did it, we still had forty days to go to Cape Town. For forty days and forty nights we would wander in the wilderness...

When I came off watch at noon I stretched out on my bunk, and my eye caught a book above Alan's bunk – a tribute to Brian Johnston, the cricket commentator with an endless supply of cakes and conversation for the long days when portions of test matches were rained off. He also had an inimitable way of saying things that unintentionally caused explosions of helpless laughter in millions of homes of avid listeners to Test Match Special on Radio 4.

Like the time when Michael Holding was bowling to Peter Willey in a West Indies vs. England fixture. Just as "Whispering Death" was approaching the crease Brian intoned breathlessly: "The bowler's Holding, the batsman's Willey..."

Or the time when he rendered himself unable to commentate for about two minutes – surely an event unheard of before or since on TMS – through helpless laughter occasioned by his own utterance. Ian Botham was at the crease, and received an awkward delivery which he tried to connect with but failed. He lost his balance and spun round and hit his own wicket with his leg and was therefore given out. Botham had tried gamely to lift his leg to clear the stumps, but had just failed and narrowly nicked one of the bails. Brian's comment on the incident ran something like: "Oh that was bad luck for poor old Botham. He got all tucked up there but just didn't manage to get his leg over..."

Being a bit of a sport fanatic, I spent a minute in silence in memory of the great man. Summers truly will never be the same again.

When I came back from my reverie, I had a pit in my stomach again with more mixed emotions. We had another thirty-nine days to go on this hellish leg – why were we doing it exactly? Why were we putting ourselves through this? I thought of home and the upcoming break in Cape Town. Although I had seen Kate in Wellington the girls had stayed at home, and Cape Town would be the first time I would have seen them since Southampton 1996. All this made me feel very melancholy as I drifted off to sleep.

We improved our position during the day with fair winds and current. But although we were twelfth at the time and gaining steadily on the rest of the fleet, we were still seventeen miles off the pace. At one stage we were also the most inshore boat trying to take advantage of the East Australia Current, which was good tactics. We were in fourth place and gaining on the others, close to *Nuclear Electric* flying our Genoa and staysail.

I was on watch at the helm for an hour with mixed seas and winds. We had fallen again to eighth place but were now closing on the leaders once more. *Toshiba* were eleven miles in front, with *Group 4* lying third at that stage. This was good news because our game plan was paying off. But it was at this stage that I almost had a calamity. That moment of inattention I had dreaded ever since catching my arm on the training sail now caught up with me. The foredeck was awash and I got picked up and washed down the deck. I was completely disoriented – all I knew was that I was being pushed around against my will by a large body of water, and I couldn't feel the boat beneath me. Then I fetched up against the guard rail as the water ebbed away around me. Painfully, I dragged myself to my feet again and staggered halfway up the deck, only to be met by a further deluge, hitting me with greater force this time and not so much lifting me off my feet as hurling me back against the guard rail with almost vindictive force.

I lay there dazed for a few moments, and then my eyes fixed on the number 2 halyard, which was waving and whipping crazily in the howling air. Suddenly it became all-important to recover the halyard, and I started on the perilous journey to retrieve it.

It was then that I had my closest ever flirtation with death. I can picture it clearly: me struggling away on the deck, with only one thought in my head – how to get that halyard back, and the possibility of death standing there at my shoulder, ready to trip my heels, standing at one branch of an infinity of split-second decision trees. And I don't know what happened, it was like a physical proximity, an entity really standing there in physical space waiting to take me down. And I think it was that physical feeling that saved me, because when I felt it, I knew something was wrong.

I suddenly realised with a rush of panic what it was. During this whole episode, I had not clipped on. I was just an object, free to be tossed around like a cork on this boiling sea with nothing to hold me to that boat that was the only barrier between life and death. I clipped on straight away, and a split second later, a third huge wave hit. It was only my line that saved me.

The experience was absolutely terrifying. For about two minutes afterwards I just stood still, gulping in air with almost pitiful gratitude – to who or what I don't know – that I was still able to do so. But once my heart rate had returned to normal, I began to see the incident as yet one more proof of my inner conviction that I was going to be all right. After all, I could so easily not have remembered to clip on in time, and then I would have been gone. It just felt as though, once again, somebody or something was looking after me. Maybe it was God, or the universe, or just my own inner strength that had taken on a separate personality of its own. But I felt once again that glowing, warm centre to which I returned time and again throughout the race suffusing me with its mysterious intimations of well being.

After this little adventure, I had an excellent sleep. Partly because

I was completely exhausted, and partly because my near escape had paradoxically made me feel more secure. When I awoke to go back on deck the storm was still raging, throwing an average of 40 knots at us over the deck. I went on the helm for an hour or so and made good progress to seventh place, only nine miles behind *Toshiba*, the current leaders. *Group 4*, normally the other great contender for the lead, was lying fourth. The fleet was some twenty miles off Tasmania, passing through Bass Strait, which divides the island from the mainland. This required regular tacking, and used the sort of inshore tactics that Richard was so used to. As a result, we were managing to move up through the fleet again.

We hoisted the Genoa, and I winced as memories of Saturday came flooding back. That was, of course, when I had caught my arm in the sheet while manoeuvring this very sail, and it still hurt quite badly. I have to say, however, that part of the reason for my wincing was the sheer embarrassment of the memory. It was one of those moments when you close your eyes and stand still and say to yourself, "Did I really do that? Was I really that stupid?" But once I had got over my flashback I managed to settle into a good rhythm, and we had a truly wonderful evening sail. Not only were we motoring along at a good rate of knots, but the scenery was absolutely perfect as well. I managed to get a beautiful sunset picture of Bransom and Ian under the spinnaker, gazing out to Tasman Island under a blood red sky.

Obviously, there were many of these moments of pellucid beauty throughout the voyage. And like beauty everywhere I suppose, it always took us by surprise. It was a bit like when you walk through a gallery of ordinary pictures, and every now and again coming upon a masterpiece. You stand transfixed before it, drinking it in, yet knowing that you will never be able to slake the thirst it has inspired. Knowing that soon you will be back outside the gallery in the greying city air, the mundane metropolitan rain, with just the afterglow of the images in your head.

Early the following morning we found ourselves in sixth place, although we were in fact only three miles behind the leaders. We started with the light spinnaker and then the promo. It was still "inshore" racing, although now we were gibing frequently rather than tacking because of the changeable winds. Richard was very enthusiastic that morning because of our position relative to the leaders, but this seemed to send his mind spinning off in other completely irrelevant directions. For instance, this was the morning that he ordered a major clean-up in the galley because, as he put it "there was something nasty growing in the mug rack"!

But perhaps I am being a little hard on him here, as we did constantly worry about hygiene, particularly in view of the necessarily compromised circumstances on board, and the possibility of getting some sort of "Delhi belly". This would probably of course have put us all out of action, me included, as I can obviously only claim immunity from the effects of motion-induced sickness. Just like anyone else, I am powerless in the face of bugs! And it is probably sensible to arrange to do these mundane tasks when the going is good, as you are not likely to have time for them when all hands are on deck battling with a storm that threatens to dismast the boat! But it did just seem a little incongruous to be worrying about the state of the galley when we were racing furiously to close an already narrow gap on the leaders.

As night fell, another school of dolphins started playing around with us. Again, we were enjoying great competitive sailing, with all the port boat lights strung out in a line like glowing rubies on a bed of black velvet. Some fishing boats hove into view, and they must have wondered what we were all about.

We left the Tasmanian coast on the 6th in beautiful, warm afternoon sunshine with a playful light breeze in the air. We were still lying 6th as we headed out into the Southern Ocean. This was it. This was the big time. It suddenly dawned on me. "No more services until Junction 13," I thought facetiously, my mind probably trying to soften the impact of the real truth, which was "No more land until the Kerguelen Islands!"

On the 7th, we noticed a definite fall in sea temperature to sixteen degrees – a sure sign that we were leaving the comfort zone. We successfully manoeuvred south of the fleet to get the best of the wind, and then from 2200 till 0200 we embarked upon what I always look back on as the "Keystone Cops" watch. I don't know if you have ever heard Gerard Hoffnung's famous speech to the Oxford Union about the misadventures of the unlucky builder, but it always reminds me of that. If you have, you'll understand exactly the desperate humour of the situation. If not, try and find a copy, because you'll probably laugh until it hurts.

As you will know from elsewhere in this book, I am not given to using strong language. I don't swear, and I even managed to win a bet with Richard that I would be able to go the whole race without swearing (the stake money of £300 went to the race charity). However, this is not out of any sense of prudishness; it is simply the fact that I never feel the need to express my anger in such a manner. And I certainly do not intend to go censoring this book and putting in blanks and asterisks all over the place. So please, as you read the following paragraph, remember that I am reporting speech as it happened. The words used are not those that I would have chosen in the situation, but they are certainly those of the protagonists!

The situation seemed innocuous enough. Everything was pitch black on a moonless night, but there was little wind and the team knew each other well. Alan was on Mother, so there were five people in the team, with the main *dramatis personae* being Bransom, Trevor and Neil. Trevor was in the cockpit and Neil was on the helm. The first intimation that something was going wrong came when they needed to gibe, and somebody noticed that the spinnaker halyard was tangled. So just as Trevor was embarking on a downhaul of the spinnaker, he realised that the sheet and guy had to be untangled as well. This meant that he was short-handed, so he called for Bransom's help.

Now Trevor and Bransom are both very capable people in their own way. A bit like water and electricity, they are fine on their own as long as you treat them with due care and attention. But put them together and you might find you're in for a shock. The sum of these two together is somehow more chaotic than the parts. I think this is because their particular character quirks act to inflame rather than offset each other. Thus we have Trevor, the "bumbling professor"— very intelligent, but has his head in the clouds a lot of the time. And this is absolutely fine when you pair him with me or most of the other people on the boat – we knew he was a bit vague, so we would unconsciously sharpen our perceptions when working with him. And again, Bransom: a very capable guy, but with a bit of an annoying voice and a tendency to worry about *everything*. This trait would have been fine, and in fact very useful, if the things he worried about ever actually proved to be worth worrying about. But, as with most worriers, the things he worried about never actually went wrong, and the things that did go wrong (and there were, after all, plenty of them) turned out to be things that he had never even thought about worrying about. For instance, had he worried about the split pins that had been missed during the last stopover, they would no doubt have been checked, and a lot of panicking could have been avoided.

Once again, if anybody else had been working with Bransom at that time, things might well have been OK. But it wasn't anybody else; it was Trevor. And Trevor's bumbling, muddle-through-and-it'll-be-all-right air was almost perfectly calculated to set Bransom off worrying on a pathological scale. So when Trevor realised that the sheet and guy needed to be untangled, he suggested, in his mild-mannered way, that he might need some help from Bransom.

Bransom, however, in his Action Man meets Old Mother Hubbard way, immediately started rushing around the deck trying to take charge of the situation. At first it was difficult to tell that this was what he was doing, because the only evidence we had was bangs, crashes and obscenities coming from out of the pitch black. Then he had the bright idea of getting a flashlight from the cockpit, which meant that from then on we also caught the odd dancing point of light in the commotion.

Presumably, however, the flashlight helped Bransom to see a lot more of what was going on, even if it didn't illuminate things very much for the spectators! And where Bransom was involved, this wasn't necessarily an advantage as it simply seemed to inspire him to higher heights of worry, which led to more uncoordinated activity, which led to a worsening situation, which inspired him to even higher heights of worry…

You get the picture.

At the height of the chaos, things went something like this:

Bransom: What the fuck's happening with this downhaul?

Trevor: Well, if you could get on with that, I need to sort out the sheet and the guy…

Bransom: What do you mean "if I could get on with that"? That downhaul needs to be done now!

Trevor: OK, well if you could just wait…

Bransom: (Panic raising his voice to a scream) Now! It has to be done now! If you can't even do a simple downhaul then I suppose I'm bloody well going to have to do it! (Sound of stamping feet hurrying along a wet and slippery deck) Here, give it… AAAARGH! (Followed by loud thump.)

At this point it seems sensible to digress for a moment in order to introduce Bransom's nickname. For those readers who know nothing about sailing, the boom is the heavy bar that runs along the bottom of the mainsail at right angles to the mast. It swings backwards and forwards across the deck as the mainsail crosses from one side to the other during a tack or a gibe. The first thing you learn on a sailing boat is to keep out of the way of the boom, if necessary by ducking. Normally there is plenty of warning that the boom is about to go across, because tacks and gibes are usually executed as a team effort. Everybody knows you are about to carry out the manoeuvre because you shout it out in an extremely loud voice, and so everybody knows to keep or get out of the way. However, dangerous situations can occur, especially if the boat crosses the line of the wind accidentally or without due warning being given. Then the boom can swing across, sweeping all before it. (This is in fact what did happen during my first encounter with sailing when I went out for a corporate day on a boat in the Solent before I ever signed up for the race – two young guys on another boat were knocked off the deck and drowned in foul conditions.)

Anyway, back to Bransom. Since a boom is something that keeps banging into things, often with catastrophic results, it was fairly natural that we should start calling our resident bull in a china shop "Boom"!

So, to continue our story, there was an almighty thump as Boom's body hit the deck. Later we found out that he had collided with the running backstay and been thrown flat on his back, but at the time the only thing we could see was the wildly gyrating light beam of his torch, spinning like some crazy miniature lighthouse as it skidded across the deck. For a moment, we thought that all the fight must have been knocked out of him, that perhaps he'd given up and decided to lie on the deck for the rest of the watch. But no such luck. After a couple of seconds' silence, he scrambled to his feet with, it appeared, new energy, grabbed his torch and ran up the deck towards Trevor, mouthing obscenities as fast as his vocal cords could process them:

"You motherfucking son of a cocksucking fucker what the fuck do you think you're fucking around at, Fuckhead…?" and so on and so on – energetically and enthusiastically exploring the linguistic permutations afforded by his apparent necessity to employ an expletive every other word.

When he came level with Trevor he turned on his heel and shone his flashlight on the end of the downhaul preparatory to taking over operations himself. And lo and behold, a miracle of incompetence was then revealed to the assembled throng! The staysail sheet that Trevor was energetically "winching" in was in fact only attached to a cleat on the deck and not the end of the sail at all! In the dark nobody had noticed that Trevor had in fact been exerting all his energy to try and detach our deck from our hull, and I suppose it could have been "goodbye deck!," with the top being ripped off of our boat like a tin of sardines! Now that would have been something uniquely special. I suppose that Oscar Wilde might have said that to lose a mast may be regarded as a misfortune, but to lose a deck would certainly have looked like carelessness!

This development sent Bransom into a kind of self-righteous frenzy. Probably conscious that he had been making a bit of an idiot of himself, he realised with relief that his idiocy had now been miraculously eclipsed by somebody else's. With much huffing and puffing, the gibe was eventually completed, then he flounced downstairs to make some drinks, obviously dazed but in some obscure way pleased with himself. (But even then he managed to mix up the drinks order!)

Whether as a result of these contortions or not, we found that we had dropped to tenth place, forty-three miles behind the leader.

At 0600 I went on watch, and repairs to the promotional spinnaker began in earnest. Obviously gibing is an essential manoeuvre, but it must be done with care, and on this occasion it was obviously not done with enough of that desirable commodity. Part of the problem was that we were used to doing it with a full team, and in this case Alan had been on Mother. We managed the situation by detailing two people only to sail the boat on each watch, with the others working on the repairs, because it absolutely had to be sorted out. This was particularly urgent with the long Southern Ocean leg still stretching ahead of us.

In the meantime we continued to peal between the light and heavy spinnakers, and so lost a fair amount of speed. I don't know who was responsible for it (do you believe me?) but an unkind piece of paper suddenly and mysteriously appeared on the wall above the chart table steps. It read: "Anyone on board with more blow-jobs to their credit than Lars?" (The point being that he was the one who had so far been responsible for blowing the spinnakers.)

Alan, our BT Mr Fixit, kindly volunteered to oversee the sail repairs. As usual, whenever he was involved in repairing anything, he seemed to have some useful experience up his sleeve. In this case, he had apparently done some time repairing tents in his past (don't ask me where or how!) Little did he know when he signed up for this thing that he was going to end up repairing the equivalent of a marquee!

At 1800 I was back on watch, and we were back in tenth place forty-five miles behind *Global Teamwork*. However our strategy had paid off in the sense that we had the wind with us and we were in the most southerly position. This is what we had bargained for, so we could hardly complain and it was now up to us to make the best of it. On the 8th we nearly had a disaster with the jockey pole (a pole which you use to hold the guy out when you are running with a spinnaker). Margot alerted us to a banging on the deck, and this was duly reported to Neil, the watch leader, and it was a good thing that it wasn't Bransom because we all panicked enough as it was when we realised that it had come adrift. I ended up going up with Neil and Alan, risking life and limb to recover it because if we had lost it there would have been a seriously major problem.

On the 9th on the 2200 watch, there was another nightmare on the foredeck. Bransom, Alan and I were completing a mainsail reef on the low side, when we were all washed down with waves washing over the deck. Bransom was trying to coil the ropes at the time and was getting very frustrated. Once again, he was using his now-famous phrase "motherfucking son of a fucker" repeatedly. Our clips got stuck and the ropes got tangled on the spinnaker pole. To say it was frustrating was a bit like describing Richard's attitude as sometimes being sarcastic! Frankly, we were all losing our patience, and Bransom was just the least inhibited about expressing his feelings!

But on the 10th I had a better watch, helming and trimming well in harmony with Ian, and making good progress throughout the afternoon. Then there was good progress again through the evening until the morning watch when the wind and boat speed both dropped, causing yet more frustration. We were maintaining our position south of the fleet, but then while working on the promo we discovered that the head had been put on the wrong way round and the tapes were all twisted, so there was yet more delay and frustration while we undid it and changed it back again.

All this time, the idea of writing all this down when I got home was boiling around in my head. I even sent a fax to Vicki, the journalist who had crewed with us on the first leg, about writing a book. It was also about this time that I started to get crunching headaches, which I ascribed to blood pressure through the worry and stress of doing something like this while I had a large family and business back home.

At this point, I discovered another potentially serious problem. It is amazing how much care is needed to keep something as apparently "low-tech" as a sailing boat moving efficiently (and I am only talking here about the "low-tech" end of the operation, not about all the

GPS navigation gizmos and stuff that we had on board – just the sails and rigging). We were about to gibe, and so I started to get the jockey pole ready. Just as we were about to commence the operation, I found the release pin, which had dropped off, rolling around on the deck. If there is one thing I learned about sailing in this whole adventure, it is that God is truly in the details: so much depends on little pins, clips and swivels. If we had lost that pin then we would have had major problems. As it was, we were extremely lucky to save it. The spring had fortunately stayed in, and if that had been lost then all would have been lost! It was only the amazing skills of Alan, our Mr Fixit, that saved us from racing disaster, because it would have been a major operation to replicate the pin. As it was, the repair turned out to be a time-consuming two-man job.

In the meantime, it was hell on the foredeck. At the time Alan likened it to being on a family holiday in a caravan in Skegness in the rain: cooped up with nowhere to go and having to put up with the people – so that tells you how bad it was! (It also tells you something about Alan's capacity for understatement!) We had number 1 headsail up, then changed to number 3 and reefed in a couple of times. All this time we were sailing in about 45 knots of breeze and heeled over at about thirty-five degrees. In these conditions working, which was difficult at the best of times, was nigh impossible.

Looking back, I have to say that a lot of the things that happened probably had a serious effect on our eventual placing. If we hadn't had to contend with so many broken and lost pins and blown spinnakers, we would definitely have been able to put up a better showing. In the cold light of day, I do have to conclude that attention to detail during maintenance in stopovers could have been improved. It would have been quite easy to institute a double-checking procedure for key maintenance tasks, and would not have added significantly to the time taken. I also feel that, as hinted earlier, at least some of the blown spinnakers could have been avoided if we had learnt some lessons the very first time it happened. Specifically, I think there was a "macho" tendency to try and get the fastest speed, regardless of the strain that this put upon the fabric, and it would have been more intelligent to settle in a little behind our maximum speed on occasions in the interests of better preserving our equipment.

Perhaps, in summary, I feel that physically we gave the race everything we had. But we could have done more to ensure that our physical efforts were channelled more effectively. We could have worked smarter, as they say, to ensure that our hard work paid off to its best advantage. The routines could perhaps have been slicker and more automatic to ensure that fewer mistakes were made. Perhaps it is true that while on board we were completely focused, but that on land we took our eyes off the ball a bit and sadly worked against the good efforts that we were putting in at sea. We were not as focused and co-ordinated in port as we should have been, and the vision and discipline were not there in sufficient supply. Richard was, of course, skipper and therefore ultimately responsible, but obviously he relied heavily on delegation to the rest of us, and to be fair to him, Ian had full responsibility for the upper diagonals and split pins. I had responsibility for winches and heads along with Tim, and we did operate a system of double checks, and of course the record shows that we didn't have any problem with these aspects. I can only think that the same degree of checking didn't go on in other teams. But so far as the pins were concerned, this could have been catastrophic, and there really should have been a system of cross-checking for them.

On the 11th there were appalling conditions on the foredeck. We were flying the Number 2 headsail and storm gib, and then had to hoist the trisail, which is a replacement for the mainsail in very tricky conditions. We continued to make good progress in spite of the conditions and moved up to sixth place, twelve miles behind the leaders. I was on the helm for two sessions, and at times we had about 50 knots of wind coming straight at us. It was extremely cold and wet on the foredeck however, and I personally was very tired. Nevertheless, we'd had had a good night's sailing with good speeds, and when the port watch took over they inherited a good situation. Eventually we were able to lower the trisail and storm gib.

On the chat show the following morning *Nuclear Electric* mentioned that they had spent forty-eight hours repairing their main and staysail, so we were obviously not the only ones having major problems. It is perhaps fair to assume that other boats were also having comparable difficulties, but that they weren't letting on.

On the 13th we encountered high winds up to 50 knots, and at the same time we saw the southern lights which were very spectacular. It was a strange juxtaposition, seeing the lights so breathtakingly beautiful, tranquil and serene while all Hell was raging across our deck! One particular tack I remember from that night, and will do so for the rest of my life, was particularly nightmarish. As we were going about, a "lazy sheet" developed, and I had to feed this, single-handed, round the rigging on the foredeck. I was cold, wet and, quite frankly, scared shitless. I look back on this episode as one of my most amazing exploits of the whole voyage even though I say so myself. But worse was to come. When I got back in the cockpit at the end of the watch, I was completely exhausted, and I believe my co-ordination must have been suffering from fatigue. Tim was sail-trimming and my final act of the watch, and almost as it turned out, of my life, was to help him by winching in the staysail sheet. I stepped over in the cockpit to do this and fell forwards. I went shooting through the rail, head and shoulders first, heading straight for the boiling seas and almost certain extinction. At the last moment, my legs caught on the toe rail, and I was left dangling over the side, almost choking on my heart which had found its way into my mouth!

After that it was extremely difficult to sleep. Once again, I hadn't been clipped on, but in this case it wasn't my fault. There had been no time in the situation. I hadn't been remiss, it was just that however careful you are, however many procedures you implement and ingrain into your subconscious, in the end you are involved in an extremely hazardous operation and you just can't guard against every eventuality. Even if you follow all proper prescribed procedures there is still a large risk.

Before retiring that night, I suffered a further mishap. Although this was not life-threatening, it did in fact result in serious physical injury. I believe it was partly due to the fact that my body was still in a state of shock, and not responding as accurately as it should have been, but it also had a lot to do with the extreme conditions we were facing. I was in the galley and decided to tidy up the cupboard. I knew I wasn't going to be able to sleep, so I wanted to do something useful with the time and hopefully also tire myself out. I put on a CD of relaxing music and started on the job, which you might have thought would have been a routine one. But the trouble is that everything you do on a boat in the Southern Ocean has a large element of risk to it, and before I knew what was happening I found myself free-falling about nine feet and fetching up against the galley wall! The boat had once again suddenly heeled over to about thirty-five degrees and gravity had done the rest!

My arm and left side were extremely painful where I had collided with the wall. Margot, our resident nurse, strapped me up but I had weals all over the affected part and pins and needles in my hand, so I was fairly certain I had broken something. Margot's advice was that I should be confined to bed with analgesics, and that I should rest and miss the 1800 to 2200 watch.

This was very unusual for me because I normally take a very stoical attitude to injury and force myself to carry on with the job. But I think the combined events of the night had shaken me up more than I had realised. Richard, right on cue with his sparkling wit, came in and started singing, "I'll Tumble For You"!

We hit very heavy seas on the 14th, and I had to end my enforced inactivity to help deal with the general pandemonium on board. "Pandemonium" is not a word that I have thought about much in my life, but as I write it now I realise what an appropriate term it is for what was happening at the time, as it did indeed seem as though "all the demons" had been let loose. I was riding shotgun, watching out for icebergs, with Bransom helming. It was a very scary situation, not to mention extremely uncomfortable, with 45-knot winds driving needles of sea water into our eyes. It was impossible to spend more than about thirty minutes on deck at a time, because your hands would turn into Marks and Spencer frozen ready meals, and your eyes would burst and freeze as they dribbled down your cheeks. Of course, we had specially designed protective gloves and jackets to shield us from these conditions, but they were basically ineffective.

At 0600 I went gratefully down to my cabin, desperate to sleep, only to find water streaming in over my bunk. It was completely saturated, and I had to switch to Eileen's on the other side. This was very little better because it was extremely hot, being near the generators. In her bunk it was like being in a sauna, and in mine it was like being in the plunge pool. Take your pick!

So there was no realistic possibility of sleep, and conditions on deck were horrendous. Number 3 and storm gib were up once again, with no main. As a prelude to what was about to happen, the gib sheet snapped. A spare one was threaded by the port watch and then...all hell broke loose. I had been wrong earlier: we were only now reaching pandemonium.

A massive wave hit us and knocked us down. As we recovered, we realised that six of our winch handles, stored in pockets on the deck, had been simply lost overboard. We were therefore down to our minimum complement of five or six, and if any more got lost or damaged we would have to get into complex swapping and sharing operations to spread them around. But, of course, such considerations were now far from our minds. First of all, we had to get through this or we wouldn't have any more opportunities to use winches even if we'd had a whole boatload of them! The galley looked as though a bomb had been let off in the middle of a chimps' tea party. There was food lying in chaotic piles everywhere: bread mix, flour, tomato ketchup, coffee, tea, porridge, McDougall's dried foods, cornflakes, mustard, dried egg, dried milk, HP sauce and broken biscuits. Much of the dried food had also started to reconstitute itself on contact with the considerable volume of water that had burst in from outside.

As I scanned slowly over the damage, one particularly large pile of foodstuffs started to move. It was Claire. She had been sitting at the computer when all the boxes had come flying over from the far side of the galley and emptied their contents over her. A large amount of food had also landed on the computers and it was obvious that there was going to have to be a major clean-up operation. I volunteered at that stage with Alan to clean up before going up on deck. In effect, we were the only people willing to do it because everybody else was too concerned and worried about what the weather was going to do next.

So here we were in the Southern Ocean. This is what we had waited for and expected and dreaded all at once. It was suddenly living up to expectations.

Obviously, everybody was very cold and wet all day. We started a routine known as the Ice Watch. I would switch with Trevor every thirty minutes in wearing goggles to protect us from the piercing rain. Thirty minutes was the maximum you could do without losing your hands, before having to go below and warm up. The wind eventually eased, and we raised Number 1 staysail and main with reefs, and started making good progress. We were currently sixth behind *Concert*. Gradually we came to learn that a number of boats had suffered during the storms, which had blown hurricane force gusts of 70 knots at times. A lot of the boats had put trisails up which had then been damaged; on *Nuclear Electric* the steering gear and mainsail had been damaged;

many boats reported radar problems; and *Pause to Remember* dropped back in the fleet while they dealt with problems with their mainsail.

On the 15th March I was on watch from 0600 – 1200 when we developed our own radar problems. Even Alan, who was normally best with these things, couldn't revive it. So Mr Fixit couldn't fix it, and if Mr Fixit couldn't fix it, it probably couldn't be fixed! So there we were in the middle of prime iceberg territory with no radar, which was not a good situation to be in. We would just have to rely on warnings from other members of the fleet.

We lost out a bit to other boats but were still hanging in there at sixth. We now had a bit of breathing space to patch over some of the damage. First we sweated Ian and Neil up the mast to repair the Windex system. Then I put in a blanker plate in the vent to stop the water coming into my bunk. Normally it's left open to allow air to circulate, but watertightness was a greater need at the moment. I had a sarcastic fax from Kate about the terrible time she was having at home, but I'm afraid I was in no mood for it and returned the compliment. Claire and Margot masterminded a culinary rising from the ashes by cooking some fresh scones for us all. They were absolutely fantastic, and just what we needed at the time.

Ian had another look at the radar, and decided that it was definitely beyond immediate repair with the resources we had available, which was a major frightener as we came to realise that we would definitely need to rely on others for iceberg information. At the time we were closest to *Concert* and so asked them to relay information to us, just before we heard that *Toshiba* and *Group 4*, who were also ahead of us, had just sighted icebergs – so our fears had been well-founded. Richard started to panic slightly, because of the weight of responsibility on his overburdened shoulders, but the rest of us were more sanguine.

Then at 1200 we suddenly found ourselves becalmed again! The worst weather we had experienced suddenly evaporated and, were it not the case that the sea temperature was only five degrees, we could easily have been back in the Doldrums! This continued on the 16th, and at 1400 we spotted an iceberg that had an uncanny resemblance to the Cliffs of Dover. Somebody up there was obviously having a laugh! At 1500 we spotted another iceberg, and a pod of pilot whales and a school of dolphins came past to pay their respects. This lifted our spirits somewhat.

On the 17th we had 4,121 miles to go. It was a very cold morning, and we passed several large icebergs about twelve miles off our port bow. Somebody also spotted another iceberg with smaller chunks breaking off it, and in a sense this was more dangerous because, although they were smaller, such icebergs were more difficult to see. They were more likely to sneak up on us without warning.

On the 18th I cooked my favourite: curry! Or at least what passes for that majestic dish on a boat! I used the standard McDougall's beef stew and spiced it up by adding chillies and anything else I could lay my hands on. Once again, though, I couldn't sleep. We were still in sixth place when some heavy winds whipped up, then they dropped off again and we were almost becalmed in fog. It was a frightening situation and not a little eerie. Then we had another amazing natural firework display as the southern lights started up again.

I was on watch again at 0600, and very busy with heavy winds that had picked up again during the night and were now gusting up to 50 knots. We had reefed the main and ran into another nightmare on the foredeck when a clip broke on the tack while we were hoisting the Number 3 sail. Eventually we managed to haul it in and reclipped, but it was another complication we could have done without. Then on the 19th a huge wave washed over the deck while I was hanking on Number 3. I flew down the deck into the sail, Bransom smashed his knee on a cleat and Ian got the forestay tangled up in his own bit of rigging, which was apparently extremely painful! We dropped the mainsail in difficult conditions, but had we but known it, this was the calm before the storm.

At 0800 on the 19th things went absolutely crazy again. The winds suddenly accelerated dramatically to over 50 knots. Bransom, of course started worrying, and went to wake Richard from his beauty sleep about helming in the conditions – even though we were flying just the Number 3 and staysail without any mainsail or storm gib. I mean, conditions were bad, but it was just one of those situations where you need to keep your head down and hang on in there. But dear old Boom always had to have something to worry about! As it happened, Richard definitely did not appreciate being awoken, and was quick to voice what the rest of us were already thinking. They had a bit of a confrontation, in which Richard was typically sarcastic. Basically he asked Boom what his problem was when we were only flying Number 3, and told him to get on with it.

We were still in sixth place, having lost out slightly to the leaders. The maximum wind speed we recorded was 68 knots coming across the deck. I was washed down while on the famous Ice Watch and reluctantly travelled all the way from the coach roof to the steps of the cockpit. Once again conditions were dreadful, with stinging eyes, freezing face and hands which hurt like Hell in spite of being practically anaesthetised with the cold. Again, it was the most anyone could do to stay on deck for thirty minutes. A problem developed with the helm when a rope got stuck under a cable and prevented movement of the support. Eventually Richard and Alan cut this away, and I am afraid that I felt so low that I didn't even help, I just looked at them. This was uncharacteristic for me, but at that particular time I just somehow felt that I had nothing left in my tank. I was running on empty, emotionally and physically, and just couldn't bring myself to get involved. I guess it's a bit like inexperienced marathon runners: they say that at about twenty miles you hit "the wall," and find it very difficult to go any further. It's not that they're tired, or broken down, or that they've suffered an injury, it's just that they haven't got any fuel left. They physically can't do any more.

From 2200 till 0200 we were off watch, and that was when a serious injury happened to Sid. Another massive wave hit the boat and the wheel and pedestal got bent backwards towards the seat. Sid got trapped in between them and was in absolute agony. He apparently sustained injury to his stomach area and it was later found that he had in fact damaged his liver, spleen and pancreas. At the time, I was in my bunk, getting one of my rare snatches of sleep, and I was awoken by his screams of pain. He was calling out for Margot the nurse, as we all did when in distress. I hate to think what would have become of us all if she had been injured!

She gave him painkillers and sedatives, and he was installed in my bunk. Unfortunately for me, it was the best one for the purpose. It was on the right side of the boat for avoiding the worst of the weather, it was nearest to Margot and, after my expert repair work, it was certainly the driest berth on the boat! As I was being ousted, I said to him in my usual black humour manner, "I'll tell you a joke... later!"

I went up on deck and was stunned to see the angle at which the wheel had been bent back along with the binnacle. Yet more evidence of the force of the beast we had set ourselves to tame. We eventually managed to winch the wheel back to the upright position with Alan's help, but all this time we were losing out. Then we found out, I have to say not without the tiniest sliver of *Schadenfreude*, that *Group 4* had also been knocked down and suffered temporary loss of radar. This might sound unkind, but it was a fairly common feeling among the fleet that *Group 4* were the boat for whom everything seemed to turn out right. It was just nice to be reminded they were human every now and again.

Once we had cleared up after the storm, we found ourselves becalmed again. We maintained sixth position in front of *Motorola* throughout the 20th and 21st, and gained slightly on the boats in front. We were now north of most of the fleet and holding our course steadily. Sid was improving and eventually managed to sit up and walk to the chart table. As luck would have it I was suffering a dreadful headache again all day with more difficulty sleeping. Since Sid was in my bunk I was moved around into various people's beds, depending who was on or off watch at the time. But eventually my head cleared up and I was able to join in some good sailing down the line through into the 22nd.

Then we had what I always think of as the Bitches' Watch. For some reason when we were on watch that day from 0200 to 0600, we were all very tired and irritable, and just couldn't stop bitching at each other! The low point was when Richard shouted at Bransom, who was complaining of being tired and (sob) being unable to go on. What soap opera melodrama! Ian was on Mother at that time so couldn't help out, and that put more pressure on Bransom and Neil and as a further concession we agreed that they could helm most of the time.

I managed to get three hours' sleep, and when I awoke my headaches had gone. I got up and chatted to Margot for a while and together we read through some letters we had received from schools through the BT education programme. I also had a fax from Zena who had had a meeting back in the UK with Vicki. As I thought about this meeting I realised that the two of them were very similar people and that they would probably have got on very well together.

On the 23rd we flew the heavy kite again… and promptly blew it again with Neil at the helm in 40 knots of wind. It was a sad reflection on our learning curve, but this was becoming almost a regular occurrence. We had to make do with poling out the Number 1 and Number 2 headsails on both sides, basically using them in the same way that you would normally use a spinnaker. At the time I remember thinking that we were nearly out of the "Furious Fifties".

We had to relay back that *Pause to Remember* had broken their boom and were having to repair it, and they thought they would probably have to put in to the Kerguelen Islands. As it was they didn't need to and managed to repair it on board. It was only when we reached land that we understood what a mammoth task that must have been and what dedication they had shown in accomplishing it. There was a tremendous change in the sea state at the time, and this put huge stress on the mast and the rig, to say nothing of the effects of the regular gusts of 40-50 knots of wind. Our thoughts went back to the other Southern Ocean leg when similar things had happened.

On the 24th, *Group 4* started pulling away from the pack again, and by this time we had begun to ask ourselves "Why?" Did it just come down to the quality of leadership in the end? Rumours did go around that they were somehow managing to get weather and other information that was different or more advanced than ours, but this was probably just sour grapes. It was, however, maddening how they almost always managed to do just the right thing.

Our heaters chose this cold and miserable time to pack up, which added to the generally dispirited feeling that had descended upon us. But Mr Fixit, wouldn't you know it, managed to get them working again on the 25th and gave our morale a great boost. Apart from that, however, there wasn't much happening. There were about 1.5 knots of current running against us, which took its toll. We were headed west with north-westerlies blowing at about 40 knots.

We set our bearing into the sun, and sailed through a period of squalls. I was on Mother until the 26th, and heard on the race radio that Sean was just then having his back operation. On the 26th we needed major repairs again when we managed to blow the medium (promotional) spinnaker as well as the heavy. I didn't go to bed all day, and once again it was a replay of the other Southern Ocean leg when I had got completely immersed in the housekeeping. I was becoming a proper little housewife, and made bread for everybody which was greatly appreciated.

We passed the way point which was (the Kerguelen Islands – remember the warning at the beginning of this leg: no more land until the Kerguelen Islands?) although we couldn't see them. At 1133 we were running down the line towards Cape Town, still in sixth place with *Group 4* 160 miles ahead. At 2000 I went off to bed and found that I was completely hyper, and at first I couldn't sleep at all. Then when I did get to sleep, I slept very well with all trace of my headaches gone.

On the 27th the wind suddenly gusted up to 68 knots for half an hour. We were about to drop the main but then it relented to 30 knots, which was in a way a bit of a disappointment – we couldn't even rely on the weather to be universally awful! We played around putting various reefs in and out but to little effect, and ended up very tired at the end of the watch again, having slept so little the night before.

Back on watch again, we were running the bearing in calm conditions. It felt very exhilarating, just like you think it should feel. We all felt a lot better. At this stage, there were 2,270 miles to go, but then conditions got suddenly rougher again.

Bransom was on Mother, so we had to change sails two or three times without his help, while it was blowing the usual nightmare on the foredeck. It was just Ian and me, and looking back on it I realise that we only just managed to pull the Number 2 headsail down successfully. I don't know how we did it in those circumstances – the force of the wind was such that I was literally swinging on the hanks trying to bring my body weight to bear on it, with Ian at the base. Then we hoisted Number 3. So that day there were basically two of us handling all the sail changes in big seas and 60 knots of wind. I must say that when I think back on it, I thank my lucky stars for all the hard training I was put through.

The next mishap was the loss of the SSB aerial (the inshore radio system), which snapped off the back of the boat. As it happened, it wasn't a major problem, but it could have been in different circumstances. We registered the lowest pressure we had experienced, at 978 millibars and our clock showed 2,150 miles to go.

The wind eased and then picked up again, and then Alan and I had to do a regular hazardous job. Before Alan had come on board, of course, I had done this with Sean, but now we were the strong arm team, known colloquially as "Red and Dare" (I don't know who was meant to be who!) Our mission, should we choose to accept it, was to go and change the propane gas bottle. Now this may not sound like a huge job, but it certainly becomes one when the boat is heeling over at thirty-five degrees in atrocious conditions. The housing for the bottle was located to the left of the seat on the helm, and we had to manoeuvre one full gas bottle from the companionway leading up from the lower deck to the upper deck, move it about fifteen feet to the helm and connect it up in substitution for the empty one.

The seas eased a bit after that, as if they had been trying to cause us maximum aggravation during the changing process. We were still lying sixth, eighty-two miles off the pace, but gaining on *Group 4*, *Global Teamwork* and *Save The Children*. Then we heard that *Group 4* had snapped their steering cable, so at last their juggernaut was slowed for a period while they replaced it from spares they had on board. Unsurprisingly, we managed to make some gains on them at this stage. Even *Group 4* couldn't make progress while they were standing still!

In accordance with Richard's clock system, we put our time back another hour to GMT + 4. I was on watch in the afternoon, and the weather had warmed up in sunny conditions. We passed the Crozet Islands on the 30th with 1,978 miles to go, and it was a happy Easter for Richard with us moving up into fourth place. The water temperature was now twenty degrees, so it was definitely warming up.

On the 31st we were enjoying great sailing down the line, but then our water maker stopped working. The low pressure pump wasn't working either, so it was time for the imposition of water rationing. To save people from embarrassing themselves being caught using water when they shouldn't, one of the head pumps was taped up so that it was physically impossible to use. So there was only one pump working on one side. It was the sort of situation that sounds like a bit of a joke, so the danger was that people might not understand the severity of it. There therefore had to be a demonstrative act to stop people using it.

We started putting our backs into medium spinnaker repairs again, and soon (we were getting quite expert at it now!) completed it, packed it and stored it. We managed to achieve some great speeds down the line, and then I had a great sleep through to the 1st. I was up at 0155 and full of the joys of April Fool's Day. I sent a fax to Sean, asking him to set up a spoof fax to Bransom, saying that the BT Global Challenge authorities were making a film starring him, and referring to him as the "Manx Yank"; furthermore, because of his sterling efforts on board *Commercial Union*, they were considering appointing him as a boat skipper for the next race!

I think it was at this stage, while sitting making further repairs to the promo spinnaker, that I finally decided that I would write all this down in a book, so that the world could know all about it. "Cruising – the alternative BT global challenge!" – or something like that. Apparently there was a good starry night's sailing up above, but I didn't appreciate it because I was assigned to repairs below, putting Dacron on the Promo with Alan (a much better alternative to stitching and sewing. See? I told you we'd been learning a lot from our experience!).

Then I had my first shower in weeks. I washed my hair, put on a clean shirt and new underpants, and felt fantastic! Then Jim the chirpy cockney started a book on finishing positions and arrival times. My original prediction was that we would be fourth, but after a sarcastic exchange with Richard I changed it to first! You changed it to first!

That day the results showed us in fourth place, seventy-six miles behind the leader. The boat was finally beginning to dry out, although Margot's bunk was still quite wet. On the 3rd, I had a great sleep from 0600 to 1200, only to be rudely awakened by a ship's rat in my bunk. It turned out that this was a present from Richard, who was getting very frustrated about the fact that it looked like he was going to lose the swearing bet he had with me. He could see that £300 cheque disappearing into the charity box faster than you could say "*Group 4*"! This was his method of trying to push me to my limit. The thing he didn't understand, however, was that swearing just isn't a habit with me. It was a bit like betting a strict Muslim that he would have a drink at some point during the race – there was just no way I was going to lose the bet because I simply don't swear!

And this is a good point to say how this famous bet arose in the first place. When I first met him, I told him a shaggy dog story. He fell for it and started swearing profusely. I told him this was a weakness, and he said, "What, so I suppose you never swear, do you?" I told him that no, I didn't. He wouldn't believe it, however, and bet that he would have me swearing by the end of the race. He might just as well have written out his cheque and given it to me there and then. Eventually back at the welcome reception in Southampton, up on the stage with Sean, the cheque was duly handed over, and I had it framed.

The closest he got was when I was playing the Romeo and Juliet soundtrack CD on the boat, which I like a lot. He criticised it, saying it was pseudo-modern rubbish and that I had only bought it because of Vicki(!). This did seriously wind me up, as he was getting very personal about it. But in the end, swearing is something I just don't do, so the bet was safe.

I remember during this phase sweating Neil up the mast single-handed to replace the Windex, so I think I must have stayed pretty fit, as it would normally take two to do this. One night I spotted some fishing boats and sent a fax to CU West End, and I had a feeling that things were starting to come together again. We were past the worst of the Southern Ocean, so in one sense we had all but made it, and now we could concentrate on the race without distraction. It was a bright, starry night with the medium spinnaker up, the repair looked good, and the future looked good. We were achieving excellent speeds down the line, holding our own in fourth place with the leaders.

I had a great sleep between 0200 and 0400, and then the wind picked up suddenly, putting the spinnaker under strain. It blew again in the most spectacular style with a clew and the head coming out and dangling in the wake of the boat, so that we had to pull it in. All hands were called on deck to recover it. Luckily we managed it and then got the Number 1 and staysail up straight away.

We managed to maintain our speed at about 10 knots. Trevor, the bumbling professor, played true to form and lost his twathat overboard. On the 5th I was on Mother watch again, and we all know what that means, don't we, children?! Curry time! Well really it should have been Lancashire Hotpot, because that's what it said on the label, but I changed it into a curry. Massive anvil-like clouds were building up ahead, and squalls were starting to come in. Alan was once again supervising spinnaker repairs, and I was doing my best in the galley. I baked bread and made a cheesecake as well (but don't look so hungry, this was all made out of various forms of powder reconstituted!).

But no sooner had I finished the cooking than my blinding headache came back again. Richard started suspecting (as he had done before) that we had mildew on board. He got this so firmly fixed in his head that he threw all the chocolate bars overboard in a fit of hygiene mania! He'd done the same thing before with tea towels after he got a bad stomach, and decided that it must be the tea towels that had done it (on evidence that certainly would not have convinced Hercule Poirot) and they all had to be thrown out!

I had another reasonable sleep but awoke again with a headache. We had a mixed day of speeds until we were finally able to raise the heavy spinnaker at 0630 on the 6th, when we got great speeds of 14-15 knots. Neil and Richard were at the helm as they were the best performers at the time. But then at 0900 the spinnaker blew again, so once more we had to fall back on Numbers 1 and 2 poled out again. Nevertheless, we did good work getting the rig up (well, we'd had a lot of practice by now, hadn't we?) and registered good speeds again. Incidentally, our on-board allowance of spinnakers was one light, one heavy and two mediums – one with the promotional logo and one plain.

I came off watch, and then Lars came on and notched up 19.5 knots which was a record at the time, and I have to admire his achievement, especially as it was achieved with the Number 1 rather than a spinnaker! We were still in fourth place but Bob (*Group 4*) was pulling away with 600 miles to go. There was a 2-3 knots current against us as well, so we were all getting a bit hyper about it. At times like this, we needed instant energy, but this was in short supply as Richard had thrown away all our chocolate bars. In the end, we were driven to desperate measures: there were "grab bags" on board which were only supposed to be used an abandon ship situation. They contained Tracker bars, porridge and so on. We broke into them to fuel our efforts and—wouldn't you know it?—Bransom was on Mother at the time and he started worrying about what would happen if we had to abandon ship and there weren't any grab bags. I tell you, we very nearly loaded him into a lifeboat and cast him adrift without a grab bag! This led to another in the series of arguments between Bransom and Richard, who was, truth to tell, getting mightily pissed off about the Manx Yank's mother hen attitudes – as were we all.

We lost out to the leaders that day through adverse currents. The sea temperature had risen to twenty-two degrees. On the 8th April we finally lost our fourth place to *Save the Children*. We were 9 miles behind them, and 190 miles behind the leaders. Richard then chose this most inopportune moment to have a spring clean! I mean, what was the point? We would be in port soon and would have to completely overhaul the boat anyway then. But nothing would do for our dear skipper but that he should immediately go bustling around the boat, throwing out old papers from the chart table and God knows what else.

Claire was on Mother, and made some excellent scones with jam. At the time, this hit the spot beautifully. We were sailing in bright sunshine, and it was now quite warm so some of us took to wearing shorts for the first time since Australia. Jim was still running his finishing book, and we heard on the radio chat show that we were making gains on the leaders. We were now six miles ahead of *Save the Children* and gaining on *Motorola*, and, in addition, we were now entering match-racing territory which, as we all knew was our dear skipper's forte! The current was with us – about 1–2 knots at last.

Then we heard that *Group 4* and *Concert* had spotted land. We were getting close with only 182 miles to go. We were cruising at a reasonable speed of 7 knots, and received encouraging faxes from Sean, Regent, and various other interested parties. Some of them were gently ribbing, along the lines of "Congratulations on doing quite well, but why can't you catch Bob?"

Twilight fell, and led into a cathedral night with a Milky Way stretched like a giant silk scarf across the heavens. I had been given a stellarscope for Christmas, and I got it out and had some fun identifying constellations with Trevor. The southern cross and the centaur were obvious ones, then we started on the more minor constellations. At 0100 on the 9th, however, we were back concentrating on the struggle for speed.

The dark gave way to a bright morning, and at 0600 we were still hanging on to fourth. *Save the Children* had dropped back, but *Motorola* were now closing nineteen miles behind us. *Group 4* and *Concert* finished within twenty minutes of each other, and this was a great achievement for the latter boat after having been dismasted in the other Southern Ocean leg – although as a result of that they had no real chance of doing anything impressive now in the race overall. Still, it showed great spirit for them not to have given up. *Toshiba* finished next, at 0548 GMT.

By 1100 that day we had gained on *Save the Children* and *Motorola*, and I had a great sleep, a shave and wash preparatory to landing. Richard appeared live on a chat show on the 10th on Johannesburg radio (a set-up by Roger and Bransom – in both senses of the word!).

We were all looking forward fiercely to getting in and finding some refreshment and recreation. Our ETA was 2100, and we actually got in at 2119 on 9th April, in fourth position after thirty-eight days at sea.

As I finish this chapter, though, my final thought is a sad and poignant one. I heard recently that Ed Harrison who crewed on board *Concert*, a bright young Cambridge graduate of twenty-eight, and a great friend during training, was recently killed in Africa by an elephant that became startled while he was trying to take a picture of it.

I mean, you go through all that adventure, successfully managing to survive losing a mast in the Southern Ocean in the worst weather in the world. Then you go on holiday, and get killed by an elephant. It makes you think, doesn't it?

I don't know what it makes you think. All I know is it does.

# CAPE TOWN STOPOVER

THE CAPE Town stopover was the one that I had been looking forward to ever since the start of the race – for many different reasons. First, there was the reputation of the city itself, as being a friendly, welcoming place where people enjoyed life in a pleasant, sun-filled climate. (An added bonus was that, as far as I knew, we weren't going near any gay areas!) Second, this point of the journey would mark the end of the terror of the Southern Ocean – once I got to Cape Town I would be past the worst of the horrors and it would be coasting downhill from then on. I think there was also a general feeling among the crew that we could now concentrate more on our sailing, without the stormy caprices of the oceans playing such a large part. And third, Kate and the girls were flying down to meet me. I would find my base, my anchor once more. Kate would bring me back down to earth and help me relax and focus on the remainder of the race.

The only problem was that, the night before I was due to pick them up from the airport, I was getting trashed in our adopted pub, the Rocking Shamrock, with Jo Hake and some of the other crew. Jo was a BT legger who apparently thought I was a reliable down-to-earth person! We got on well and on one occasion she asked me to drive her to Cape Town airport at five a.m. in the morning to pick up Neil, her husband. As she put it, she felt that she could rely on me to get up! As it was, I nearly destroyed my reputation by not getting up after a late night session with Rob the BBC cameraman. The Rocking Shamrock was yet another of the Irish bars that we seemed to be drawn to on our travels. We seemed to find them all over the place and they were without exception dens of the deepest iniquity. I shouldn't have driven Jo on that occasion because I had only got in at four and had to get up at five! In the end, it all turned out OK and Jo was very grateful. She was apparently completely oblivious to my situation, although I must have been positively reeking with alcohol. She must have thought it was my aftershave.

Anyway, I just got up and did the job, no problem. I suppose I had done my apprenticeship on the many weekends when I was first married. Kate and I used to go out every weekend without fail to various pubs before any children arrived, and would invariably drive home on about four or five pints. I suppose I might feel guilty about it, but Kate certainly never demurred. In my view, that almost halves the responsibility.

So the night before I was due to meet Kate and the girls I was in a strikingly similar situation. I was out drinking until four a.m. and was due to collect them at six. The crew, very trustingly, lent me their minibus and I wove my way out along the motorway in a state of semi-consciousness. When I got to the airport I dived into the cafeteria, ordered four pots of double-strength coffee, drank them all and sat in the arrivals area with a stupid grin on my face, intended to convince everybody that I had just arrived fresh from an untroubled night spent between freshly laundered sheets, followed by a healthy breakfast of fruit and cereals.

It seemed to work. Certainly nobody said anything, but I'm sure after twenty years of seeing me in a state Kate knows the signs when I'm covering up. But maybe not, and maybe it's no different from when we used to drive home from certain pubs all those years ago. Anyway, if the end doesn't justify the means, then at least it goes a long way towards it. Well, doesn't it? Everybody got back safely and we had a great time.

There was more than enough interesting activity to keep everybody happy in Cape Town. We went on a garden route trip which Kate and the girls really loved, and I was in my element among some of the most stunning golf courses ever made. We went to visit a local girls' school where I had been invited to give a presentation about the race, and I did my usual exhibitionist bit by performing a striptease (ostensibly to show off the full range of kit that you have to wear when sailing a boat on a round the world race). It was just like The Full Monty, although we didn't have the soundtrack, which was a shame. I also didn't make too much of the tattoo as Kate and the girls were in the audience, and the tattoo, as I have mentioned before, has always been a particularly sore point with Kate.

One of the people that I remember most fondly from this stage of the race was Jim Desmond, who we jokingly referred to as Mr Mischief. He was a BT legger who joined us from  Sydney to Boston. Jim was very much the cheeky cockney sparrow, a lovely guy with a great sense of humour and not an ounce of malice in him. He was excellent company on the tricky second Southern Ocean leg and showed true strength of character during his time with us.

I first got to know him on a team-building motor sport event in Salcombe in Devon as part of the race preparation. We stayed for three nights in a charming old manor house hotel called Bovingdon Hall. After dinner with the crew, a small group of us inevitably retired to the bar. Jim and his future wife, Mary, were among the group, but then gradually people started disappearing. At the death, there was just Jim, Vicki and me left, and then Vicki also fell off the perch. I certainly don't remember going to bed, but Vicki reliably informed me later that when she left us we were in that exalted state of inebriation known as alcoholic glossolalia – she could hear us talking, and she could understand our individual words, but when she tried to catch the meaning of the sentences she found it impossible. We were basically speaking a language that we could presumably understand between us, but which no other sentient being (or at least not Vicki, as a fairly representative member of that class) could comprehend. That would have been interesting enough after a single night, but the strange thing is that the same thing happened the following night. This time Mary was also in on the speaking in tongues and once again Vicki couldn't understand it. (Come to think of it, maybe that says more about the effect of drink on Vicki rather than us!)

Mary reminded me very much of Kate at that age—a sensible, dependable primary school teacher, with a similar gentle manner and outlook on life, who had somehow managed to get hooked up with a complete madman!

On the final night, we continued much as before, but hatched a cunning plan to wind Richard up. At two-thirty, we decided, Mary would ring up to Richard's room, panting breathlessly to appeal to the manly Richard's chivalrous instincts, and saying that I had gone berserk in the bar because the barman was refusing to keep the bar open. I was threatening him and Richard was the only man she knew who could control me. Please could he come and help as otherwise the police were going to be called…etc., etc. You get the picture.

The beauty of this was of course that it was entirely believable, and it fitted precisely with Richard's character to see himself as the Man of Action, the Knight in Shining Armour, the Saviour of the Universe and all that.

The upshot was that Mary made the call, I stood near the barman as if threatening him, and Jim stood on the lookout. We heard Richard coming down the stairs, and I duly grabbed hold of the barman's lapels and started shaking and abusing him. Richard swallowed the bait whole, and started trying to reason with me, with Jim and Mary backing him up. It was great fun. Then finally I let go of the barman raised my arms in the air, turned round and said,

"Sorry, Richard, only joking."

Richard, however, was the only person in the room who didn't seem to be amused. To this day I don't know if he was seriously upset

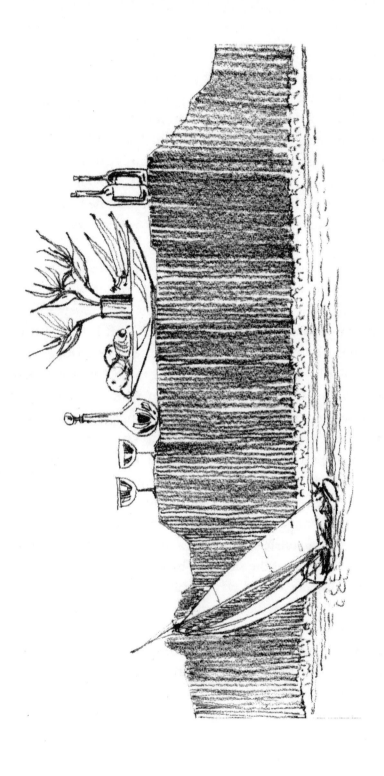

or just embarrassed at being taken in, but either way he stormed off back to bed. He certainly made a passing remark to Jim:

"I want him f★★★ing well out of here by the morning."

Personally, I think that the reason for Richard's reaction was that we had understood him too well, and had cooked up exactly the sort of situation that he would get seriously involved in. When he realised it was a wind-up, it was presumably a double disappointment to him. First, he had been taken in, and second he had been deprived of a situation in which he could show his assertiveness and diplomatic tact.

These situations I get myself into are a permanent puzzle to me. Anybody who knows me would tell you that I would never harm anyone, and yet I am always putting myself in these scrapes. My father was the same, and no doubt that is where I get it from. I really don't know how far I'm going or how far the other people are getting emotionally involved in the situation. I think I probably have a sort of antenna for the types of situation in which people are going to get stressed out and then I play on them mercilessly. I always go too far and then somebody always steps in to save the situation.

There is probably only one situation in which I have nearly hit someone. That was in Amsterdam after a football trip. We had just finished a game, and this guy kept on and on at me about how many chances I had missed. He made one remark too many, and my hand drew back – fortunately there was another guy with us who grabbed my arm and defused the situation by diverting us off on a pub crawl (and that's usually a good way to calm me down!).

Anyway, Jim, Mary, the barman and I all had a good laugh afterwards, and this firmly cemented my relationship with Jim.

Another great friend from that stage was Alan Thomas, whom we variously called Mr Fixit or Mr Impossible, because some of the handyman jobs he took on and succeeded with were positively miraculous. He was a BT legger who was scheduled to join us for the Cape Town to Boston leg, but, in the event, he hopped aboard at Sydney because Sean wasn't able to rejoin us as he had hoped. He was a great asset to the boat because of his magical way with all things mechanical, but he also had a wicked sense of humour. I served as his unofficial apprentice during the legs in which he took part, and, as a result, I was involved in the hair-raising situation when our gas supply ran out in the middle of a storm in the Southern Ocean (described in my account of the 4th leg).

Another interesting character was Trevor Corner, whom we called Mr Clever or the Nutty Professor, depending on our prevailing perception at the time. He certainly led a very insular existence while on the voyage and kept himself very much to himself away from the boat. He was obviously a very clever person who had an infectious dry sense of humour. I have a great respect for him although he obviously wasn't really my "type". He was very relaxed and laid back, and admitted that, although the 'sixties were his heyday, he feels as though he never really got invited to the party. He says that he lived a simple life and wasn't really exposed to the excesses of sex n' drugs n' rock n' roll. We shared the same watch for three legs of the race, and I like to think that we hit it off in a quiet sort of way.

We shared a fondness for the *Hitchhiker's Guide to the Galaxy* and shared the strong conviction that the answer to the universe was definitely forty-two. I remember sitting with him on the foredeck coming into port at some point and looking forward to the first alcoholic drink in – yes, you've guessed it – forty-two days, and one thing led to another and by the time we made landfall we had to admit that we had just spent half an hour talking the most concentrated purée of rubbish that had ever oozed from our orifices. But that was again rubbish, because we had enjoyed it so much!

He inhabited the character of a bumbling professor. Personally, I don't think he was naturally that persona; it was just a useful social shorthand for him. It meant, among other things, that:

he could do much as he liked;

he could say things to people that would have sounded offensive from other people who were considered to be more in touch with the world; and

he wasn't ribbed for not joining in the prodigious drinking sessions that most of the rest of us went in for.

He once apologised to me for being so bumbling, but I winked and said to him, "That's fine – you can be as bumbling as you want to be." I think he understood then that I knew that it was partly an act, a flag of convenience, because he smiled his dry smile at me and nodded his head slightly as if to say, "OK, that's our little secret."

For all that I got on well with him, I must confess to having left him, rather unkindly, in a difficult situation. He Sean and I had been watching a cricket match back in Wellington and we all then repaired to a bar afterwards. We went in and ordered drinks, and only then did it slowly dawn on us that the bar was populated by a lot of very strange people. Specifically, there were a lot of men dressed in women's clothes, and also a few women dressed in men's clothes. Sean and I began to think it was not a very good place to be, but Trevor seemed to be quite at home, and started up a long conversation with one of the cross-dressers. I truly have no way of knowing whether in his private life he might have been drawn to that sort of thing, or whether he just had a natural academic's curiosity about this particular aspect of the world around him, but either way Sean and I just walked away and left him. We don't know what, if anything, happened after we left, but he seemed very happy just sitting and talking and, after all, he was a big boy for all his bumbling professorship which, as I say, may or may not have been as bumbling as it seemed. There was one occasion when Richard and most of the crew absolutely crucified him for a petty offence which was perhaps a typical "bumbling professor" misdemeanour, when he took the keys to the minibus in Cape Town and forgot to return them the next day when Richard needed access to unload some equipment. But anyone can forget about keys and I often think that it was partly Richard's fault for not having a spare set anyway. I do think that on that occasion he was unfairly censured because it was seen as a failing that was peculiar to his character, whereas we've all done things like that. Personally, I think Richard was very petty about it. But having said that, I did think that in other ways he was very pragmatic and sensible, for instance about my little snoring dispute!

All in all, the Cape Town stopover was my most stable and restful. We had finished the Southern Ocean, and my family were there for a large part of the time to keep me on an even keel. I found that, instead of my usual drinking antics, I did some healthy things, like taking part in a "Surf and Turf" run.

Things were working out all right. I was through the worst of it, and my family was through the worst of it. And then, just before we set sail once more, a complete bombshell fell on me out of the blue — more of this later.

## Cape Town to Boston

---

THIS WAS the leg where we knew we could do really well. Or at least we had thought we could before the experience of the previous legs! The point was that we perceived one of our main strengths as being spinnaker work — running before the wind. However, as you will have realised by now, our tendency had been to attack our spinnaker work a bit *too* enthusiastically, with the result that we kept on blowing holes in our spinnakers before we could get the best use out of them. The question facing us in this leg was whether we could use our spinnakers to the utmost without ripping them to shreds!

But for me it was hardly the ideal situation to be setting off. I have already mentioned that the state of both my business and my family back home in London were continually preying on my mind, but during the Cape Town stopover a further burden was added. This burden was physically very light, only about seven pounds, four ounces to be precise, but emotionally very heavy, and had been delicately placed on the top of the pile by Zena's sister, who had unknowingly let the cat out of the bag.

I had been making final phone calls just before starting out, and she had let slip that Zena had just had a baby on 4th May by Caesarean section. And I hadn't even known she was pregnant! She must have known before I had even set off on the race, but in her typically selfless way she had decided to keep it from me, and determined to manage the business single-handed in my absence and manage to have a baby at the same time. Her plan was to turn up on the docks to welcome me home and present me with the baby to hold!

I felt like one of those fairytale heroes who goes on a long journey and meets some weird magician in his travels who helps him out of trouble, but only if he promises to give him something in his house that he doesn't even know he has. This, of course, turns out to be the baby that he didn't know his "wife" was carrying when he left. My normal pre-embarkation telephone calls therefore changed from their usually mildly panicking character to frantic gibbering and stammering. I know I go on about Bransom worrying a lot, but I think in those final hours before setting off on that 5th leg I could easily have rivalled him for head worrier! I was in a terrible state, with a patina of shock laid over my normal shredded nerves. The more I thought about it, the wiser I thought Zena had been to try to keep the secret from me. In the end, I don't think it affected my racing, because once you get into the swing of it you tend to forget about all your external pressures. But it certainly had me jumping around like a speed-fuelled springbok for a few hours.

Notwithstanding all this personal turmoil, the leg got off to a fantastic start. Well, it was hardly surprising when Archbishop Desmond Tutu himself turned up to give us a direct link to God for his benediction, but everybody else turned up as well for good measure and gave us a wonderful send-off from Cape Town Quay. The Commercial Union support was, as usual, brilliant, and, of course, all the other boats had very vocal and demonstrative support from their own various sponsors. The quay and harbour was a chaos of colour, with crowds of people on the quay and on various boats, all shouting and singing and waving things. It was a bit like a football stadium set up by the waterside with fourteen sets of supporters cheering on a game with the same emotional supercharge as an England vs. Germany fixture.

For me it had been one of the best stopovers, partly because the percentage of it that I could actually remember was relatively high, and partly because the memories themselves were so enjoyable. Everything had combined to make it a great experience. It had been a fantastic city, full of activity and atmosphere, particularly along the waterfront, and the scenery had been so breathtaking that I was still gasping as we pulled out of the harbour. The Cape Grace Hotel had been superb, and of course it had been my first reunion with the children since setting off. It was strange to think that, before we had parted, the whole of the Southern Ocean and all the perils that lay therein had been ahead of me, and now here we had met again and it was all behind me. The following legs were going to be tough sailing, certainly, but they were not going to be nearly as dangerous, and there was a great feeling of having got through the worst of it. In fact, looking back on it, it was very fortunate that I had received the news about Zena when I did – if I had heard about her pregnancy before one of the Southern Ocean legs, the stress would have been unbearable.

One of the highlights of the stopover had been giving a talk to a local girls' school, simply because of their obvious enthusiasm and interest. There was also a "Surf and Turf" run along the coast for about thirteen miles, and I was very pleased with my performance, particularly as I hadn't had a run for ages. It was a welcome change from working on the boat, and gave me a different kind of exercise, using different sets of muscles.

So we pulled away from the Victoria and Albert waterfront, in bright and sunny weather for once, but with variable winds as usual. The gin and Jag brigade in their luxury powered palaces tagged along with us until they got bored, then at 1330 the real race began again in earnest. Everybody hoisted their headsails for the first mile, and then, one by one, up went the heavy spinnakers. I was feeling very tired, thrust straight into rough confusion of work on the foredeck after the relative calm and relaxation of the stopover. My particular workload was bigger at this point as well because Tim had cut his arm while working on the foredeck. It started swelling quite badly, and I was reminded of how I had caught my arm while tacking on the training sail just before the previous leg.

As I have said, this was the long spinnaker leg, and our crew was really keyed up for it because we knew we could do well. Whenever we had been involved in "match" racing conditions we had been extremely competitive and given a good account of ourselves. Obviously, our big test would be against the infamous *Group 4*, who had so far shown themselves to be extremely strong (with a little help from their supernatural weather forecasting abilities, of course), and we really felt we could give them a run for their money. As usual, I was feeling quite emotional and, truth to tell, a bit ill. I had my customary pit in my stomach, but this time it was exacerbated by a real gastric upset that I think was caused by the farewell dinner we had had the night before. As we gibed out past Roban Island, we caught a tremendous view of the whole fleet in sight against the dramatic backdrop of Table Mountain.

At 0400, like a troop of schoolboy virgins fumbling with their Fetherlites for the very first time, we decided to hoist our new medium spinnaker that we had acquired in Cape Town. We held our breath as it filled out, and felt very fortunate when there was no immediate sound of rending canvas. Incidentally, it is customary at the Cape Town stage for all boats to be issued with a new medium spinnaker, as the likelihood is that they have all taken something of a battering by this time, and the interests of good, competitive racing are served by giving everybody a new lease of life. *Courtaulds* and *Nuclear Electric* were just off our starboard, sailing up with full main, staysail and heavy spinnaker. That night we found ourselves in fourth place, but for some reason we couldn't see many lights in front. Perhaps they had all managed to find sets of *Group 4*'s special conveniently dimmable lights during the stopover and get them fitted. Certainly, things like sail plans were successfully cloaked in secrecy that night. Only 6,636 miles to go!

On the 4th at 2300 the poll results came through and…we were in first place! Well, we were actually first equal with *Concert*, but that didn't detract much from the spirit of jubilation which suddenly seized the crew. At least it wasn't *Group 4*, and we had never yet been in first place throughout the race. It was all coming true! Our spinnaker leg was going to work for us, our strategy had been right, we were going to overhaul the insufferable smug buggers on *Group 4* and win! It was as though everybody had received a sudden shot of adrenaline direct to the heart just from this news alone. We could do it! We deserved to be here, competing in this high-quality, high-tension, high-danger race! It was fantastic news, and major whoops of excitement flew up into the night sky. I imagine they could have heard us on all the other boats!

Then we all settled down to a concentrated determination. Now everything we did had an edge to it. Every sail change, every tack, every gibe was executed with a new enthusiasm laced with confidence that we could do it. We could win the race. We had always known that this would be the crucial leg for us, the one where we would take over if we were going to. Like a long distance runner who lies off the pace in order to conserve himself for the final push, we had the added confidence that our strategy was paying off.

We were achieving good speeds, notching up 14 knots at times. I was feeling very emotional for a number of reasons: high because of the good showing in the race; missing the family after the wonderful holiday we had had in Cape Town; wanting to get this whole thing over so that I could get back to be with them all, and to take the strain off Zena a bit with her new baby; and finally a little bit euphoric, because I could see the end in sight. I could almost feel Southampton under my feet. I sent a fax to Kate putting down my feelings, mentioning that there were another thirty-eight days at least of this leg to go. Then a fax came back from my eldest daughter, Juliet, saying that there were "only" ten weeks left in total, and not to worry. That was very comforting, and when she sounded so positive about it I felt that it was the least I could do to stop my melancholy mooning around and get back to work!

On the 5th we had a frantic watch. We had to manage two peals during the night – that is to say we had to change from the heavy to the medium spinnaker and back again. This would have been easier had I been in the team to which I had become accustomed, but I had been switched round onto a new watch. I was one of the adaptable, flexible people who didn't mind being chopped and changed a bit, which of course meant that I got chopped and changed a lot!

This meant that I was now teamed with Sid and Lars, and I must say that when I had been teamed with them earlier on the foredeck we had worked very well together. Without trying to sound big-headed, I think this is just a mark of the professionalism that had been instilled into us amateur sailors. Whoever we were paired with, whatever our personal differences, we all had the same set of procedures and standards which we automatically worked towards when put together. Obviously, certain teams had a particular magic to them that meant that they produced more than the sum of their parts, but I think it was true that you could have mixed any combination of us up together and got a good return out of us. Sid was bowman, and I slotted into the team as his Number 2. We worked very well together, I sweated him up and down the mast with no problem. During one particularly heavy stretch I realised that it was a Bank Holiday back in the UK, and spared a moment to think about the folks at home relaxing – but then realised that they were probably enjoying just about the same weather as we were, i.e. wet, grey and gloomy! The only slight problem was that I noticed that Sid was a bit anxious about certain procedures. He was obviously still remembering the fear and pain of his injury on the previous leg, and I noticed that at times he was worried about going up the spinnaker pole to any great height. Sometimes I would sweat him up and see his body tense, and I would know that he was inwardly fighting back a tsunami of self-doubt.

I should perhaps clarify here that sweating is a process in which somebody is attached to a halyard and hoisted up to the top of the spinnaker pole. Once on top of the pole, he executes whatever manoeuvre is required, and then is let down again. Being on top of the pole is a fairly harrowing experience if you have any kind of fear of heights, and even if you don't it takes quite a strong nerve. There are no reference points up there and it simply feels like how it is: you are literally stuck on top of a pole like old Simon Stylites. The only problem is that you are doing this while the boat is performing its unpredictable motion beneath you, and in even in moderate seas this can be very disorienting to say the least. And when you have had a nasty experience with being injured in a sailing accident like Sid had, the spectres can be very real indeed. Still, at this stage he was bearing up well. He obviously had a fear, but he was dealing with it and getting on with the job. I admired him intensely for that. As for the pain of the injury, I think he was now over that. It was just the mental scarring that was giving him trouble.

After the watch, I had an excellent night's sleep (for once). There were fantastic stars of all types all over the sky: shooting ones, milky way ones, bright ones, sparkling ones, different coloured ones all poured out across the sky in rich profusion. One of the compensations of this mad adventure, I thought, and how strange that such an apparently insubstantial compensation should feel so substantial and comforting. I mean, why is it? Why are there these things of universal beauty that can take us out of ourselves, take us out of our situation, literally transport us? How is it that we can be stuck in awful weather in a dangerous corner, and suddenly we see the Southern lights or something and, for a few moments, everything is OK? This is one of the mysteries that my voyage left me with. Unfortunately, or perhaps fortunately, it didn't provide the answer.

We were making good speeds with Lars at the helm, Tim was looking mean and moody with his massive black eye; we really looked like a band of high seas pirates. I remember Tim taking a shower and thinking that his black eye was going to wash off – it looked so good that it looked like a fake!

At this stage, we had the heavy spinnaker up most of the time. There was too much wind for the medium, and the virgin sailors were wary of having to take their morning-after pills. At 1100 the results came through. We were equal second with *Group 4*, but trailing only a mile behind *Concert*. This was good match racing, although it was a shame that *Group 4* was back up with us. We just couldn't shake them off! Funnily enough, we couldn't see them, even though we were supposed to be so close together.

I went off watch and had a body strip wash (the usual shower substitute on board ship). Afterwards I was greeted with the news that we had covered 247 miles in the first twenty-four hours of the leg, which was quite an achievement. (Most people should be able to work out that's just over ten miles an hour, which may not be shattering in Formula 1 terms but for sailing it's pretty good!)

I took over a new communications role on the chat show today. *Group 4* were hosting it, but there wasn't a lot of news. A number of boats seemed to have an outbreak of a stomach bug which was keeping them all unnaturally quiet, and I wondered if it was the same thing that I'd had as we set off. But I'm fairly convinced it was the crew dinner we had on the Friday night before setting off.

*3Com, Ocean Rover* and two other boats had had major spinnaker blows (again, why does this never happen to *Group 4*, I asked myself). So *3Com* were down to 2Com and very depressed. The skipper was definitely not his usual self. For once, we were able to say that there was no stitching going on on board *Commercial Union*, and this didn't go down too well with the other boats. But surely nobody could deny us our bit of *Schadenfreude* after all we had been through? We had, of course, had our own near miss with Tim's eye, which could easily have required some stitches – or even some Dacron!

On every leg, you tend to have fresh food for the first couple of days. The limiting factors are 1: Sell-by dates; you have to be more scrupulous than you might be on land, because an outbreak of food poisoning could have much more serious consequences at sea; and 2: Weight; fresh food weighs a lot more than dried and powdered stuff. Thus today we found ourselves drooling over the news that *Time and Tide* were having real bacon sandwiches for breakfast, and lamenting the fact that we had already guzzled all our real food.

In spite of hoisting our medium spinnaker for long periods of time without mishap, we slipped down to third behind *Group 4*. The same old story. The euphoria that we had felt during our leading period had evaporated, but had left a thin crust of determination to get back there again! Nevertheless, it was another night of beauty for a fabulous night's sailing. The night was sparkling like a diamond, Leo was very clear and also the Southern Cross along with many others. I was tired through, having done a lot of spinnaker trimming, but it was the right sort of tiredness: it was wearing me out – making me sleep well and awake refreshed. And of course, the Southern Ocean was now out of my head. I would never have to go back there again. I had met and conquered my fear, and that was enough for me. I knew that I could do it, but I certainly never wanted to do it again unless I had to! The two thoughts of having been through those legs and of being on the way home combined to lift me to a plane of contentment that I hadn't felt for months.

On the 6th we were still in third place, one mile behind *Concert* and about four behind *Group 4*, so we were still in very close sailing conditions. We put the clocks back one hour in accordance with Richard's system, and then we noticed a small hole—just when we didn't need it. There we were, challenging *Group 4 Toshiba* and *Concert*, some of the best boats. They were all on our horizon, and we developed a small hole in our medium spinnaker. What should we do with it? Once a hole appears, it concentrates the stress and makes a massive tear more likely. But taking it down, hoisting another one and fixing the tear all takes time – when time is the thing you've got least of. What should we do with this small hole? Get the sail down and fix or not?

Apart from that, it was another lovely night for sailing. The sort of night where you just wanted to enjoy the privilege of being allowed to plunge along through the velvet darkness, with the majestic panoply of stars overhead, without having to worry about holes in spinnakers. *Group 4* were once again sailing near the wind (metaphorically, that is) because they didn't have any lights on. Apart from being illegal in terms of the rules of the sea, it was also gaining them an advantage in racing terms, because other boats couldn't see what sail plan they were using. In spite of this we managed to gain on them and overtook *Concert* during the night and were now lying in second place.

Although *Group 4* were invisible on the water, they weren't invisible on the radar. We could follow their motions on the shadowy screen. We saw them gibe, and then gibe back again ten minutes later. They kept crossing our line, and it was truly exciting, particularly having to battle with an adversary we couldn't see. It was an excellent spell's racing. At one point, we were in line with *Group 4* and *Concert* with *Toshiba* slightly off the pace to starboard. Then, slowly, *Group 4* started to fall behind and we were once again first equal with *Concert*.

At this point a fax arrived from Zena. She was very unhappy that her sister had thrown the cat out with the bath water or let the baby out of the bag or whatever she had done in telling me about her baby! The chat shows were on, and talk was of other boats and their positions – and since we were doing so well at that moment we were more than happy to join in on this topic! *3Com* had a crew member who looked like Johnny Mathis, and I asked him to give us a song. He retorted by insisting that we had a song from Gary Glitter first! (I should mention here that many people have commented on my striking resemblance to the "Leader of the Gang"!) All the crews commented on the fact that the processed sea water we were drinking had a funny chemical taste and we came to the conclusion that there must have been some residue left in the tanks after they had been cleaned during the stopover.

We tried to raise *Group 4* to get a position but they were radio silent. *Concert* came on the air to say they might be able to give an approximate position, and we retorted that we could give an *exact* position because we had seen them just off our starboard bow but they couldn't be raised on the transmission channel. It was just another subtle instance of how *Group 4* were not quite "in the club" with the rest of us. *Concert* and *Group 4* were both very close off our starboard bow, but there was no infringement.

Lars was on Mother, and of course he was too macho to be on Mother so everybody had to watch out. The other mean and moody hunk – or should that be hulk – was at the helm: our good captain Richard Merriweather. Still, I suppose all this meanness and moodiness was having a good effect, because we were still hanging in in second place only two miles behind *Group 4*. This leg was turning out just as we thought it would, with us holding our own in a tight match racing situation, but *Group 4*'s "gamesmanship was getting just a little bit irksome. It seemed like they would stop at nothing short of actually infringing the rules to gain an advantage. Thus, at the height of the excitement, while all of us leaders were gibing backwards and forwards trying to catch the best winds with our spinnakers, we "accidentally" received *Group 4*'s BT weather report.

This extremely interesting document referred to *Commercial Union* and *Concert* "swaying around behind them in the darkness as if they were drunk". It also referred to *Group 4* themselves having their heavy spinnaker up, although it was obvious to all of us, and particularly to Richard's experienced eye, that they were flying their non-promotional medium. It was obviously a ploy to get the followers first to lose time pealing to their heavy, then to lose ground through using the wrong sail, then to lose yet more time pealing back to their medium again. Richard sent a fax back saying that we had received their fax by mistake but applauded their choice of a heavy spinnaker, telling them it was "indeed prudent to keep their heavy up – wind up more like!"

On the 9th there was a lot of gibing about again but it was very frustrating because every time we executed a manoeuvre it seemed to be just the wrong situation and we had to go back again, so there was a lot of time wasted. The result was that although we were still reported as second, we were having to do a lot of work just to keep our place – we were running to stand still! In the meantime, the boats to the south-west were gaining on us. Through sheer hard work we found ourselves at 1000 first placed with *Group 4*. They were of course still ahead in the overall race table but it was all good cut-and-thrust racing. The team spirit came back again in a repetition of all the whoops of delight, back-slapping, hugging and hand-shaking that had gone on before. There was a real buzz in the air, I think because we realised that the earlier high placing hadn't been just a flash in the pan. We had hung in there and maintained our good showing, just like our strategic planning had told us it would be.

I went off watch at 1200 but as you can imagine, I didn't really want to. We were in first place by now, a clear four miles ahead, and this was the first time it had happened in the whole race. Once again, it was a victory for our strategic thinking, and there were faxes flying in all directions urging us to keep it up. Obviously there were also quite a few saying things to the effect of "keep up the good work now that you've worked out how to make the boat go in the right direction at last"! We went on the chat shows and read out ditties and basically made the most of it, and our internet report said that it was a long time coming, but after 20,000 miles sailing we had finally gone into the lead. It was a long time coming but well-deserved. We'd always known we had it in us and we'd certainly be on a high for a long time to come.

I exchanged long faxes with Sean, agreeing that it was a great achievement to be leading the field at some point, whatever happened later. And with hindsight it often makes me think that we really did have it in us. We could have done it if we'd been sharper on maintenance and more careful with our spinnakers. In a long haul race like this, consistency is the name of the game, and it is instructive to look at *Group 4*'s performance, where there was only one leg out of the six in which they didn't come first, and in that leg they came second! Sean was winding me up about "taking his place" (as if I ever could have), but I had after all ended up on the foredeck watch with Sid and Lars which was where he used to be. I faxed him back saying good luck on the dole.

On the 10th we were still six miles ahead. Our strategic theory was still holding out, although it was a tiring watch and it did begin to occur to me that staying in the lead was simply a lot harder work than hanging around in the middle of the field. At this stage Alan, our Mr Fixit showed great foresight and installed some electric fans on the boat, rightly pointing out that they would be invaluable when we reached the Doldrums.

Crossing the Tropic of Capricorn, we somehow managed to lose four miles back to *Group 4*. Conditions were fickle, and it was frustrating gibing backwards and forwards trying to find the right line, but the tension was relieved somewhat when Tim, the Watch Leader, walked forwards in front of us all to the port halyard to bring the spinnaker pole down. We could all see that the halyard was on a winch, and not attached to the pole at all, but apparently he couldn't! Realising his mistake, he returned to the cockpit with his head bowed sheepishly, to be greeted by the inevitable massive cheers of us all!

Well, when you start getting frustrated in one area of life, something else often happens to compensate. This time it was a fax from Steve and Lyn, friends of mine back home. (Steve is a major football supporter, but inexplicably chooses to spend all his energy on propping up Gillingham.) Anyway, Steve came through with the news that my team, Wolves, had made it through to the playoffs against Crystal Palace, and also offered his congratulations on being in first place. So obviously everybody knew about it back home and it was making quite a buzz in the news. But the main thing was, of course, that I could possibly have a season of First Division football to look forward to when I got back! Steve was so excited that he offered me a curry in either Boston or Southampton to celebrate!

At 2000 hours we were all standing waiting with baited breath for results. We were no longer in the lead, but were only a mile off the pace in second place. I began to think about Boston and what a great time we were going to have there. In a sense, it was going to be just like a version of England, with the beer just being quite a bit colder. I had heard about Boston's "microbreweries" – small brewing companies that produce a wide variety of local beer, very like what still happens in parts of England. I was looking forward to tasting all the different types of beer, and going to all the fantastic restaurants, particularly the seafood ones on the waterfront. I also knew that Commercial Union was very well represented in Boston and that we would be accommodated in very up-market, luxurious apartments. The perfect prelude to going home!

But in the meantime, back to life, back to reality. The weather was beginning to get very hot again and life was beginning to hang heavy on the hands. On the 12th it was particularly hot and boring, and I was on Mother. I decided to give everybody a system shock and produce a bumblaster of a chilli con carne with some real chillies I had smuggled on board in amongst the powdered stuff. But at the last minute I chickened out and did half of it mild for the tendertongues.

Well, Mother does have to cater for all the divergent tastes of her little children! But at least I managed to get a good hot foretaste of the heaven that awaited me in Boston. I mean, it's one thing to do without alcohol while at sea, but spicy food is quite another matter altogether!

But later that night, I began to wonder if I had overdone it on the chillies. They do say that some of these spices can have hallucinogenic effects in large enough quantities. I don't know if that is true for chillies or not, but something strange definitely started going on inside my head. Or at least I *hoped* it was inside my head. Because if it was *outside* my head then I would have been very worried indeed.

A friend of mine tells a story about how he once took a holiday job as an undertaker's assistant while at college. At one point they were looking for a new driver, who would be capable of driving the various vehicles that the undertakers used in the course of their daily business: the van, for picking up the bodies from the places where they had fallen; the limousines, for taking mourners to and from funerals; and the hearse. In between driving these various vehicles, he would also have to do a fair amount of humping bodies around.

One day, a driver came in who seemed perfectly suited for the job. He was an ex-bus driver, so had the necessary experience to drive all the vehicles. He was big and burly, so he obviously wouldn't have any problem with the lifting. Straight away that afternoon, the boss sent him out with my friend and another driver to pick up a body from an old people's home.

My friend's name is Don, the new driver was called Bert, and the old-established driver (who apparently looked very similar to Lee Marvin) was called Fred. These three musketeers walked into the deceased's room at the home, and the dialogue went something like this:

Fred:   Oops, this one hasn't got any legs!

Don:    There they are in the corner.

Bert:   …!

Fred:   OK, Don, you get the legs, Bert and I'll get the rest of 'im.

Don:    Right you are, Fred. [Don goes to the corner to pick up a pair of prosthetic legs standing in the corner.]

Bert:   …!!

Fred:   OK Bert, you get the head end as you'll find it easier to get a grip. On the count of three, lift 'im up and into the shell. [A shell is a temporary fibreglass coffin used for carrying  bodies back to the "shop".]

Bert:   …!!!

Fred:   Come on, Bert! Get a grip on 'im under the armpits and heave…

Bert:   Ulp!!!

Fred:   Oh no! Outside, Bert, get it outside…

Immediately on his return to the office, Bert told the boss that he didn't think he was suited to the job after all.

The point of this little digression is that appearances can be really deceptive. Just because you are big and burly doesn't mean that you don't have irrational fears that play upon your mind. And I am afraid that I am the same way (apart from the fact that I don't throw up, as mentioned before), but not so much about actual dead bodies, but about the fictional stories that people make up about them and turn into horror films. I try not to watch them, but every now and again one of them slips through the net, and when it does, I get hyper about it. Examples from my past are *Carrie*, where a hand reaches up out of the grave to grab somebody in the very last frame, and the

Cybermen from *Dr Who*. Kate is the same, so we make a right pair, I can tell you. Sometimes we both wake up in the middle of the night, each unable to reassure the other that the clown figure from *It*, or Freddie from *the Nightmare on Elm Street* series isn't prowling around downstairs. Sometimes I can manage to sleep, but, even then, it will prey on my sleeping mind. I have to be consciously on the watch to make sure I don't start watching something like that, because it's like a fascination with me: I won't be able to stop, and then at the end I know I won't be able to sleep.

Thus, in spite of my being extremely fit and physically very well developed, my mind is prone to sudden attack by any one of the horror film monsters that I have seen at any time in my conscious memory. I know it's irrational, and I know they're only films, and that the monsters don't really exist, but these words of wisdom are of no use to me whatsoever when this phobia (for that is what I suppose it is) takes over. It's a bit like being afraid of spiders (in England at least). It is a matter of record that there are no poisonous spiders indigenous to the British Isles. There is therefore no need ever to be afraid of any naturally-occurring spider in this country. But saying this to somebody who is afraid of spiders is just no use whatsoever. There is no way that you can convince them to feel any better about meeting a spider without deep analysis and therapy. And even then it's difficult.

Anyway, on this particular evening, I was on watch on the foredeck when I suddenly saw a shadow moving at my elbow. I froze, fixed my peripheral vision on the point, and slowly turned my head to see if I could see what had moved. There was nothing there, however, and I dismissed it as a trick of the light, not yet suspecting that my mind was about to go into horror hyperdrive.

A few minutes later, again out of the corner of my eye, I saw the end of one of the neatly coiled sheets rise up in the air, as if lifted by an invisible hand. This time I turned sharply to see what was happening, but when I looked at the sheet directly it was still lying, undisturbed, on the deck. Then I sensed something standing over by the staysail. I turned slowly and, sure enough, there was a black shadow clearly outlined against the night and staysail, looking like the form of a small human. Nightmare images from the films I had seen and the books I had read flickered through my mind: the dwarf from *Don't Look Now*; the ring-wraiths from *Lord of the Rings*; the homunculus from the *Dr Who* TV series. I had leaped from my rational world into one where shadowy ghouls were out to get me.

As I looked at the figure by the staysail, it slowly became less distinct. It faded until I could no longer be sure that it wasn't just a trick of the light. I dragged my eyes away, but kept darting them back time and again during the watch. There were no more incidents, but you can bet that I had a terrible time sleeping when I came off watch.

The next day was the 13th – Kate's birthday. She was forty-two, and had been born on a Friday, so inevitably everybody always jokes that Friday 13th was definitely an unlucky day for me! Putting a call through to the UK from the boat was a very lengthy process and not something to be undertaken lightly. It could be done, however, if you really persisted, and many of us did when we needed to phone home for special occasions. I was glad that I did, because it was great to hear her voice again. I had sent a present from Cape Town and she had received it, and she told me that Juliet, our eldest, was off to Germany on a school trip, so I was able to wish her Viel Gluck as well.

The same day, I had a fax from Sean with more than a note of wistfulness in it. He said he was missing all of us and me particularly, and he really wished he was on the boat with us when we were doing so well up against the leaders. Touching, but of course he'd left himself wide open for my reply: that it was only because we'd got rid of him in the first place that we had managed to get into this situation, and that the boat certainly went a lot faster now that we'd got rid of some dead weight! This is the sort of banter that has carried on between us since we first met, and neither of us can get too deep and meaningful before the other cracks up. I think it has a lot to do with the fact that I am about the only person he has ever met who hasn't been completely fazed by the fact that he is a massive (in all sorts of sense of the word) star of a popular TV series. He says it's refreshing to meet people who just treat you as a person rather than a persona – to which I reply that I really didn't have any choice because (a) I'd never seen the series and didn't recognise him at all, and (b) if I'd known he was a luvvie in the first place I would have steered well clear of him and stood with my back to the nearest wall! (In our relationship it is completely acceptable for either of us to insult the other's profession in whatever terms we wish, and in fact Sean opened the hostilities by making it clear what he thought of insurance brokers the very first time I met him!)

Anyway, the results showed that we were still second just as I was finishing my fax to Sean, so I added that in just to make sure that I poured the maximum possible amount of salt into the wound!

Apart from that, we all felt that the fruit flies that appeared on the chart table were the height of the day's excitement. You could tell we were heading towards the Doldrums, psychologically as well as geographically (although naturally I gave no hint of this impending despondency in my fax to Sean).

I went on the chat show speaking to Mark Lodge, and for some reason he brought up my Buzios experience, which I felt was a little below the belt. It put me off my stroke a bit on the show because all the terrible memories suddenly came piledriving back into my head. I wonder if that's what people mean when they talk about flashbacks after taking acid; if so, I sympathise. But it certainly wasn't going to put me off the race. It was all firmly in the past now, and I was finding it easier every day to focus on the task in hand.

We received mixed news when the race positions were announced.

We had gained on everybody, but somehow *Group 4* had managed to pull out thirty-two miles in front. How did Bob (our pet, if that's the right word, name for the *Group 4* skipper) manage it? Didn't he ever take a day off? How on earth (or, for that matter, on sea) was he managing to get an average of 9.3 knots in this part of the ocean, whereas the rest of us were well down on that? The wind was so unpredictable, up and down, hovering between 10 and 5 knots, that we started to suspect him of having a wind machine on board!

Sunset came, and Lars for some inexplicable Scandinavian reason thought it was a ship! At least, we were all sure that's what he said, but who knows – his original words might have lost something in translation from the Swedish. Needless to say, for the next few days, whenever we wanted a little light relief while Lars was around, we would start stumbling around the boat, shading our eyes with our hands as we peered out to sea exclaiming, "I see no ships!" in our best Lord Nelson impersonations. All very silly, and from all the moody scowls we got I don't think Lars entirely appreciated the joke. Which, of course, made it all the funnier! How we laughed.

From the 13th to 15th we had the Andy Pilkington saga. At the time, I thought he must be the unluckiest crew member of all. He was sailing on *Heath Insured*, and had already had an accident at the start. Now he had apparently suffered a burst appendix and the boat was going to have to put in to St Helena so that he could be taken off and transferred to Cape Town or Ascension Island for surgery. I particularly felt for him because I had done some training with him and I realised how dedicated he was, and how much the race meant to him.

On the 14th I put on a CD of sea shanties and songs to try and cheer everybody up and get a bit of team spirit going again, but it didn't work because the wind was too light and fickle to get any momentum going. At 1000 the clouds were clearing and the sun was shining, but the conversation was definitely heavy weather with Richard back on the helm being very depressed and sarcastic, as he was whenever things were going slowly. In the evening there was a bit of cat-and-mouse racing with *Concert*, pushing and pulling, gaining and losing, but with no real bite to it.

On the 15th at 0300 we had gained against whole fleet, but *Group 4* were still thirty-one miles ahead. We were moving towards the equator now, and beginning to pick up the south-east trade winds. Suddenly everybody started appearing on deck in swimsuits – unfortunately minus the refreshing influence of G & Ts, but Boston was beckoning! While preparing a script for the chat show, I found out that the FA Cup was happening on the 17th, so I arranged to receive the broadcast on the radio. Entertainment is very scarce on board, and you need to grab opportunities where you can!

That meant I had to toil through the 16th until my football fix! There was a heavy current flow against us, but we seemed to have lost *Concert* who had been quite close to us, so they must have managed to pull away. Lars was on Mother again, and Mother was definitely suffering as a result. The chat show I had been preparing for turned out to be the longest in history. Like entertainment, I was having to take my claims to fame as I found them! 2000 brought us news of great results. We had made gains across the whole fleet, but most gratifying of all was the plus-seven mile dent we had made in *Group 4*'s lead. At 2100 the temperature was reading eighty-five degrees F, so the heat was really on in more senses than one!

On the 17th we had a very tiring watch both mentally and physically. We were ploughing through lumpy seas, but we were gaining again so it was worth it. The clocks went back an hour in accordance with Richard's system, and we had to crack open the sun cream. Listening to the FA Cup final while sunbathing was the most exciting thing going all day. As usual, the Cup didn't live up to expectations. Chelsea were playing Middlesborough and won with a pair of "bookends" goals, Di Matteo scoring after forty-three seconds and Newton after eighty-two minutes – with eighty-one minutes of scrappy play in between.

On the 18th it started getting extremely hot. Alan, our famous Mr Fixit, erected a canopy over the helm to keep the sun off. Unfortunately, it seemed that he had erected it too late to save Lars, who was already more than touched by the sun when he stepped up to the binnacle that day. This was evidenced by a sudden fascination with the "music" of Barry Manilow. I tell you, being stuck on a boat thousands of miles from anywhere in the sweltering heat and being forced to listen to "Bermuda triangle, try to see it from my angle" and other equally strained rhymes would be enough to turn the Dalai Lama into a homicidal psychopath. As it was, our confined space and the way we were all having to climb over each other to get as far away from the music as possible made me think of an old expression of Vicki's: "madder than a box of frogs". Having been reminded of her, I thought that a good way to take my mind off the excruciating pain of "Could It Be Magic" would be to send her a fax. So I wrote to her about writing a book, and possible serialisation in her new paper, the *Mail on Sunday*.

Lars seemed to relent a bit and offered us all some sweets. The only problem was, could he open the packet? The answer was yes, but only with much difficulty. After the matron of the Mother watch had wrestled with the stubborn packaging for a full minute, the whole packet suddenly exploded, scattering Lars' sweeties all over the deck! Of course, everyone else exploded at the same time – with laughter! Lars just couldn't take it – he looked like a big schoolboy about to burst into tears because he'd lost all his sweets! We were all just doubled up and screaming with laughter, but he just couldn't see the funny side.

Jo, our new BT legger, did her first chat show. I had a fax from Kate that Wolves had lost to Crystal Palace and not made it through the playoffs to the First Division. Some things just aren't meant to be. The current was teasing us, playing around with us, sometimes with us and sometimes against. I got bored and went to send some faxes to our group of supporting schools.

On the 20th when I came off watch, it struck me how much Alan had done to improve our quality of life. While on deck at the helm, I had been shaded from the fierce sun by his canopy, and now that I was off watch, I was able to keep cool with one of the fans that he had, with great foresight, installed while we were in cooler latitudes. We crossed the equator on a gibe while I was on Mother, toiling in the sticky sweatbox that was the galley down below. I was putting together breakfast for everybody, consisting of cereal, porridge and toast. I had tried gamely to persuade everybody that they really didn't want porridge because we were running out of sugar, my real reason being that I didn't want to add to the sum total of heat in the galley by cooking. But practically everyone insisted on it, saying they preferred it with salt anyway! But the toast was fantastic. I made it with bread that Margot had made the night before, in spite of Richard slagging her off because he thought the noise was because she was doing her washing on deck! We almost didn't let Richard have any for that! Once everybody had been fed I knocked off for three hours' sleep, and woke refreshed and ready for one of my chilli con carne specials for lunch. I somehow managed to drop in too many chillies, and upset Lars by making it too hot.

Now was the time for the mysterious initiation ritual that sailors invariably perform when there are people on board who are crossing the equator for the first time. In this case, the lucky noviciates were Jo, Alan and a couple of others. We had in fact been secretly planning and plotting for a few days for the ceremony by storing leftover food in a large pot that Richard would use for the ceremony. There was quite a lot of apprehension in the air about what was going to happen. The noviciates knew that something was going to happen, but didn't know what; the rest of us certainly knew what was going to happen, having been through it ourselves, and we wanted to make sure that everything went as well as possible to ensure that the new sailors "enjoyed" their initiation every bit as much as we had!

We were enjoying superb sailing while King Neptune (Richard) was below deck getting ready. Then he appeared bearing port and whisky which he had once again managed to keep secret and happy hour broke out on deck. Then, just when the new transequatorials were sipping their drinks and thinking this wasn't going to be so bad after all, out came the lovingly prepared pot of goo, and they were suddenly covered in two days of culinary history of the good ship *Commercial Union*!

I went back to the galley and cooked chicken curry with rice once more in my trademark three versions: mild, hot and one single plate of extra flaming double hot specially for Lars! While I was doing this they were washing down after the ceremony, and water started coming in through the hatches, which I had opened because of the heat. I shouted up "Oi," or some other meaningless syllable to warn them to be careful, and Richard pounced on it, thinking that I had sworn and he had won his bet! But it was quickly obvious that there was no possible swear word he could have mistaken for "Oi" and I realised he was winding me up as usual.

At 2000 things started going our way again, as we started to make gains on the fleet once more. I had my first (much needed) shower and hair wash. When I came out I found a cup of sugar on top of the oven, and suddenly I was a hero, because it meant everybody could have porridge again! (And poor old Mother could get back to sweating in the galley!) It hadn't been my devious machinations entirely that had struck it off the menu a few days earlier – we had in truth been running low on sugar. Everybody was ecstatic, and I don't think I will ever again see such enthusiasm for porridge (although it was of course immaculately prepared!) It just shows how values are distorted on ship, where porridge was really one of the only "natural" foods you could get.

But my celebrity status as Supermum didn't last long. Before long I was back to the mundane and unpleasant jobs that Mother normally had to do. Thus, just before going to bed at 2100 I had the delightful task of pumping the slurry tank because somebody had left the valve open. As I eventually teetered on the brink of sleep, I realised that I was going to wake up with one of my headaches because of the hot conditions. I tossed and turned fitfully and, sure enough, woke up with a thumping head.

At least we were racing well, however. On the 21st at 0100 we were moving along with exhilarating speed, and were anticipating the results announcement with great optimism. Sure enough, when the announcement came at 0200, we had made big gains on everybody, and closed the gap on *Group 4* to twenty-six miles. There was a bit of current against us, but we were still managing to log speeds of up to 14 knots. We were gibing around all over the water trying to find exactly the right setting that would deliver us the maximum benefit. I thought at the time that we could easily gibe for England, but then with the state of the nation's sporting endeavours at the time we were doing ourselves a disservice! The enthusiasm was white-hot, the team was going like a hamster on speed, morale was higher than a giraffe on acid and the boat hardly touched the water as it was propelled along by the sweet, inexhaustible breath of our guardian angels. We were invincible, unsinkable, unstoppable, unbeatable!

One last gibe before I was able to go off watch. The racing was fantastic, and my mind really wanted to keep on going as long as possible – but my body was crying out for sleep. The spirit was willing but the flesh was well and truly knackered and I needed my bunk. Sid was on the helm, Claire was trimming and Tim was on the winch as I began to let the spinnaker forward.

And at that moment, before our helpless and uncomprehending eyes, our race hopes collapsed. With a sigh that voiced all the despair that gathered in our breasts in that single instant, the spinnaker died.

We watched as it deflated and refused to fill again. At the time we had the spinnaker net up, trying to keep it from wrapping around the forestay, and the spinnaker seemed to catch on the net hanks. Then came the sound that we were all dreading: a terrible ripping and tearing that sounded like all our guardian angels getting together and ripping up their celestial lottery tickets. We hadn't heard a sound like that since the previous leg, and we had all hoped we would never hear it again. But we all knew what it meant. As the horrid truth sank in, all hands appeared dejectedly on deck to haul in the spinnaker. We pulled it in gently, handling it tenderly, as if we all knew that this winding sheet held the remains of our dreams, that we were here to perform the last rites. For all our care, however, we only succeeded in damaging it even further as we dragged it in. In fact, this is what always happens with a torn sail, but at that moment we could have done with a bit of damage limitation.

We hoisted the heavy spinnaker in double-quick time, fighting back with the energy of those whom Fortune has slighted, but we were all feeling terribly upset. Activity didn't really make us feel any better, but at least it anaesthetised us from feeling so bad. Personally I felt sick when I thought of the fifteen days of good work that we had put in to get to where we had, and the dreams that we had had of playing to our strengths in this leg and of putting up a great show. This, more than any amount of rolling seas, brought me closer to throwing up than at any other time on the voyage.

The first thing that we had to do was to put the repairs in hand. Richard delegated the task to Eileen and Claire, who immediately started assigning people to repair teams and putting together a programme to get the horrible task finished as quickly as possible. At least there was one thing that was going to make it easier for us, and that was that we had acquired supplies of a wonderful material called Dacron, specially developed for repairing torn sailcloth. The tears would be held in place with Dacron strips and glue, and then the strips would be reinforced with heavy staples. The process would be completely different and a lot quicker, and no stitching would be required. We got started straight away, and although the situation was very disheartening, the new system certainly alleviated the mechanical boredom of the repair process considerably. Squalls were blowing up at the time, so as it turned out that the heavy spinnaker was the correct sail for the situation after all. This made us all feel a lot better, and managed to convince us that we would soon be through the worst of this latest setback and back at the top slugging it out with the best of them. I started work in the galley with Margot and Claire, stitching and gluing. The smell of the glue was overpowering, and of course the heat didn't help. We all had to wear face masks to protect us from the fumes (but hey! With little alcohol and no drugs on board, surely sniffing glue was about as good as it was going to get?). Eventually I went to bed, stoking myself up with aspirin because I had another splitting headache. What's more, Margot and Claire had awakened old spectres of Dr Who monsters with their face masks, and I kept waking up with night-time hallucinations in which the Fly was coming to get me!

On the 22nd at 0115 we found ourselves back in familiar territory: in fourth place, seventy-two miles behind the leaders. Who were, incidentally and as if you needed telling by now, *Group 4*! Why? We had had a setback, it was true, but we had ended up flying the right sail for the conditions, and surely we hadn't been sailing badly enough to lose another forty miles! Still, there it was, you couldn't argue with the actual results. The only person who thought he could change the facts was, as usual, our resident King Canute, Richard Merriweather. He wrote an entry in the log book that read: "What a load of bollocks!" as if he thought that expressing his displeasure to the universe in general might bring about a recalculation and consequent adjustment in our ranking. But whatever else it revealed, it certainly told us that our captain was feeling the strain!

We started ringing the changes, using Number 2, gibing backwards and forwards, trying to find that elusive sail formula that "Bob" seemed to tune into time and again without any apparent effort. Meanwhile, repairs were continuing non-stop in the galley, putting the sail back together again. Conditions were choppy and confused – and that was just the crew! At 0800, we found ourselves 110 miles adrift. Later the gap had widened to 140 miles, and we had slipped to eighth place. We couldn't believe it, couldn't understand it. Why was it happening and how did *Group 4* always manage to profit, whatever the situation?

At last the medium spinnaker was finished. As we slipped it back into its bag, we examined it minutely for further damage and found two more small tears. Well, it was far better to discover them at this stage than after we had hoisted the sail and started relying on it once more! We repaired these quickly, and we were back in business! It was a great feeling to have completed it. I suppose it was similar to what people felt after Dunkirk – the uplifting feeling of overcoming adversity!

On the 23rd we had some breeze, which helped us fight back at last and also helped us through the heavy swell we were having at the time. We were now 177 miles behind in seventh place. Lightning was flashing in the distance as the current turned against us once more. The weather was hot and sticky and tempers started getting short. Someone wrote in the log, "There is a Hell – and it's here," which I think summed up the feelings of frustration that were niggling at us at the time. After doing our very best for so long on this leg, we now found ourselves back in our usual position, and we couldn't really understand what had gone so wrong.

I had been involved in a lot of other activities on board during this leg and I hadn't managed to do any helming, so today I took the helm for the first time. In the famous words of the one that everybody says I look like, it was "good to be back!" We sighted some strange white blobs in the water, most of them about eighteen inches in diameter, and eventually worked out that they were Portuguese Men o' war.

At the time I was reading Tim Severin's book, *The Brendan Voyage*, a fascinating account of how he had set out alone in May 1976 to try to reach America in a boat made of oxhide leather. His purpose in doing this was to prove that St Brendan could conceivably have done this in the sixth century, as there is some evidence that America could have been "discovered" 1,000 years before Columbus. I was reading it for about thirty minutes at a time to calm me down when coming off watch, and although it was very interesting, I can't say that it did a lot to take my mind off the problems of the day! I went into a silent phase – I was receiving lots of faxes but wasn't replying to them. It just didn't seem fitting at the time, when we had been receiving all the congratulations on our progress and now we seemed to have squandered our lead again. Now we were falling behind again, it was difficult to look people in the eye.

Of course, we, and of course Tim Severin, had the great advantage over St Brendan that we knew our modern geography. If we set out west and went for long enough we knew we would reach America, but poor old St Brendan had had nothing but myths, rumours and his own faith to sustain him. It's always the same for someone who does something for the first time. When Chay Blyth first sailed around the world "the wrong way" in 1971, on the voyage that gave birth to the current BT Challenge, nobody knew if it could be done. And Chay is somebody who really dislikes sailing! In that sense he was a bit like me on this voyage: he only wanted to do it for the challenge, and not out of any love for boats or the sea. And of course in his day there was no such comforting convenience as satellite navigation!

The current was still against us, killing us slowly by sapping a lot of our efforts, but we were nevertheless managing to make good speeds. We put the clocks back an hour in our continuing scheme to try to keep ourselves oriented when crossing the time zones. I helmed for an hour, and kept us trucking nicely down the line. It felt good, but at the back of it all was a sense of futility, a feeling that however well we did we still seemed to lose out to the leaders.

On the 24th, at 0843, (1043 GMT), we passed another landmark (seamark?) when we crossed our outward track. It had been October 15th, 1996 when we had last been here. And I fervently hoped that I would never have to be here again! I was one of eleven new members that Richard was welcoming to the select club of circumnavigators (or trackcrossers or, or crosstrackers – he couldn't really make up his mind what to call us). He got quite emotional, and said he had never sailed with a finer bunch of people (etc, etc). He also said that he felt choked because we had all worked so hard at our forte on this leg but something seemed to have gone wrong. He admitted to being extremely depressed about it all, but said it wasn't any fault of ours. We had done our best, but not caught the right weather, the right currents, the right luck.

On the 25th we had an improvement in our results while I was helming (so it must have been my magic touch, surely?!) Then the current turned against us once more, and we were slopping around again trying to find any gust of wind that would help us. To tell the truth, we were all tired and fed up. We wanted a bit of entertainment, a bit of excitement, but where was it going to come from? At midnight, I was on Mother again and we were running with the spinnaker up. But, if the truth be known, the wind angle and course were not ideal for this. Looking back, I am sure that this was one of the roots of our problems – that Richard was prejudiced in favour of using the spinnaker, even when it wasn't strictly the best thing to do. It all went back to his soling days, where the spinnaker was the main weapon in his armoury.

When I came on the 0200 watch on the 26th, Richard was in his lean, mean and sarcastic mood. At times like this, we all observed an unwritten, unspoken agreement to stay well clear of him, but on this occasion Sid managed to snag on one of the rough edges of his mood. When Richard came on deck Sid had been helming for an hour, and Margot had taken his place. Tim suggested that Margot should have a rest and asked if Sid would like to take over again. Sid refused, but Richard intervened and said he thought it would be a good idea. It was then he made the mistake of declining again, on the premise that he was tired!

Richard immediately started throwing all his toys out of his pram. He grabbed the helm, spitting out words to the effect of: "Oh, I see. Well, if the crew are too tired to do their jobs, then I suppose it falls on the captain's shoulders to just take on all the burdens. Doesn't matter how many, it's OK. I was originally thinking of doing this voyage on my own anyway. I would probably have done a lot better without all the dead weight…" and so on. Then he said that he hoped it wouldn't be too much trouble for Sid to make him a cup of tea before he went off to have his beauty sleep. Claire tried to make the peace by saying that she was just going on Mother and could easily do it, but Richard was having none of it. He was making his point, and nothing but a cup of tea made by Sid would do. In the end, Sid did do it with very bad grace. If it had been me, I would have loved to have taken the opportunity to wind Richard up somehow, perhaps by taking it to him on a silver tray or something like that. But Sid just dourly delivered it and went about his business.

I came off watch at 0600, with 2,649 miles to go. We were battling it out with *Toshiba* on our port beam most of the afternoon, so were very busy doing the sort of racing we liked best. It was a busy afternoon, with the heavy spinnaker up for two hours and then switching back to Number 1. We logged some good speeds, and then hoisted the heavy spinnaker again. But then you know who started worrying about whether we should keep up the spinnaker or go back to the headsail. Worry, worry, worry, would the virgin sailors blow out their heavy duty again? Helming was tricky, because we were being dragged to windward, and then overcompensating and diving off to leeward.

On the 27th we started gaining again – at last. But this still meant we were in 6th place and 157 miles behind the leaders. As Richard was getting ready for the chat show he was in a disgusting mood, so I really didn't have the heart to show him the daily report as usual. Then he suddenly started berating me for not showing it to him! I had only been doing it for his own good because he was having serious difficulties maintaining a sense of proportion, and if I had shown him he would have embarrassed himself even more by mouthing off at the whole crew rather than just me! I still think that the confrontation was a wind-up, and that he was still hacking away at the old chestnut of trying to get me to swear – which I never would. (He really didn't seem to understand this about me – that it was just something I didn't do and would never do, whatever the provocation.) To this day I am honestly not sure if he was serious or not, but I think in the end I come down on the side of the wind-up. But then, as you've probably noticed, I usually do. As far as I can tell life is just one big wind-up, and if anybody's looking for a deep and meaningful message out of this book, that might as well be it!

We sailed on into an extremely hot afternoon, with a lot of sail trimming so that when the cool night fell and enveloped our weary bodies we were very grateful. The stars were shining for the first time in days, and the general pleasantness of the evening must have mellowed Richard somewhat, because he emerged from his sulk to make quite a funny proposal for an on-board competition. Old Grumbleguts had a sense of humour after all. In effect it was just a sweepstake, but with a fairly individual idea for the prize.

For a start, it was a reverse prize, a booby prize, a wooden spoon prize. It would be called the Berk Trophy. The sweepstake would be on the estimated time of arrival in Boston. Each crew member would provide their ETA, and then an average would be determined for each watch. The furthest watch away from the actual time would have to take the new Boston legger on their team, who would be a joy-riding journalist – and therefore a berk! (Funnily enough, her surname was Burke!) In addition, the *individual* with the worst prediction would also have to share a cabin with the berk! Well, you have to do something on board to liven up your evenings. (Apologies to the journalists out there who have excellent personal qualities, but I'm sure both of them will realise that it's no worse than what gets said about insurance brokers behind their backs!)

On the 28th I was on Mother. And at this point, I would like to break off my narrative to provide a "taste" of what it's like to live on ship food for forty-odd days. Here, therefore, are a couple of main course recipes for your scrapbook, as well as one dessert. Alternate them in your diet for the next six weeks and make sure you have porridge for breakfast every day, and you'll have a fair idea of whether you've got what it takes to "stomach" life on board ship!

## Claire's Spaghetti Bolognese

Serves 14

Ingredients

*1 sachet McDougall's powdered dried minced beef*
*1 sachet McDougall's mushroom soup*
*2 sachets McDougall's oxtail soup*
*½ pt white wine vinegar*
*1 bay leaf*

**Method**
Boil 10 pints of water.
Throw in all the ingredients and simmer for half an hour.
Serve with spaghetti (you know how to do that, don't you?)

# McDougall's Mediterranean Chicken

Serves 14

Ingredients

*1 sachet McDougall's Chicken Italienne (don't worry – this is
magically transformed into Mediterranean Chicken by the addition
of powdered garlic, dried mixed herbs and lemon juice!)*
*3 sachets McDougall's chicken soup*
*1 tbsp dried garlic*
*1 tbsp dried mixed herbs*
*4 fl oz lemon juice*
*½ pt white wine vinegar*
*1 bay leaf*

**Method**
Boil 10 pints of water.
Throw in all the ingredients and simmer for half an hour.
Serve (no spaghetti needed).

PS: If anybody from McDougall's is reading this, I would
like to thank you for providing the excellent powdered
comestibles that sustained our fleet throughout its voyage.
Might I also suggest that it would be an ideal promotional
activity for your company to sponsor a boat on the next
race?

# Orangefresh Rehydrated Dried Fruit with Lemon Juice

(NB Orangefresh is an orange powder which when mixed with water produces an approximation to orange juice)

Serves 14

Ingredients

*7 sachets Orangefresh*
*4 lb dried mixed fruits*
*4 fl oz lemon juice*

**Method**
Place all ingredients in a pan.
Add enough water to cover and leave to stand for 2 hours.
Serve.

On this particular day I prepared Bolognese for lunch and Mediterranean Chicken for the evening meal, with the dried fruit rehydrated in Orangefresh for dessert. As you will have worked out, the amount of chef interaction in these recipes is minimal, and in this case I was able to spend most of the afternoon writing up my log notes on a bright, sunny day. I did help out at one point with a peal on the heavy spinnaker, and this was the sort of thing I used to do periodically: although technically on Mother, and "relaxing" between domestic tasks, I would generally get involved and lend a hand when necessary. In a sense, though, I wished I hadn't got involved in this particular peal, because we messed up the drop and damaged the medium spinnaker as we were pulling the sheet through the boom. Claire, as the main architect of the repairs after the last accident, was naturally and justifiably disgusted. Fortunately the damage was only minor, but at the time we all resolved that we should spend some time getting the spinnaker drops sorted out, as they were wasting a lot of time one way and another. The medium spinnaker was quickly repaired, and Sid was somewhat scapegoated as the helmsman at the time. He was demoted from his position because it is crucial when doing any sail-changing to keep the boat steady into the wind. He was judged not to have been steady enough by the mean and moody powers that were!

At 0200 on the 29th there were officially only 2,000 miles to the end of the leg, although this showed up on our instruments as 1,982 because of some trouble we were having with the technology. A huge vessel loomed up on our starboard bow, and certain elements started to worry that we were going to hit it. There was little chance of this as the radar showed that it was actually 7.1 miles away, although it did seem a lot closer!

On the chat show, Richard got into a conversation with James Hatfield, the skipper on *Time & Tide*. He made a bit of a howler which James quickly took advantage of – much to the merriment of the rest of us. *Time and Tide* was, of course, the disabled boat, and one of their crew, Paul, was deaf. Forgetting this, Richard asked if he could speak to him. Without batting an eye, James said, "Yes, of course," and the next thing we heard was James appearing on air again, putting on a "deaf accent" voice. All of us understood what was going on, but our poor dear skipper had to carry on gamely with the show while distracted by our uncontrollable laughter. In fact, I laughed so much I actually cried, and when it was my turn to speak I was unable to speak and just had to come off (shades of Brian Johnston again!). James told Paul about it all later on and he apparently loved the joke. We later found out that this was a set-up between James and Richard – and therefore even funnier! After recovering from the chat show we had an excellent morning's sailing. At 1700 we put the clocks back an hour, so that we were now GMT –3 hours. Mackerel skies appeared, with fluffy cloud scudding along, just as we were revving up for another chat show (inspired by the quality of the earlier one!). I made up for my inability to speak earlier, and broke the previous record for the longest chat show ever (forty-five minutes of high-quality banter and one-liners!) Tim and Margot were, in fact, very upset because they had been on watch and missed it, which is high praise indeed!

On the 30th, I came on watch in the middle of what I thought must be a Yankee Bingo Master's Breakout. As I stuck my head above the deck, I could hear a series of seemingly random numbers being dragged through the wringer of Bransom's twanging drawl: "thirdee-fay-aahve, fordee-doo, twennee-nay-aaan". He was on the helm, calling out wind angles to Ian. As I came up the steps I shouted, "House!" in my best imitation Bransom accent – and I think he was very unimpressed! A quick reading of the instruments showed that the current was with us, which was great news, and put us all in a good mood to celebrate Neil's fifty-fifth birthday. Someone had smuggled some South African whisky on board, and Alan, whose Mr Fixit skills obviously extended beyond the utilitarian to the artistic, produced a trophy, complete with banners and candles. We had Shepherd's Pie and peas for lunch, after which a magnificent chocolate cheesecake materialised, courtesy of Margot and Claire. A little bit of a drunken atmosphere then descended on the boat, but true to the oath that I had taken against drinking spirits any more – even in these very moderate amounts – I didn't get involved. In spite of this, I was convinced that an aeroplane passing overhead was actually a UFO, so perhaps the atmosphere affected me even though there was nothing in my bloodstream! Bransom, Neil and Trevor had all obviously had a fair amount, and Sid drew a suitable line under the proceedings by putting a message in the empty whisky bottle and throwing it overboard. We put the Genoa up for the first time, and I took the helm for about forty-five minutes, achieving some reasonable speeds. Then some excellent results arrived, showing that our alcohol-fuelled efforts were paying off. We were making gains on everybody, as well as holding off *Motorola*, who were coming up strongly through the fleet at the time.

On the 1st, things had fallen back to a state of glorious inactivity. We were slopping around in a flaccid sea, and there was a telling log entry at the time that ran: "Are we ever going to get out of this?" Just for fun (as I've said before, you've got to do something to keep the brain cells active) we made a calculation of our ETA based on our current speed, and were dismayed (but not surprised) to find that we were due to reach Boston on 14th June 1998! Lars was on Mother, and at the time I wrote that he was behaving like a bear with a sore head. Everybody was puzzling about which way to go: the boats to the north were going slowly, and the boats to the west were going even more slowly, but the difference between them was so slight as to whip up nothing but complete apathy for any proposal to change course. Every direction was equally useless.

The high point of the day was the unintentionally entertaining spot on the radio where Richard and James Hatfield were competing for the "Mr Happy" Award. I don't think I ever heard a more dismal and gloomy chat show during the whole voyage. I was on watch at 1330, and we used the spinnaker pole to "pole out Number 1". This improved the speed slightly, but the only real contribution that it made to the cause of water sports was involving us all in a game of "Golden Showers". As was her wont, Margot (never one to take things sitting down) was just at that moment taking advantage of the lull in activity to have a leak out of the cockpit, and my manoeuvre with the Number 1 therefore resulted in us all getting covered in Number 1 (as my youngest daughter might say!)

At 1700 we were eagerly awaiting the results, but they were disappointing when they arrived. We had gained a little on the other boats, but there was no rhyme or reason to what was happening. When we calculated it at the end, the average speed for the leg was 7.6 knots, which was pretty dismal. We spotted a huge black shape in the water, but nobody could tell what it was. We were just fervently hoping it wasn't a boojum! By 2100 there were still no changes in the situation, and everybody was getting very frustrated. As often happened when there was little activity, Richard started tinkering with things and sticking his oar in where it wasn't wanted – well, he was only the captain after all! Who did he think he was? He started charging around issuing orders on what to do and really only succeeded in causing havoc!

We were heading north, and Richard started gambling to try to get more breeze out of the situation, but had no idea whether this would pay off or not. The other watch kept gibing to try to find the best course from 1200 to 1600, but without much success. They also pealed the spinnaker three times, but again without any joy, and it was all very frustrating. Once again we had to fall back on our feeble methods at entertaining ourselves. This time we fell to discussing our most embarrassing experiences. Margot recalled once that she had spat on someone's birthday cake, but I told her it could have been worse – given her recent record she could easily have pissed on it! Sid said that when he was seven, someone had asked him what 3 x 6 was, and he had answered 20. I mean really! Were these the most embarrassing things that had happened to us? And then when we came to Lars, he said he wouldn't tell us because it was something to do with sex! Ridiculous! Surely that was the point! That was exactly what we were looking for! A story about a filthy sex session that went wrong with suitably embarrassing and rapidly detumescent results! But then I was no better. I simply couldn't remember a situation where I had ever been embarrassed. Certainly, I had done a lot of things that would have made a lot of other people feel embarrassed, but somehow embarrassment just isn't a reflex with me, the same way swearing and vomiting aren't. The boredom was alleviated somewhat by a fax from Zena saying that she had named her son Elliot, and that she had started putting things on my desk already (with six weeks to go!) In fact, the real work was going to have to start in Boston, when I would have to call her to discuss the year-end salary reviews.

On the 3rd we were still juggling with the light and medium spinnakers, trying to get the best out of the situation, when the medium spinnaker blew again. There was no sense of shock or surprise this time, however; it was just becoming part of the routine! We had to put up the headsails instead, but the great thing was that we started gaining on everybody! Who needs spinnakers? Nevertheless, we had to start getting ready to repair it again. This time, however, we decided to work full-time on the deck rather than go down below. The main reason for this was of course the weather, which at this latitude could generally be counted upon to be fine, and it would mean we would have more space to spread ourselves out. On investigation, we found tears across the head and halfway down.

It was about this time that I woke one night with one of my horror film hallucinations. I had awoken one night imagining there was a mummy standing beside my bunk, and for some obscure reason I believed that the mummy was me! That is to say, I was partly terrified of the mummy itself, and partly terrified because it was me inside the mummy! I reached out of my bed to grab some of the bandages to try to unwrap them and find out if it really was me inside – if it was, then I knew I would have to unwrap the whole mummy to stop myself from suffocating! In my half-waking state, I reached out towards the shadowy figure, grabbed a bandage and pulled. It came away in my hand, and I looked at it more closely. And then when I saw what it was I immediately woke up screaming. I sat up in my bed and tried to bring myself back to reality, tried to remember what it was that had frightened me. And as I thought about it, I realised that the "bandage" had been a piece of Dacron! This mummy that was wandering around the boat terrorising my dreams was dressed up in Dacron, and what's more, it was Dacron that was suffocating me! I promise you, if I never see another piece of Dacron in my life it will be too soon!

Hallucinations notwithstanding, we were attaining good speeds on the watches again, typically about 10 knots. Our ETA on the automatic calculator had now improved dramatically (by about a year) to 9th June 1997. Anyway, we were on track now, sailing fast down the bearing and maintaining good speeds. It must have been the thought of all that ice-cold beer in Boston!

On the 4th at 0100 our instruments showed less than 1,000 miles to go to Cape Cod, and we were keeping up our good speeds. During those days, it was a real pleasure to come on watch. We would hand over with the jubilation of a successful relay team, happy in the knowledge that we were clocking regular speeds of up to 11 knots. At one stage I managed to turn in a top speed of 11.6 knots when we were running a helming competition, which was equal fastest with Sid. And it wasn't just the speed, but also the accuracy that was pleasing. We spent a wonderful fresh morning running straight down the bearing, and it was great fun! "Bob," the captain of *Group 4*, was on the chat show, and relayed a message to *Toshiba* that conditions were grey and miserable. I said, "Enough about you, tell us about the weather!" At some point during all the excitement of the helming competitions and so on, I found time to send a fax back to Zena about the six-week work lead-in she was piling up on my desk back in London.

On the 5th the wind started whipping up again, and a pertinent question appeared in the log from Eileen: "Who remembers how to do a reef?" Well, it was a good job that someone remembered, because we had to put one in that very morning. The whole watch was very tired and wet, and everyone was feeling itchy because the boat was heeling over to thirty degrees for the first time since Cape Town. Everybody was stabbing each other in the back because of the conditions, and niggly comments were appearing in the log about being fed up and so on (as well as some fairly sensible ones like "Lars is a twat"!).

The wind started getting up again, and Lars had a go at Tim for putting a reef in because the previous watch had said that Richard didn't want a reef in. This was the sort of silly argument that tended to blow up whenever things started getting frantic. Then Claire was seasick, and she had a run-in with Margot. Then there was friction between Lars, Claire and Tim, because Lars and Claire had been assigned to serve under Tim after he had been appointed watch leader, whereas they had previously been watch leader and No 2 respectively. Basically, there were all sorts of little gunpowder kegs all over the place and it seemed like everyone was on a short fuse. Eventually Margot and Sid came and took over on the foredeck while I was trimming. I was very tired, and grateful to be able to go and nod off. Mother was really hot and sweaty down below (perhaps I should rephrase that?) as I passed through the galley to my bunk. For once I had no trouble getting off to sleep, and as my eyelids dropped I was thinking, "Oh well, not long to go now."

I slept well for two and a half hours, then I was up at 1000 replying to letters from schools who were following our race effort. Lunch was tuna salad, pasta and peach delight, then we hoisted the heavy spinnaker again, but only for about fifteen minutes because the conditions were so fickle. The average log speed had dropped by about ten per cent (to 10-11 knots), but the distance to go was now only 663 miles and decreasing rapidly. But then the barometer started going down like a lead balloon, and our speed started going up again. We were heeling over at thirty degrees again with the wind gusting up and a current running with us. All in all it was good stuff.

At 0300 it was back to the good old days with poor old Trevor the dithering professor on Mother. I was on watch after a restless sleep, getting high as a condor on kwailudes because my only clean shirt had fallen in the diesel/water mixture that had come through onto the floor of the cabins for some reason. So I was standing there in a cloud of diesel fumes, and not enjoying the experience. The wind was all over the place and for a couple of hours we couldn't get the sail plan right. The mood of dissatisfaction was epitomised by the childish exchanges that Sid and Lars were leaving in the log, for example: "Sid is a wanker;" "Well at least I don't wear plastic underpants," and other such adult observations. Instruments registered less than 400 miles to the way point, and at 1900 we were able to change our clocks onto Boston time (GMT -5 hours). The current had turned against us but we were still getting good speeds.

On the 7th I was on Mother while we were logging good speeds again at around the 10-11 knots mark. The water temperature fell about ten degrees, which was an excellent sign that we were heading for the favourable currents of the Gulf Stream Labrador current. 327 miles to go and we were really eating up the distance! I sent a jubilant fax to Kate and girls, and got faxes back saying not long to go – so I wasn't just imagining it! I also got a fax back from my brother-in-law and his young son Dominic. I was his hero at the time and he'd been following my progress all through the race.

Then we heard the news that "Bob" and *Group 4* had finished at 0920 local time. Gnashing our teeth, we settled in to carry on with the racing that we still had to do. We put in a second reef after the watch change, and then changed down to the first reef with full mainsail. This formula was getting us good speeds, but we were deviating from the line somewhat. As I put it at the time, we were managing "15 knots – towards Bermuda"! But then we managed to rectify the course and maintain the good speeds once we were back on track again. Claire was on a health kick at the time, and eating a lot of prunes. The rest of us, however, thought it was a very bad idea, particularly with conditions being as cramped as they were. From Richard's point of view, of having to share a berth with her, the main problem was that it was very noisy when he was trying to get to sleep! There were also other undesirable consequences which became obvious when Sid got in on the act. Not only did they start competing with each other for the honours on the gaseous equivalent of the Richter scale, but they also started staging "prune stone spitting contests". The idea was to spit the stone from the seat on one side of the cockpit at least as far as the seat on the other. It soon became apparent that Claire could only just reach the other seat, whereas Sid's range was far greater, so people quickly lost interest, but it whiled away a few minutes of this last trudge into port.

At 0600 I came off watch with 223 miles to go. There had been another big drop in sea temperature, down to eleven degrees. At 1900 there were 212 miles to go, and at 2200 we drew up a scheme showing the lie of all the boats that were still left on the water. *Motorola* still had thirteen miles to go. We started picking up and monitoring the local fishing boats on the radar, as there was a fair bit of traffic as we approached. We put the heavy spinnaker up again, but didn't know if it was the right strategy or not. Richard was in his sarcastic mood, getting a bit fraught because he thought that he ought to be able to pull some last-minute benefit out of the situation. The stars were out and it was a clear, cold night.

On the 8th I was back on Mother again. Our speed had slipped from 10 knots to 4.4. We were basically back to slopping around again, so we reasoned that we *must* be near port! We put the promotional spinnaker up for a while but it didn't do anything, so we dropped back to the Genoa again, with our speed right down to 2.1 knots. At 1200 I came off watch, with the boat still on its mandatory go-slow whenever we reached the end of a leg! With eighteen miles to go our ETA was 3.35 GMT, but at least that was the next day rather than next year!

At 1300 the wind picked up a bit at last, and we were able to tack for a bit along the Cape Cod coast line at a speed of 7.7 knots. Eileen had started filling out the arrival forms so we knew we must be getting close. At 1700 I was having a great sleep, when suddenly Margot woke me up with a big dig in the ribs because I was snoring! I was startled, thinking it was time to go on watch, and then realised that I didn't have to because we were so close. I tried to go back to sleep but couldn't, because Eileen and Jo were making so much noise scavenging around for food. There wasn't any left, but you would have thought they could have waited!

We finished the leg in seventh place, which was of course very frustrating considering our high hopes for the leg, and especially after the good performance we had put in for much of it. We finally put in at 1628 on 9th June.

# Boston Stopover

AS SOON as we arrived in Boston we went through the essential, and by now familiar, procedure of making sure that the boat's alcoholic requirements were catered for. And for fourteen thirsty people who had spent the previous forty-odd days jammed up against each other shoulder-by-buttock in a boat without a drop of comfort oil in sight, these requirements tended to be fairly hefty – as you will have already gathered.

So this was obviously top of the priority list. An advance party was despatched (yours truly naturally straining at the leash out in front) to make a quick reconnaissant bar crawl to find the baddest, roughest, most drink-sodden hole in the city, dive into it and only emerge once we were happy to certify on solemn oath that no greater opportunities existed within a five-mile radius for testing the upper limits of the human body's tolerance for alcohol.

The bar that we eventually found was the Roisin Dubh – the Black Rose – and, like most of our stopover haunts, as Irish as they make them. Mission accomplished, I started my usual hunt for methods of self-destruction. The one that came most naturally to hand, as usual, was that of alcohol. Not, you understand, from the possibility of alcoholic poisoning, but from the way it seemed to transform me from a mild-mannered guy who would never raise a hand in anger to a – well, a mild-mannered guy who would never raise a hand in anger but who would say anything or do anything just to wind someone up to the point of – yes, you've guessed it – laying me out!

Anyway, the Boston instalment all started when we had settled in to this bar and got down to some serious drinking. By the small hours of the morning, I wasn't going anywhere without major assistance, and this time it came in the shape of Margot Douglas, our resident nurse and my cabin-mate for the whole race. She managed to earn the nickname "Bag Lady" from the crew because of two quirks of behaviour: the first was the habit she had of storing all her possessions in plastic carrier bags. The second was the way in which she used to get terribly over-concerned and worked up about the way in which we folded and stored the sails in their bags on board ship. She was convinced that neatly folding the sails before storing them would bring us extra speed when they came to be used. It reminded me a bit of how butlers used to iron their employers' copies of *The Times*. Little foibles like these set her up as a typical target for Richard's merciless ribbing, but she took it all in her stride.

Margot was the one who had looked after me and nursed me so attentively and professionally through my injury in the Southern Ocean. That night it was she who took me under her wing and made sure that I got back safely to the apartment. But in this case, getting me back to the apartment didn't exactly mean getting me safely tucked up in bed with a cup of cocoa and a hot water bottle. The big problem was that my apartment was actually a powder keg in serious danger of explosion at any point. This was because I had been assigned (presumably after a black mass in which BT Challenge's high priests had offered up sweet-smelling sacrifices to their malicious god of permutations) to share quarters with Lars. Sooner or later someone was going to light the blue touchpaper and retire!

Anyway, as I say, I was escorted back to the apartment that night by Margot. As we walked, I remembered how I had lain in my bunk in agony while she was looking after me and called out "Margot! Margot!" whenever the pain got too much. Now, as we staggered on our way through the unfamiliar streets of Boston, we got talking about the adventures we had been through and I reminded her of how I used to call out for her. Before long I was walking along with her calling out her name the way I used to do, and things developed from there in the facetious manner that they usually do with me. I added into my act (completely without justification) the idea that Margot was molesting me. Thus what started out as "Margot! Margot!" quickly became, "Margot! You incorrigible vixen! Unhand me! Take your hands off me! I will not be taken advantage of! Margot! Get your hands away from my trousers! I'm too young and innocent for this debauchery!" It was all good fun, and she was having a good laugh about it because the idea of either of us wanting to be more than just friends with the other was just ludicrous. And in fact, that was the whole basis of my larking around like this.

I mention the incident, because it gives you an idea of the sort of spirits in which we burst in upon Lars' splendid isolation. As I have said elsewhere in this account, I am a "confrontationophobe". I hate confrontation and I don't like to get involved in it. This may sound contradictory, because there are many incidents in this book where I have wound people up to the point where they were about to "lay me out". But the point is that none of those incidents started out as confrontational – they were just wind-ups. I never had any disagreement with anyone, just used my instinct for finding psychological Achilles heels to get under people's skins. They were never situations where I disagreed with someone about something and we both stood our ground and things escalated from there.

And it may have been that there was something deeply psychological about my relationship with Lars. You see, it may have been that old chestnut of us really being rather alike ("You see, Mr Bond, we are really rather alike, you and me. We are both very accomplished killers. The only difference is the justifications we give for our activities..." etc., etc.). I must say that I never really got any strong feeling of this, but there was one time in Rio when we sat out together in the pouring rain in the early hours of the morning and exchanged stories about our fathers. By the end of our talk I was crying freely. I hope that Lars didn't see because of the rain, but I rather suspect that he was going through the same experience and hoping that I hadn't noticed. He has apparently also written a book about his experiences on the voyage, but I don't imagine anyone will want to read it because it's all in Swedish!

We had out first humourous experience before the race even began. At the time he was having big problems with his girlfriend. Unwisely, he introduced me to her and I made the sort of comment that anyone who knows me will tell you is typical:

"There must be some mistake. You can't be Lars' girlfriend, you're far too attractive!"

Now I would call that fairly straightforward, par-for-the-course banter. But I'm afraid Lars couldn't take it. Admittedly it was at the wrong time for him because they were going through a break-up, but then again I wasn't to know, and we surely have to be able to deal with our own relationships and not expect everybody else to tiptoe around them? I suppose this is part of what I mean about needing to grow up. Once again I found out afterwards that he had been close to "laying me out" on this occasion.

We were completely opposite in temperament. We did discuss our senses of humour at one point, and he told me that the Swedish sense of humour was similar to the British, and apparently they love *Monty Python* and *Fawlty Towers*, for example. So we did discover some common ground there, but we had to accept that we were different and that, unfortunately, we would never really see eye to eye (or did we?).

Anyway, there I was, rolling into the apartment, blind drunk at four in the morning, laughing and joking raucously with Margot while Lars was trying to get his beauty sleep. We encountered each other in the corridor, where he had emerged in a bath robe.

"For God's sake, Nicholas, don't you ever stop playing the idiot?"

Once again, it was nearly "laying out" time, but Margot stepped in to save me – led me off to bed and tucked me up warm and snug where I slept like an innocent baby until the morning.

And "innocent baby" is really how I think of myself at these sorts of times. I cannot pretend that during my adventure I was not approached by a fair number of attractive women looking to get involved with me on a physical level. How much of this was due to my looks and personality and how much was due a "groupie" syndrome born of the fact that I was in a fairly high-profile position as a member of one of the BT Challenge crews I cannot say, but the fact is that I was often put in a difficult position *vis-à-vis* my family situation. It sounds ridiculous, I know, but I felt that I was very often walking a line where I was getting involved with an attractive woman without having to do anything. I was just sitting there and getting drunker and drunker, with my will power slowly seeping away. But then when things got serious I would realise from one perspective I might be seen as having led on a very attractive woman, and I was left with the difficulty of having to brush her off – but all my instincts were that I had to do the *polite* thing. In these situations the problem was that the most polite course of action would have been to have gone all the way with them, but of course I couldn't. I had to find a way of bailing out. Very often, fate gave me a helping hand.

For instance, I had been warned by Margot that the manageress of our adopted bar had her eye on me. She had been asking questions about me behind my back and one evening, apparently satisfied with Margot's replies, she had made a beeline for me. We talked for ages, and then suddenly I realised with a kind of familiar shock ("here I am again") that it was just me and this woman and Trevor Corner the nutty professor. It suddenly dawned on me that I was marked. Like a fighter pilot must feel when his sensor confirms that an adversary has "locked on" to his aircraft, I felt a sinking in the stomach. Sure enough, Trevor eventually evaporated and it was just the two of us walking past a park back to my apartment.

It was a beautiful evening, and it seemed to have made my companion come over all romantic. Luckily, it was this that saved me on this occasion. She looked at the breaking dawn, and said,

"Oh Nick, isn't it beautiful? Let's go and lie down in the park."

This was, of course, a total *non sequitur*. If we wanted to look at the beautiful sky, we would get a far better view by just carrying on walking in the same direction. Nevertheless, my mind still hadn't managed to get itself around the problem of how I was going to get out of this without upsetting the good lady. For want of any better course of action, I followed where she was leading me, and we lay down on the grass together.

Now things started to get serious. I felt her fumbling with my shirt, and, at the same time, I felt her position my hand firmly on her breast. Quick! How to get out of this? Should I pretend to need to urinate? Should I feign a sudden back injury? Should I suddenly "confess" to being gay? Wild ideas, all of them initially seeming like the answer, but then equally quickly revealing their manifold flaws. There was nothing I could do except go along with it as slowly as possible and hope either for a brilliant idea or for some *deus ex machina* to come swooping down from the wings and rescue me. And eventually, believe it or not, that is what happened!

More layers of clothing were breached, and I had just about made up my mind to throw myself into an artificial rictus of pain and claim that my back had gone, when suddenly I was granted mercy in my predicament – just like in *The Merchant of Venice*, it was dropping literally "as the gentle rain from Heaven". Within a minute we had been drenched, and my companion's ardour had been dampened.

We rose to our feet, she cursing in fluent Gaelic, and me getting as close as I ever do to cursing in order to keep up appearances. It was not, as I had thought at first, a sudden shower, but the photoelectrically operated sprinkler system – as soon as it had become light enough the trigger had tripped, with very fortunate consequences. The mood had been broken. We walked to my apartment, but there were no further advances.

On another occasion, Andy Homer, a Commercial Union executive, came over to visit the crew. He was known to be "a bit of a boy" and somebody had to be detailed to make sure that the entertainment came up to scratch. The lots fell my way for two reasons: 1: I was the only crew member who was actually involved in insurance (I don't know what everyone thought – that we were going to sit together all night and discover a deep mutual interest in roofing contractors and subsidence claims?), and 2: They thought I was the only crew member who was likely to be able to keep up with him!

So I duly went out with Andy, and, what with one thing and another, I gradually began to feel myself going off at a tangent. At one point, I went to the bar to get some drinks and that's where Andy and I lost touch because I was taken in hand by these two very attractive Argentinean ladies.

It transpired that they were mother and daughter. The daughter was one of those girls who would have been hailed by the *Sun* as a "scorcher," in spite of her undeniably Argentinean extraction and extremely cool demeanour. The mother, for her part, had obviously been just as attractive in her time and could certainly still pack a punch.

Anyway, to cut a long story short, so far as the mother was concerned, I was obviously the biggest hit since the *Belgrano*. I ended up outside with her on the wall, desperately trying to extricate myself from yet another situation. As we sat there, she peeled down the top of her dress and revealed a very presentable pair of breasts with aureoles like Portobello mushrooms, with nipples that completed the illusion by standing up as thick and erect as stalks.

"Make love to me now!" she gasped.

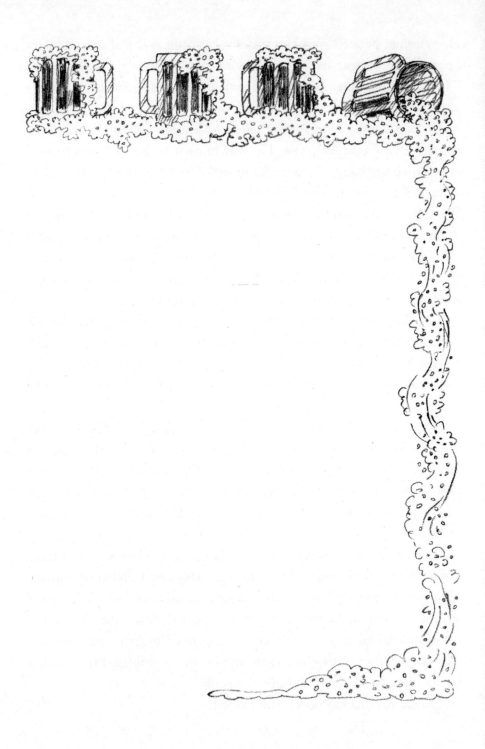

What could I say? Time for English embarrassment and confusion:

"Well, actually, I don't feel much like it tonight. I think I've, er, had a bit too much to drink."

"Oh you English are impossible! How can you look at these beauties and not want to shower them with your kisses…"

"Er, OK then. Perhaps I'll do a bit of kissing, but anything else will have to wait until another time."

So I ended up escaping with fondling and kissing her a bit. What she did not know was that, had it been her daughter in her place, I would have had a much harder time controlling myself. But her daughter's affections, from her demeanour earlier on, obviously lay elsewhere, so there was no danger from that direction. As it was, I was able to get away from the situation relatively unscathed, and somehow I managed to forget that I had promised her a rematch!

One very happy event in Boston was when Mark Lodge, the *Motorola* skipper, decided to get married there, and I went to his reception. Daniel, a young guy who had previously worked for my company, came over to visit me on his way to Camp America, and he ended up coming with me. I don't think he was quite prepared for the excesses of the occasion (and I'm not talking insurance here!). As Trevor put it, after meeting up with us he decided there was no point in going on to Camp America as he'd seen it all with the CU crew!

Another not-so-happy event occurred when we were visited by somebody I can only describe as a woman with an interesting agenda. I had been out on a corporate day enjoying the local beer and oysters. I returned to the boat to find that it had been invaded by pestilence in the form of the mistress of a former England cricketer who, although famous for his ability to score runs, is sadly equally famous for his slowness in doing so and his concern with his own batting averages rather than the performance of the team. This woman ran a computer and communications company, and was testing a satellite telephone link on our boat. I tried to put through a call to Kate but it wouldn't work, but then she started dropping large hints that she wanted one of us to go and buy her a bottle of Champagne. Thankfully the crew showed great team spirit and, to a man and woman, ignored her completely. Eventually she left with her satellite link well between her legs.

After she had left, I got to thinking how her name would have been savaged if she had tried that stunt while Vicki Harper was still with us. Vicki, or Miss Naughty and Trouble rolled into one, is an extremely talented journalist who sailed with us on the first leg. She is completely mad ("madder than a box of frogs" as she herself would say), knows how to enjoy herself and wields an absolutely deadly pen. She used to write for the *Daily Express*, and filed very entertaining reports during the race build-up and first leg. Her no-nonsense, true-to-life lifestyle won her the Young Journalist of the Year Award a few years ago. She was a firm friend during the first leg and we shared a cabin, and while I was going through my hyper phase she was brilliant. She talked me down patiently and helped get my sleep pattern in order.

Her stories were superb, witty and well told, and there is one particular column that made me laugh until I cried. It has passed into journalistic lore as the "Sainsbury's Better Than Sex" story.

During her period as a journalist on the *Express*, she met and got involved with a guy one Saturday night. They got on really well, went home to her place and had a fantastic night of passion together.

The next morning they got up, and he started putting his clothes on. When she asked him where he was going, he said he had to go. She said that after having such a great time the previous night she had thought they would at least spend a relaxing Sunday together.

But he was adamant. So she asked him:

"What have you got to do? What could be so important that you have to leave straight away?"

"Oh I don't know. I have to sort myself out for the week."

"By doing exactly what?"

"Oh, you know, shopping and stuff. I have to go to the supermarket and get my shopping for the week."

"Which one?"

"Sainsbury's"

"OK, fine. Off you go then if you have to."

And in that moment she had crystallised in her mind what she was going to do. A few days later there appeared in the *Express* a column under her by-line with the bold headline: "Is Sainsbury's Better Than Sex?" One can only guess at the poor guy's embarrassment.

For my last night in Boston, and in fact my last drinking night of the voyage, I chose my wardrobe very carefully. It was a present that had been given to me by Neil's girlfriend back at the naming ceremony at St Katharine's Docks. A beautiful white T-shirt with "Betty Ford Clinic" emblazoned on the front, and "Clean and Serene" on the back. That about summed it up really.

## Boston to Southampton

THE FINAL leg from Boston to Southampton started on 28th June. It was an amazing feeling to look out at the Atlantic, to think about crossing it, and to think that this was a small thing to do. This time last year, I had hardly done any sailing in my life. Now I had done so much of it, and in such perilous conditions, that I could gaze across this great expanse of water and contemplate its crossing with as little concern as if I were taking a cross-channel ferry.

Once again, we'd had a great time in a great stopover, and there were many sad farewells to be said. Among the people there to see us off were Vicki, Daniel, Rob (the BBC cameraman), Andy Homer (the CU Finance Director) and last (but certainly not least – well, in terms of bulk even if nothing else) Sean. Personally, it had been particularly good to see Vicki and Sean again. Vicki had only signed up for one leg in the first place, but Sean had, of course, had his race rudely cut short by his back injury.

At 1130 we were due to depart from Rowe's Wharf in Boston. And the most important thing I had to do before we left was to make sure that I had my Teddy Bear with me! Well, it was really Sean's Teddy Bear, but he had to make sure that it went all the way round the world, got its passport stamped in each stopover and then ended up safely back in Southampton. This bear was called Captain Wishbone, and he was travelling with us as the representative of the UK-based "Make A Wish" Foundation, which exists to help terminally ill children to realise their final wish. Since Sean was out of the running personally, I was to play the part of "Uncle Nick" to Captain Wishbone and escort him back home.

Sean had originally got involved with the Foundation when they had contacted him on behalf of a young boy who was dying of cancer in Northern Ireland. This boy was a fan of the *London's Burning* television series in which Sean played a starring rôle at the time, and his last wish was to meet Sean. Of course, Sean was equally eager to meet him, as he'd always suspected there was someone out there who enjoyed watching the series! But, joking apart, Sean went over to Northern Ireland to see this boy. It made his day, and I rather think it made Sean's day as well, which is why he decided to get more involved. The result was Captain Wishbone, who was making his way around the world and who would be auctioned on his return to Southampton to raise money for the charity. When we eventually did make it home, there was a six-foot model of Captain Wishbone and the charity auction was a prominent part of our homecoming reception.

From 1230 to 1330 we were involved in the pre-start manoeuvring – the "jockeying for position" to determine who would have the best wind and position when the race proper began. We acquitted ourselves well and crossed the start line in second position behind... *Global Teamwork*! So at least we weren't behind *Group 4* for once!

We hoisted the promotional spinnaker, as much really as a salute to the CU team in the support boat as out of any real sense of furthering our race effort. It had the desired effect, and an enormous cheer went up behind us as it was raised. Alan (Mr Fixit), Sean's replacement, had now left the boat, and we found a souvenir from him on the galley wall: a picture of Mr Impossible with a caption: "First into Southampton – Mr Impossible fixed it!" Thanks, Alan, for your vote of confidence! He had also given me, as his Mr Fixit apprentice on the previous leg, a nut without a bolt. I now solemnly taped this to the poster. His cryptic parting words had been, "You might need this at some stage," so I thought the least I could do was to put it somewhere where I could remember where it was!

As usual, it was a beautiful sight to see all the boats sailing together at the start with their kites flying. No doubt, they looked very calm and serene to the onlookers – only the crews knew what real chaos was going on on board! The old analogy of the apparent serenity of swans as they glide over the surface of a tranquil millpond comes to mind – you can't see the furious activity of their legs beneath the surface! At 1700 we were sharing first place with *Toshiba* and *Save the Whale*, and it was a wonderful feeling to realise that "Bob" was nowhere to be seen. I came on watch at 1800 when we had the Number 1 and staysail up with the full main. It was a sunny evening, with a blue sky, a flat sea and a brisk wind. In short, excellent sailing conditions to gladden the heart of any enthusiast (and even some people who just couldn't wait for the thing to be over, like me!)

At 2000 we spotted some whales and a basking shark. The wind had stiffened, so it seemed like a good idea to swap our promotional spinnaker for the heavy. Everything was on our side: we had a single knot of current with us, and at 2300 our ETA readout was 8th July! I think we'd all have settled happily for that, which would probably have earned us a world record – but of course these automatic calculations are really just an extra function that the manufacturers add on to the machinery. They bear no relation whatsoever to real life! Far more relevant was the readout that said that we had 2,918 miles to go – and that, of course, was to the end of the race, not just to the end of another leg. Unfortunately the instruments also showed that we had dropped back to fourth place.

On the 30th I came on watch at 0200 after a great sleep. (It was strange how much better I had been sleeping recently!) Margot actually had to wake me up three times because I was snoring. I know to most people that is a sign of possible danger, of sleep apnoea or whatever, but to me it's simply a sign that I'm very relaxed and enjoying life! Another thing that benefited from my improved sleep and general state of mind was the quality of the chat show. It was now full to brimming with my wit and wisdom, and I had even graduated from awful one-liners to passable two-liners!

On the 1st July we were navigating through a patch of fog. Visibility was very low, and the atmosphere was really very eerie – particularly for someone like me who has seen more horror films than he would have wished to. But after a couple of hours the fog cleared to a brilliant starry night. At this point, the rest of the fleet seemed to realise what a great job we had been doing in getting the best out of the conditions, and suddenly we found ourselves surrounded by boats, all wanting to get whatever it was that we were managing to get out of the conditions! We were doing very well on the route that we had chosen and everybody else knew it. It felt great to be acknowledged as the crew in the know for once instead of *Group 4*.

From 1200 to 1400 we listened in for contact with the British Airways flight from Boston which was carrying Roger Boyd, Mabel and Peter Ward (a CU Executive) back to the UK, but for some reason we were unable to establish contact. At 0200 I went on watch while we were in third place, just as the lightweight spinnaker was ready for hoisting. That was my first job, followed by poling out Number 1. Then at 0600 I was on Mother. I grilled the last of the fresh bacon for Richard, who had missed the previous day's porridge, cereal and bread, thinking it might cheer him up. But I don't think it did. He was a bit frustrated and sarcastic because we were still drifting around in fog, but this time we seemed to have lost the inspiration that we had had during the previous patch of fog, where we had emerged to find everybody following us around like journalists on the trail of a scandal. We didn't even have the right sail plan at the time, but eventually managed to find it.

On the 3rd I came on Mother again at 0600, and started preparing chilli con carne with rice and fresh apples and oranges for lunch at 1200. (On the 2nd I had agreed to do a choice boil-in-the-bag buffet, with chicken casserole, beef stew and bacon and beans instead of chilli, because people were a bit bored of my speciality, but now we were back to normal again after everybody had realised that it all tasted the same anyway!) For a time I had toyed with the idea of smuggling some fresh steak on board and adapting an old Keith Floyd recipe I had once read, called Outback Steak or something like that. (I don't have the book to hand, but the following is an approximation):

Ingredients

*1 generous piece of sirloin steak*
*1 carrot*
*1 onion*
*½ pint beef stock*

**Method**
Tie the steak and vegetables into a bundle, place in a large tin can and pour in the stock. Seal the can, strap it to the top of the engine of your 4 x 4 and drive across the outback for 5 hours. Remove contents of can and eat.

The only trouble with this recipe, of course, was that we would have had to use our motor, which would have had us disqualified from the race. But there were times when people might have been willing to make that sacrifice in favour of a good solid meal! And disqualification would have freed us from the burden of having to maintain enthusiasm during periods when there was practically nothing to be enthusiastic about.

For instance, at about this time, when we were drifting in and out of fog patches, much of the time without any sail plan or anything approaching a coherent strategy, drifting further and further back in the placings and averaging a speed of about 0.6 knots, Sid put a simple but heartfelt entry in the log: "This is crap." Many of us read it and had to agree.

At 1600 hours things mercifully changed, and we got up to about 4.1 knots. Probably still suffering from the boredom, however, I got involved in a chat show and offended a lot of people by dealing out a two-liner (remember − I had graduated to these by now!) from my "tasteless" deck. I suppose it could have been anything: famine victims, air crashes, Princess Diana (although I think she was still alive at the time), or any one of the "shocking" targets for humour. In the event, the joke that came to the top of my mental pile was about Hitler and the Jews, and it didn't go down very well at all. (Funnily enough though, there was a German guy on *Pause To Remember* who absolutely loved it! Who says Germans don't have a sense of humour?)

But then, of course, people wouldn't leave it alone. For a joke which most people apparently found abhorrent it subsequently received a surprising amount of attention. I think that if the Pope had chosen that day to announce that he approved of contraception he'd have probably had a hard time finding space on the airwaves to tell us all about it. The *Courtaulds* team followed me on the chat show, and straight away Julian (from *Pause To Remember*) asked them if they liked the joke. Then Suze, a girl I had done some marine kit modelling with at the Boat Show prior to the start of the race, said that she hoped the *London Tonight* viewers would enjoy it, because it had been captured on video for later broadcast. My attitude was: "Oh, well, what the hell. They've already seen my BT-branded right buttock."

Soon enough, of course, it was all forgotten, in the way that these things usually are.

At 1800 there were about 2,540 miles to go, and we were averaging 6.17 knots. Our ETA had slipped back from the 8th to the 20th, which was less optimistic and far more realistic! At 0030 we started making better progress and, in a sudden fit of elation, I wrote a fax to Vicki about writing a book when all this was over. (At that stage we were still thinking of doing a joint venture on the project, but we sadly drifted apart after the race.) I had a luxurious shower and then put on a clean shirt, which was absolute bliss.

On board ship there are strict limits to how much water you are allowed to use, and how you are to use it. Just as fire is the seaman's greatest danger, so fresh water is his most precious commodity. Showers could only be taken when there was general agreement that an individual was due to have one, and even then it was dependent on enough water having been made since the last one. Because of the communal nature of the water supply, it was relatively difficult to flout the water regulations, but I think just about everybody bent the rules of sea efficiency in some way or other, usually by smuggling some sort of "luxury" item on board.

My particular "sin" was my electric razor – which I personally don't look on as a sin at all. Certainly, if you are looking at it from a serious weight point of view, then an electric razor is heavier than a wet razor. But then, of course, it uses less water than a wet razor. Besides, with me, an electric razor is not a mere matter of convenience as it is with some people: I simply don't use a wet razor and never have done. And then I would also plead in my defence that my razor was my only luxury and that I didn't take any other "illegal" items on board. Certainly, other people were found out taking things on board of which Richard disapproved. For instance – shock horror – Claire and Margot each smuggled a sarong on board. Now, I ask you, if you are going to smuggle something on board ship for an arduous round-the-world yacht race then what are you going to choose? Something useful and practical that makes a positive contribution to the user's morale and sense of self-respect, or a useless piece of decorative clothing?

It is true that shaving (i.e. to shave or not to shave) was purely a matter of personal choice. But I happen to be quite meticulous about personal hygiene, and for me that includes regular removal of facial hair – although I accept that it is quite reasonable to grow a beard if you want to. It's just not something I choose to do, and I personally feel dirty if I don't shave. At the other end of the scale was Trevor, who at one point for example was quite proud of not washing for a week and a half! Sean wasn't pleased when he had to share a cabin with him, but then he was very similar to me in his hygiene standards.

Then we had one of our surprisingly rare on-board arguments. We had just managed to find the wind again, and were moving along nicely almost along the bearing on a beautiful sunny morning. I came on watch at 0600 to find that we were battling it out with *Toshiba*, who were about 3.8 miles off our port beam. Trevor was with me on watch, and was engrossed in typing up the team reports which we had to send back to race HQ each day. This may sound like a routine task, but the idea was to try to put as much humour and character into them as you could, with comments and asides and little "in" jokes. They were thus much more personal than you might expect, much more than a dry account of the day's events. So Trevor finished typing the report on the screen, then Eileen used the system to write down the results – the actual dry statistical information, and finally Margot went on the system to check all the messages, faxes and so on that had been received. Unfortunately, mistakenly believing that Trevor had in fact sent his report, she deleted it.

Understandably, Trevor was not very happy, but he seemed to take it OK. He pursed his lips slightly but said absolutely nothing, and just calmly walked away. But the next thing we heard was a torrent of some of the choicest and bluest language I think I have ever come across drifting down the companionway. Margot, of course, was hugely apologetic, but for a long time Trevor was inconsolable and couldn't speak to her.

As if to try to cheer us all up, the fog began to clear and we found ourselves trucking straight down the line. *Toshiba* were now 3.1 miles ahead on our starboard bow, but we had the current with us for once and were hanging in there in joint second place whilst grappling with that eternal question: to peal or not to peal? At 1800 *Toshiba*, *Motorola* and *Heath Insured* had all gone over to headsails, and there was a big debate on board as to whether we should do the same. Eventually we did, and switched over to Number 1 and staysail. By 1900 the current had turned against us again, and I was in desperate need of some light relief, which I found in the form of a *Blackadder* tape which Kate had sent me.

At 2100 our speed was up again to 8.3 knots with Margot at the helm. We were making small incremental gains on the other boats, and I came off watch at 2200 feeling that we had acquitted ourselves well. At 0200 I came on watch again in foggy, damp and cold conditions just as we were gaining on *Courtaulds* and starting to pull away from *Global Teamwork*. We were also, fairly incredibly, still ahead of *Group 4*, which was certainly a cause for celebration, but somehow Bob had managed to worm his way back up to third place. We just had to keep asking ourselves over and over again: "How does he do it?" He'd wrestled his way back up through the field but we just couldn't understand how he'd managed it.

It was the 4th July, and there was one person on board who certainly wasn't going to let us forget it! So we had a substantial American-style lunch in honour of Bransom, and I have to say that I was very thankful that nobody ever thought to remind us when it was Sweden's national day! On the chat show, there was a lot of banter about Independence Day, and I made a special lunch in honour of the occasion. We feasted on hamburgers, hot dogs, grape preserve and marshmallow spread sandwiches, with fortune cookies for dessert. Mine read: "Take advice from your true friends," which would have all been very well if I'd only managed to identify who they were! Our daily report showed that we were once again sailing straight down the bearing, with the fog clearing and the temperature and barometer falling as we forged our way into iceberg territory once more (although this time it was the northern "*Titanic*" variety!)

With 224 miles to the way point, rain started falling at 1600 as we continued our 4th July theme with more hamburgers for tea. This time they were courtesy of Lars who was back on Mother again, much to his unfeigned disgust. *Toshiba* was the chat show duty boat at the time, and I dusted off another one of my two-liners about a Native Indian and a Jew for Bransom's and Drew's (another American on board *Toshiba*) benefit. Thankfully, it seemed to go down much better than my previous offering. Then the results came in showing us nine miles behind the leader who was…*Group 4* again. We were all so excited by the news that we nearly fell asleep and dropped overboard.

At 1800 I came off watch after a miserable afternoon's sailing. I had been helming on and off, and had been achieving some reasonable speeds of about 8 to 9 knots, but the weather had been foul and I had had to dress up in full weather gear with my heavy boots. When conditions were like that, it was easy to feel demoralised because you weren't making any progress, whereas in reality you were moving along at quite a creditable speed. We had to put a reef in the main for the first time since the previous leg, and at 1900 our instruments showed that we were only about fifty miles from the nearest ice, with 2,234 miles to go to Southampton.

Bransom was Mother's helper that day, and he pointed out to the duty Mother (Lars) that the galley was extremely messy, with thick grease on the cooker. Lars, fairly typically, was in bed and resolutely stayed there while Bransom arranged the clean-up. There was no way he was getting involved in any more motherly activities than he had to!

At 1900 Sid sent a fax to Anna, his girlfriend at the time, who was staying over with Kate for a few days for mutual moral support. I also tried to send a fax to Vicki, which I couldn't get through. I started getting a bit hyper about her and worrying that something might have happened to her, bearing in mind the mad sort of person she is. All sorts of things went through my mind, but I don't really know why. I received a fax from Zena, who was off on holiday for a week, confirming that she had duly sorted out my new car, but that it unfortunately wouldn't be ready for my return. I had asked her in Boston to order me a new BMW Z3, the little brother to the famous Z8 that was currently starring in the latest Bond movie. (Yes, OK, I admit it, I'm just a little kid when it comes to cars, but it seemed like I was in good company, as the waiting list was six months long!)

At 2100 we were fast approaching iceberg territory. We were thinking about instituting the iceberg watches as we had done in the Southern Ocean, with one person helming and one standing lookout. It brought back fond memories for me of that place that I never wanted to visit again! On the 5th at 0400 I was on just such a shotgun watch. It was wet and miserable, but growing steadily lighter. Somehow, the threat of icebergs here just didn't seem so perilous. We wondered whether it might be because we were in our home hemisphere, but eventually came to the conclusion that it was probably more the fact that the conditions weren't nearly so bad. In the Southern Ocean, icebergs were just one more hazard on top of all the other things that we had to deal with. But here in the North Atlantic we could pretty much concentrate on just keeping out of their way. We also had our radar, of course, which helped considerably!

At 0600 I came on watch in (according to Margot's log entry) "yucky weather, very damp". At 1900 we made our gibe around the waypoint, with *Save the Whale* and *Courtaulds* in sight. We had made up a lot of ground on *Save the Whale*, who had surged ahead of us recently in the positive current. It seemed to us that they might have managed to catch the Gulf Stream, and we started fishing around to catch some of it for ourselves. At 2000, we almost had a fantastic disaster at the hands of Lars. He had attached the head of the spinnaker to the end of the pole, and this was actually partly hoisted before Sid luckily spotted what was happening. You can bet we didn't let Lars forget about this easily. In order to mark the occasion of the great cock-up, I composed a special song. Henceforth we all started to sing this whenever Lars got on his high horse:

Red, white or blue
What is Lars to do?
He can't tell the difference
Between the helm and a sailing shoe.
Guys and sails and sheets
Halyards and rails and cleats
And reefing and keeping her trim
Are all the same to him.
He can't tell a spinnaker
From a model of Gary Lineker.
Still, perhaps it's not his fault
It's only what he's been taught
Because in Sweden it's quite phenomenal
They think the difference is only nominal.
So poor old Lars hasn't a "clew" in his "head"
In fact he doesn't know the difference between them
Or so it's said.

At 2120 Richard was on the chat show, talking to Andy of *Save the Whale*, and he let slip that the starboard boats had lost out (wind-up of course). But when confronted, he hit back with his own complaint about Margot, which related to our boat's adopted song. Although this sounds petty, it was a fairly important element of the boat's public image. Each boat had to nominate an adopted song, which would be played at high volume when the boat eventually put into Southampton. Our song was "Things Can Only Get Better" by Dream. Margot decided, however, in consultation with our watch – but crucially *not* Richard – that this should be changed to "The Boys Are Back In Town" by Thin Lizzy, and then took it upon herself to fax HQ on her own with the request. Richard went ape when he found out that Margot had done this without consulting him. For at least a day he stomped about the boat muttering words like "Insubordination" and "Mutiny," and I think I even once heard him say "Keelhaul". Margot was not allowed to forget it in a hurry.

On the 6th we had the medium spinnaker up in foggy and damp conditions, then the fog lifted gradually as the sun rose. There was an impressively eloquent log entry from Lars: "fog – sun". I imagine the entry lost a lot in translation from the Swedish. The current was once again being kind to us as we sailed along through the sunny afternoon. At 1600 we were travelling north, awaiting the results and getting ready for the chat show. It turned out to be a good decision to go north, as we quickly encountered some better winds, and at 1900 I actually wrote that we were cruising. At 2100 we gibed and set a new bearing with 1,660 miles to go to the Isles of Scilly waypoint. At 2200 I was on watch, making good speeds down the line. The night was clear and we managed to pick up a school of friendly dolphins, who started following us eagerly. Sid made me a cup of tea, and luckily I was clipped on – I nearly fell overboard with the shock!

At 0000 conditions were difficult, with the wind all over the place and the trimmings a nightmare. Nevertheless the results weren't too bad, and our good progress continued. At 0300 we were still getting good speeds in spite of fog. We put the clocks forward one hour to keep us acclimatised to the time difference, and executed a series of gibes in bright sunshine. Our speed was still good, although the current was fluctuating. We were awaiting the latest results eagerly, but when they arrived they were a disappointment, as we had slipped to seventh place. The dolphins obviously thought we were doing OK though, as they were still keeping up with us and cheering us on. There were only 1,742 miles to go now, but the current had turned against us once more.

On the 8th we executed more gibes to try and find the right course. *Save the Whale* were 7.8 miles off to port, and 2 miles behind. We were going very well and hoping to take over fifth place shortly – we were still very much looking for progress and staying positive. At 0400 we passed a large tanker to starboard. Margot made contact but the reception was bad. They were apparently carrying chemicals and were stationary, and it did cross our minds that they might be dumping. The more we thought about it, the more the bad reception seemed slightly suspicious – very convenient if you just didn't feel like talking to anybody!

We found an entry in the log which read: "Get the pace up or f*** off in the dinghy." We all thought this was written by Richard, so, never one to take the undisputed Satrap of Sarcasm too seriously, I wrote in reply: "I would have done it long ago, but I can't find the dinghy!" Then I made a serious note to the effect that we seemed to have lost out to some of the northern boats. At 0800 we were still flying the promotional spinnaker with new, interesting and previously undiscovered wind angles. And after we had tried them we realised why they had remained undiscovered. The current was with us, but dull and dreary – and that was just the crew! The crew party (and that was going to be one hell of a party) was scheduled for Friday 18th, assuming we got there, of course. Zoe Ball was due to host the evening session, and each boat was going to have to send several crew on stage to recount the most amusing incidents from selected legs. In our absence, the rest of the crew somewhat predictably decided to nominate Sean and me, so I sent Sean a fax of the good news and sat down to write the sketch straight away.

At 1100 I noticed a cryptic entry in the log. "Te deum," I thought it said, but when I realised that not many of our crew were particularly religious I looked at it again and came to the conclusion that it must in fact have said, "Tedium"! The entry continued plaintively: "When is the wind coming back?" Eventually the wind did come back, and whoever it was must have wished they'd kept their mouth shut, because it came round at 270 degrees and the current turned decidedly against us, giving us a new ETA of some time in August!

Bransom was trying, with the help of Manx Radio, to gather support for an Isle of Man entry in the next race. The promotional possibilities were endless really, if a little painful. For example, everybody would have to do at least three legs, and no tails would be allowed! Bransom was getting extremely enthusiastic about it, and sent a long fax to Chay with his proposals. Part of his plan was to have one of the current boats to visit the island as a promotional exercise and to gauge potential and public support.

But, of course, in our crew nothing like this could go on for long without it turning into a massive wind-up. Sure enough, before too long Richard had sent a fax to George Ferguson of Manx Radio asking him to write to Bransom "confirming" various arrangements for the trip. And the killer punch would of course be the suggestion that, because of the good reports he'd heard, and the obvious experience that Bransom had gained on the current trip, his name would be put forward very strongly as a potential skipper! Now that *would* be something for Mr Worry to worry about!

On the 10th the winds were very light. I was on watch, trimming, with 6 to 7 knots of wind. We were still in fourth place, although we were holding straight to our bearing. The clocks went forward another hour, and the wind was still swinging around unpredictably, with speeds varying from about 6 to 8 knots. Sid and Lars were about to do a chat show, when the results came through showing that most of the fleet were closer together, apart from Shhh! You know Who, who was 100 miles out in front. We were all in despair, asking each other, "How does he do it? And every time as well!"

But then our spirits were raised by a fax that arrived for Bransom from George Ferguson, referring to the recommendation that he should be put forward as skipper for the Isle of Man boat in the next race! This threw Bransom into a panic straight away. But then after the first shock, he calmed down and said he thought that George was probably winding him up, which, of course, he was.

But then, at just the right psychological moment, Richard stepped in and said that, yes, as far as he was concerned, it was a good idea. He said that he, Richard, would personally endorse him, that he would be the best possible ambassador for the Isle of Man, that he had obvious leadership qualities (of course, these would need a bit of development, but the raw material was there), and so on. Now, if there is one quality that Bransom has in spades, it is yesmanship. So when Richard started ladling all this on with a trowel, with plenty of laying of the skipperly hand on the shoulder and confidential whispering in the ear, Bransom all but lay over on his back and asked Richard to tickle his tummy. He went off to bed, and was obviously feeling so pleased with himself that he awarded himself a glass of whisky. He was last seen sipping it as he floated into his berth on his own personal cloud. Richard then lost no time in sending a fax off to Miriam, his wife, letting her in on the joke and asking her to go along with it. As for the rest of us, well, we all thought Bransom had exactly the right qualities for the job:

No sense of humour;
Boring;
Overweight;
Spent most of his time below deck;

Couldn't sail;
Never been forward of the mast; and
Richard would happily lend him his carpet slippers!

At 1100 we were making good progress, averaging 8 knots over the last two hours. At the watch change we were travelling due north flying Number 1 and staysail with full main. The good speed meant that we weren't going to run as low on supplies as we could have done, so we probably wouldn't have to eat a crew member after all! At 1600 we had 1,002 miles to go to the waypoint. Although it was a beautiful afternoon with a fair breeze, it wasn't giving us enough lift to fly the kite.

At 0800 the next morning, there were 983 miles to the waypoint and 1,196 to the finish. I was on Mother, so out came the special curry: McDougall's chicken curry with added chopped red chillies, tinned coconut milk, tomato paste and curry powder. It was very well received, and I think Sid even had a mystical experience: he closed his eyes, and for one fleeting moment believed himself transported to an English curry house. We agreed there and then to have a curry lunch in Southampton on the day we arrived back. (Come to think of it, I don't think we even had to agree it; it was simply taken as read that that was what we would do!)

We were now very much getting the feeling that we were dealing with "last things". I settled down to answer various letters from schools, sent a fax to Mabel at CU with a draft letter to type – it was almost like being back in the office! On the chat show that night we found that we had made some gains: six miles on *Group 4* (as if it made any difference!), one on *Save the Whale* and two on *3com*. At 2100 we were storming along, flying the Number 1 staysail, at speeds of about 10.2 knots, and I went to bed feeling on top of the world and had a great sleep, in spite of the fact that the smell of diesel was encroaching again. What was happening was that when the boat heeled over, water was pushing up under the boards with diesel residue lying on top. But although it was an unpleasant smell, I could put up with it more than other people could because of my iron stomach.

Motivation was high on this leg, as it had been on the previous one, because of the anticipation of a large amount of spinnaker work. But the problem we were finding was that, although our spinnaker work was fine once we had found the wind, we were having problems with weather interpretation. Whenever we found ourselves actually in the match-racing situation, battling it out with other boats hand to hand, we could hold our own and do extremely well. The problem was reading the conditions accurately enough to get us into that match-racing situation in the first place.

The next day I came on watch at 0600, and got involved with the chat show and the day reports. The weather was squally, but the current was with us. Some trawlers passed us by on the port side, headed for Morocco, while Margot was at the helm. She was managing to squeeze out some good speeds in spite of the variable winds between 3 and 5 knots and the tricky helming conditions. We had another 915 miles to go in a variable sea state, and just as we were motoring along nicely, our speed suddenly dropped to an average of about two miles an hour. This wasn't brilliant, but then we managed to pick up and start doing well again, making gains on other boats. But once again the conditions changed. The wind was fluctuating wildly, and no sooner had we hoisted the heavy spinnaker to take advantage of a strong breeze than it would die away again. It was a case of Sod's Law all the way.

But one way and another, we kept making good progress, averaging about 10.7 knots, pretty straight down the bearing. A tremendous, dramatic cloud formation lowered over us to the north, looking like a massive hammer and anvil. Our ETA was improving all the time, and people were offering to buy each other beers on Wednesday – and not forgetting the curry, of course.

Then on 12th July, at about 0200, we hit an adverse current of about 1.5 knots, and the winds became more variable. By 0300 the current was neutral, but the wind had slackened to a light breeze. "When have we been through this before?" we started asking ourselves. The morning broke cold, crisp and uneventful, and at 0600 I came off watch and listened to the chat show, but, once again, reality flew in the face of our experience, because our results turned out once more to be good! *Save the Whale* were breathing down our neck, five miles behind us with 842 miles to go. We hadn't hoisted our kite yet because there were still problems reading the weather. The pressure was rising in more senses than one!

Sid and Margot hosted a very funny chat show, in which Sid played the Master of Ceremonies, introducing me as Lord Lucan hosting the show from on board the *Amoco Cadiz*! He played various "recordings" from each boat, and everybody had to guess what the sounds were. For example, *Motorola*: silence, representing the crew hoisting their staysail on the last leg – because, of course, they'd lost it overboard! *Group 4*: recording of two crew dragging a sail across the deck, referring to *Nuclear Electric's* protest against them for having a bagged sail on the high side of the boat not in use, when they were suspected of using the weight to flatten the boat. *Nuclear Electric*: sound of somebody typing away at a keyboard typing out protests! *Courtaulds*: a series of bleeps, representing skipper Boris swearing at someone on a spectator boat in Sydney (a protest was later made against him by the spectator involved).

At 2000 we were still fourth. The wind had died, and there was an adverse current. At last we managed to hoist our promotional spinnaker...and promptly blew it in a squall at 2300. We had to put the heavy up, but luckily the breeze rose to the occasion. But with only 797 miles to go, do you think we were particularly bothered about the blown promo? Not really, is the resounding reply. On the 13th the wind was rising and falling and shifting around, but we were still hanging on in there at fourth. With only 665 miles to go, a rat obviously got over-excited and fell on Neil from above the chart table. On the chat show everybody was now winding down and thinking about dry land. I suppose it shouldn't have been like that, and we should have all been "professional" amateur racers to the end, but that's human nature. We pealed to the medium when the wind died to a light breeze. Claire and Margot started some desultory repairs to the promo spinnaker, but their hearts weren't really in it. I think they were really more concerned about having a nice display to make for the homecoming than about race efficiency. The Dacron was out again, but hopefully now for the last time.

We were moving smoothly down the bearing. My sister-in-law Margaret (the nun) was flying to Rio at 1200. She and her community had kindly prayed for us throughout our voyage, and I sent her a fax to say that the whole crew, irreligious band of miscreants though they were, would be reciprocating by praying for her on her travels. From my experience, she would certainly need our prayers when visiting Rio! Between 1400 and 1700, we had to lower the medium spinnaker for repair when a small hole appeared. We hoisted the heavy spinnaker in its place, and then switched back to the medium as soon as it was repaired. We were getting good at it now, and the repair and swapping process was becoming routine!

From 1700 onwards we continued on deck with repairs to the promotional kite, and in the meantime managed to bring our speed back up to about 9.1 knots. Then at 1830 I was on watch on a cloudy but bright evening when suddenly there was a huge explosion. We wondered if all the sails had blown at once, or if our boat had hit a stray sea mine, but then we realised that it was only Concorde breaking the sound barrier overhead. From 2000 to 2100 we once again thought we were making reasonable progress, until the results came out and revealed that we had slipped to fifth, seven miles behind *Save the Whale*.

Repairs to the promotional kite were proceeding apace in the galley, with only 527 miles to go. At 0000 we pealed to the heavy, and then on the 14th at 0200 I was back on watch, with the heavy still up but with the promotional repairs nearly finished. It had taken us only a day and a bit, so we were obviously still motivated in spite of the fact that our minds kept getting crowded with things like beer and curry!

At 0300 we were achieving some fantastic speeds. Lars was doing particularly well, and clocked 14.3 knots. Our ETA was decreasing all the time, and those beers were getting more attractive by the minute! At 0400 we witnessed a beautiful sunrise, with *Save the Whale* on the horizon, but only partly visible through the mist. The great speeds continued in spite of the fact that the wind dropped off suddenly with 459 miles to go. At 0600 I came off watch and we were still getting good speeds down the bearing.

When I came back on again, we had two reefs in the main, and it was raining. Visibility was poor with the wind getting up again. At 0940 clocks we put the clocks forward one hour for the last time, to GMT. We lowered the heavy spinnaker and hoisted the Number 1 and staysail and managed to maintain good speeds through the rain. Our ETA was falling with 418 miles to go, and we were really putting on our last-minute show. At 1500 we were flying the heavy spinnaker and made two miles gain on *Save the Whale*, with a top speed of 15.9 knots logged by Lars, who was obviously very focused. I came off watch with *Save the Whale* 3.9 miles off our port bow, 333 miles to go, and only 121 miles to the Scilly Isles waypoint. *Save the Whale* were 3.2 miles ahead when we pealed to the medium on a very foggy evening. The result was that *Save the Whale* widened the gap to 4.4 miles.

At 2200 it was very foggy, and watching shadow shapes on the radar took me back to the Southern Ocean all over again. For a moment I closed my eyes and drifted into a daze, and the jerked myself back to reality with a start when I started to imagine that I was in fact back in the Southern Ocean again. We passed an Irish naval vessel, and traffic of all kinds was starting to appear now. On the 15th at 0100, visibility was still very poor, and *Save the Whale* had inched up to 4.6 miles ahead.

I came off watch just as the wind pulled back about twenty degrees and we were about to gibe after *Save the Whale*. They gibed back in their turn, so this was a last spurt of real match racing. I was back on watch at 0200, but very tired after the labours of the previous day. Our racing skills had paid off, and we had narrowed the gap on *Save the Whale* to 2.6 miles. The seas were becoming very crowded, with fishing vessels all over the place. In fact, we just managed to avoid one. At 0900 the penultimate BT daily report arrived. Visibility was improving all the time, and the current was slightly with us. Richard was in a good mood, and we exchanged quite a lot of happy banter. I think he was coming to terms with things a bit (especially things like Bob and *Group 4!*).

We put the traditional ETA chart up in the galley with our predictions. I guessed 1430 (I always do, if possible, so that I get the chance to go to the dentist when I get in. I promised my children I'd get their favourite one-liner in somewhere – tooth-hurty!) The range was from Lorna (0615) to Claire (1930). But then Richard crossed off Claire and Margot (at 1830), because for some reason that only he understands, he wanted to be the latest at 1800. That's Richard for you!

We sailed past the Cornwall, Devon and Dorset coasts, and passed Portland, which awakened memories of my childhood and my father. I suddenly became very emotional, realising that he knew nothing of all of this big adventure that his little boy had got involved in, and never would. I wondered what he would have thought about it all. My uncle was still alive, however, and he followed the race avidly.

Eventually we lost out on our final bit of match-racing with *Save the Whale*. They came fourth at 1432 and 23 seconds, and we arrived in fifth place at 1433 and 59 seconds, on the 16th July 1997.

That means that I won the sweepstake. But quite understandably we all forgot about it in all the excitement, I never even knew what the prize was anyway, and I certainly never got it, whatever it was. All I know is that we got Captain Wishbone home safely, ate huge amounts of tongue-flayingly hot curry and drank copious amounts of beer. Then the drunken haze came down. Kate of course was there and exerted some degree of stabilising influence, and I do remember more of it than I might have expected. But still, accounts of the events of my homecoming are pretty confused. As they say about the 'sixties, if you can help me piece together those hours…then you can't have really been there.

# Epilogue

I AM often asked how the experience of sailing round the world on one of the yachts completing in the BT Global Challenge, the world's toughest yacht race, has affected me. I am usually stumped for an answer. I find myself saying that only those who knew me before and after the event can answer the question.

But writing this book has made me re-examine the situation in a little more detail. And, if I cannot provide a full answer to the question, at least I can try to put together a few fragments of thoughts about the experience which may serve to give a partial answer.

First of all, I have to repeat what I have said elsewhere—that I don't even know why I did it in the first place. How I jumped from a single outing on a day's corporate sailing, with no previous experience, to applying for the race, being selected for it and going through with it, I don't think I will ever know. I can only say that I felt that there was a kind of "rightness" about it. That it was somehow my destiny to get caught up in it, and that it all seemed to fall into place.

My feeling of "destiny" is only heightened by the fact that the odds were stacked so heavily against the operation. The day's sailing I had been on had resulted in two deaths. And this was close to home, in British waters, albeit on a fairly rough day. The dangers would be magnified many times on a race around the world. On the face of it, it was just insane to leave my business in the sole control of my partner, to leave my wife behind with four daughters to look after, and go sailing around the world in extremely hazardous conditions. But then again, to take such a decision is only human. All sorts of people do seemingly irrational things on small and large scales all the time.

You read about the old granny who decides to do a bunjee jump; the schoolteacher who decides to go on a space shuttle mission. Come to that, what about the people who first decided to fly to the moon with less technological help than you now find in the average Ford Fiesta? And the hordes of people who risked life and limb when the world was younger and relatively unexplored to go and carve out a precarious living in a foreign country? Humans do stupid and courageous things all the time. Looked at in that light, my actions appear perfectly normal.

While on the race itself, I experienced a degree of companionship in adversity which I have never felt before or since. I feel privileged to have worked with all those people and pulled together as part of a team to bring off a very creditable performance in the race. Sharing that experience alone would have been a strong incentive to take part, had I thought about it. But I didn't. That was just an incidental benefit I picked up along the way, something rationalised after the event. I never set out to find that sort of fellowship.

I have to face up to the fact that there was no tangible reason for embarking on the adventure. All I can say is the usual explorer's adage: "Because it was there". But even that doesn't explain it fully. I mean, there are lots of challenges out there. Why the BT Global Challenge particularly?

In the end I think I have to say that I had reached a point in my life where I needed an extraordinary challenge. Something that would test me to my limits and show me what I was capable of. I think the suggestion of joining the race just happened to be the challenge that first presented itself at that psychological moment. If that hadn't taken hold of me, I think something else would have done.

Probably the single most important philosophical injunction is the Ancient Greeks' "Know thyself". This has echoes all the way down through western history, famously occurring in another guise as "To thine own self be true" in Shakespeare's *Hamlet*. And again, many further examples surface in twentieth-century literature. During this book, I have alluded many times to the poetry of T S Eliot. And once again, I find that he speaks to me through the lines of his "Little Gidding":

*"We shall not cease from exploration*
*And the end of all our exploring*
*Will be to arrive where we started*
*And know the place for the first time."*

All the best adventures bring you back where you started eventually. But as they say, not only can you never get into the same stream twice, but it can never be the same you getting into the same stream twice. The experience changes you, and next time "you" try to do it, you are different – both mentally and physically.

Hence I arrived back from my adventure, and truly felt that I understood life anew. My relations with my family and friends were enriched. My relationship with myself was enriched. I knew the place that I had come back to for the first time. And I now feel that I enjoy a greatly enhanced "inner life".

I heard recently that there has been some psychological research done on the survivors of plane crashes. Nothing seems to bother them. They are calmer than other people, their pulse and blood pressure don't rise so much in stressful situations, they tend to get less upset with friends, family and colleagues. They take life in their stride.

Unfortunately, all this evidence must remain circumstantial for the time being, because the sample of available survivors who were willing to enter the study was too small to be statistically significant – only fifteen! But you can see where they're coming from.

People always used to describe me as laid back. Since the race, people have told me that, if anything, I have become more so. And I put that down to the fact that I have seen real danger, albeit in a diluted form compared to the terror experienced by plane-crash survivors. After that, it is a lot more difficult to take family and workplace squabbles seriously. (Having said that, there were certainly times on the boat when we didn't exactly behave in an adult fashion over disputes!)

Our experiences are laid down like rings of bark on a tree. We are weathered and worn by what has happened to us. *Patched and peeled*, as Eliot would say. And what has been most recently laid down is what governs mostly our outward show.

However, an experience like the BT Global Challenge works its way into the depths of your psyche, and sits like an inner glow inside you. And you know that, whatever happens, you will always be able to look inwards and know that you once faced something in your life that took every ounce of courage and physical stamina you had available. And that through your own will and determination, and the companionship of others, you came through it, even with great credit.

The only sad thing about the adventure is that Kate has never really come to terms with my decision to do it in the first place. After all is said and done I did it; it was a great worry at the time but it was a great achievement and I came through it. And now it's over. But at home I sometimes think it's like having had an affair—something I did wrong, which, although Kate has learned to live with, she has never been able fully to forgive. And there on my buttock is the permanent reminder of the love affair – my BT Challenge tattoo.

I am branded with a mark that can never be erased without some fairly drastic surgical intervention. Kate has nevertheless said that she has come close to taking a knife to me on occasions when I have been completely anaesthetised by drink. But even if she could ever erase it from my buttock, she would never be able to cut it out of its place in my heart.

As a footnote I feel I must add that what I have said earlier does apply equally to Kate. "On the face of it", she thought, and still thinks that my action was "insane" – and her distress and anger would not only have been on her own account and that of the girls' but also out of concern for me.

On the level of "inner life", as I have put it, I wonder if Kate doesn't to some degree recognize the pull/drive that made me do it (and makes for instance my second daughter, Lucy do things!). And I do believe that Kate has become a stronger person for having had to cope alone for ten months, however difficult a time it was.

As I have also said at the beginning of the book – "And I thought about heroes. I was confused. Were they the ones who went to sea, as I'd always thought? Or were they the ones that stayed behind?"